ADAM M PINE

Sovereigns, Quasi Sovereigns, and Africans

BORDERLINES

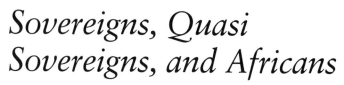

Sovereigns, Quasi Sovereigns, and Africans

Race and Self-Determination in
International Law

SIBA N'ZATIOULA GROVOGUI

BORDERLINES, VOLUME 3

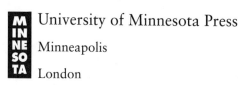

University of Minnesota Press

Minneapolis

London

Published by the University of Minnesota Press
111 Third Avenue South, Suite 290
Minneapolis, MN 55401-2520
Printed in the United States of America on acid-free paper

Library of Congress Cataloging-in-Publication Data
Grovogui, Siba N'Zatioula, 1956–
    Sovereigns, quasi sovereigns, and Africans : race and self-determination in international law / Siba N'Zatioula Grovogui.
        p.   cm. — (Borderlines ; v. 3)
    Includes bibliographical references and index.
    ISBN 0-8166-2666-9. — ISBN 0-8166-2667-7 (pbk.)
    1. Self-determination, National—Africa.   2. Decolonization—Africa.   3. Racism—Africa.   4. Self-determination, National—Namibia.   5. Decolonization—Namibia.   6. Sovereignty—Social aspects.   I. Title.   II. Series.
JX4054.G77   1996
320.1'5'096—dc20   95-24824

À la mémoire de Goua Grovogui
To Bill Johnston, for his commitment to equality

Contents

Preface

Initially, I intended to write a strictly jurisprudential analysis of sovereignty, colonial rule, and the reestablishment of sovereignty through postcolonial self-determination in Namibia, formerly South West Africa. The Namibia question — its United Nations (UN) appellation — was particularly suited for studying the practicality of the standards of the international system and the norms of international law. This Southern African territory was proclaimed a German protectorate under dubious but legally binding circumstances. Then, responding to local resistance, the German colonialists nearly exterminated the second-largest ethnic group, the Herero, during a war dubbed "pacification." In the aftermath of World War I, Western colonial powers placed the territory under an "international mandate," appointing the British dominion of South Africa as its administrator. The mandate system collapsed with the dissolution of the League of Nations, but South Africa, then under apartheid, rejected the UN request to submit its administration to the supervision of the newly created Trusteeship Council.

South Africa's defiance was perceived differently by opposing sides who grounded their judgment in their interpretation of conflicting international legal dispositions. Africans and other critics judged South Africa's continued occupation of Namibia to be a case of colonialism. South Africa and select but powerful Western nations, some of them permanent members of the UN Security Council, held a different view. Over the course of forty years, this case was periodically reviewed by the International Court of Justice. Beginning in 1947, at the request of the General Assembly, the Court issued several advisory opinions in the case. Later, starting with the 1966 action initiated by Ethiopia and Liberia, the court rendered a number of judgments in the matter. The Namibia question also received the special attention of both the UN General Assembly and the Security Council. Finally, a Western coalition mediated the conflict, leading to general elections and national independence in 1990.

During the initial phase of my investigation, I read pertinent official documents (charters and resolutions) as well as position papers of the participants in the forums that defined the structures of the post–World War I international system. The result was not surprising. The postwar settlements, in particular the mandate system, radically rejected the humanity of Africans and other colonial peoples. After reading their reports and speeches, I had no doubt that George Louis Beer, Edward House, Jan Smuts, Paul Hymans, Leon Bourgeois, and other seminal colonial experts intended by their mandate only to proclaim themselves "masters of the possessions" vacated by the defeated powers. I was bothered by their language and attitudes, but I expected them to place their national security and economic interests above the very lives of the colonized.

Nonetheless, I was disturbed to discover that the rhetoric and ideologies that permeated post–World War I discussions of Africans and other non-Europeans had been at the core of Western philosophic systems since the Middle Ages, and of international legal constructs since the Protestant Reformation. Indeed, Western notions of self and sovereignty have been grounded in claims of superiority, a higher knowledge of civil institutions, and a mission to elevate the other. These perceptions and philosophic assumptions have sustained distinct discursive traditions that have suppressed or simply erased non-European subjectivity. Only when I concluded that there were connections between historical philosophic systems and the structures of the international order did I decide to shift the focus of my investigation. I turned my attention to Western colonial and neocolonial strategies in the larger context of both theory and political culture.

In 1987, while I was reading resolution drafts and final versions at the UN Dag Hammarskjöld Library, I began to wonder about the strategies of the anticolonialists themselves: Third World coalitions, the socialist bloc, and nongovernmental Western groups and individuals. Were they not operating in a hostile cultural and institutional environment to which they were, after all, marginal? Why was it that four decades after the UN Charter had superseded the League Covenant, the independence of Namibia was still subject to legal contestations and political maneuvers? Was it just an aberration that in this case the norms of international law and the rules of the UN system undermined the anticolonial views of self-determination and sovereignty? I left New York with the conviction that most legal dispositions that applied to non-Europeans, including the procedures of conflict mediation and resolution and the rules of decolonization, were founded in colonialist assumptions regarding social evolution. As a result, I decided to combine my analysis of the historical debate over sovereignty and self-determination with one of the structures of the international order.

My graduate school professors at the University of Wisconsin at Madison equipped me for my initial project, that is, the dissertation that provided the basis for this book. Professor Fred M. Hayward, an experienced West Africanist, was my first academic adviser. When I consulted with him about my thesis proposal, he advised me to seek guidance from Professors Murray Edelman and Diane Rubenstein, both theorists and non-Africanists. This advice proved most beneficial for the development of my ideas. I am forever indebted to Professor Edelman and to Professor Rubenstein, who became my Ph.D. adviser. I also received valuable direction from Professors Hendrik Hartog, a legal historian, now at Princeton, and Mary Layoun, a literary critic. They reinforced my inquisitiveness and skepticism. He cultivated my curiosity and opened my intellectual horizons; she taught me that one person's light may blind another. Although Professor Allen Isaacman of the University of Minnesota was not an adviser in an official capacity, I might not have completed this project without his assistance, counsel, and critical comments. My gratitude to him and to his wife, Barbara, for their friendship and encouragement.

This book took shape during my 1989–90 tenure as a Du Bois-Mandela-Rodney fellow at the Center for Afroamerican and African Studies at the University of Michigan. The center's material assistance was critical to the project, but not as crucial as the collegiality of

Professors Frederick Cooper, Earl Lewis, Michael Awkward, Gracia Clark, and Rafia Zafar. I also received valuable comments from Professors Lemuel Johnson, Uzoma Esonwanne, and Babacar Fall.

I owe many of my insights to countless individuals who cannot all be listed here. However, I wish to thank particularly Kris Garvey-Mwazi, Lucia P. Hamutenya, and Yobert Shamanpande from the UN Council for Namibia for hosting me during my visit at the Hammarskjöld Library; Betsy Landis and Bill Johnston for providing me with valuable information and inspiration; Albert J. and Kathryn J. Schmidt for their moral support; Dr. Joanna Scott, Paula Sanch, and the entire department of political science at Eastern Michigan University for their understanding; and my student assistants, Doug Gordon and Michele Molitor.

Finally, I would like to express my gratitude to Michael Shapiro and David Campbell, the editors of the University of Minnesota Press's Borderline series, for their insightful comments and their invitation to contribute to the series. My gratitude to Lisa Freeman for her support, and to Todd Orjala and the many other employees of the University of Minnesota Press who have helped bring this project to fruition. Many thanks to Lynn Marasco, my copyeditor, for her sharp eye and her diligence.

As an adviser, critic, and editor, Dr. Elizabeth Suzanne Schmidt, my wife and companion, deserves special credit for the realization of this project. Jann, our son, compelled us to put everything into perspective. I alone bear responsibility for any shortcomings.

Introduction

This book was undertaken in light of the shortcomings of decolonization in Africa. It refutes the established theories of postcolonial independence that equate the transfer of political power, however limited,
from the colonizer to the colonized with African self-determination
and an assumption of national sovereignty.[1] These explanations have
construed self-determination (or self-affirmation and expression by
an autonomous entity) and postcolonial sovereignty (ordinarily, the
absolute internal authority of political entities and their capacity to
secure external recognition by like bodies)[2] to mean the application
of the rules of decolonization according to the procedures of international law.[3]

The proponents of these views have presumed decolonization to
be an end in itself. They have defended their position on the grounds
that the new law of nations, expressed in the United Nations Charter, was based upon universal principles.[4] Such scholarship has considered the availability of legal instruments with which colonial powers have manipulated the process of decolonization to their own ends
to be a juridical oddity within the present international system. According to most of these accounts, the only requirement for decolonization is the elimination of the legal instruments that provided
for direct foreign rule. This last proposition is particularly inadequate
because the United Nations Charter and related juridical and political dispositions remain silent on the most contentious issues of de-

colonization, including the extent and limits of colonial claims. In fact, the colonized have been compelled by the former colonial powers to satisfy unspecified demands as a condition for independence.

My purpose is not to demonstrate that the African struggle for sovereignty and self-determination was, or was not, hampered by deliberate Western commissions and African omissions, or vice versa. The actions and inactions of the negotiators of decolonization have been fully explored in the past.[5] My interests rest with the structures of the discourses of both international law and politics.[6] I am also concerned with the dilemmas involved in the application of existing communal rights to the formerly colonized.[7] For instance, prior to decolonization, the rights and privileges related to sovereignty and self-determination were the exclusive domain of colonial powers. During the process of decolonization they remained grounded in historically constituted Western views of themselves. These views formed the basis of a multitude of imperial claims that were central to the conquest and colonization of non-European peoples.

Although this study considers the African continent in general, I have chosen the Namibian experience with colonialism and decolonization to illustrate my findings. This case is particularly important because Namibia received the special attention of the UN General Assembly and the dubious support of the UN Security Council. The International Court of Justice issued several opinions on the matter. It also adjudicated the case, following an action initiated by Liberia and Ethiopia. Finally, a Western coalition mediated the conflict, after it had effectively manipulated the rules and procedures of the UN Charter. As a result of these interventions, the process of Namibian independence consumed several decades. Yet the outcome was not different from that in other African nations: the process of decolonization transferred rudimentary political powers to the formerly colonized, but it did not transform the structures of domination — that is, the institutional and cultural contexts of Western hegemony in the global international order on the one hand, and African marginalization within it on the other.

The disappointing outcome of Namibian decolonization has been the result of contradictions inherent in the international legal system. The rules of international law have afforded the "founding" nations of the present global order the means to continue to subordinate the rights of the colonized (and the postcolonial state) to the requirements of their own self-defined "national interests" and "security." Still, most theorists have been blinded to this central issue by their preoccupation with secondary and relatively recent factors such as the cold war in order to explain Western attitudes toward Namibia's independence.[8]

Another importuning issue regarding decolonization has been the persistence of political and juridical mechanisms that served the requirements of the dominant Western political economies. These requirements, which have taken precedence over the collective rights of formerly colonized communities, have been legitimized by systems of thought and operation that have anchored the discourses of international law and relations in the Western ego. Here too, legal scholars have provided less than satisfactory answers. In the case of Namibia, Solomon Slomin viewed South African defiance of both UN resolutions and the decisions of the International Court of Justice as extraneous obstacles that merely delayed the inevitable independence of Namibia rather than as a demonstration of the flaws of international law.[9] Likewise, the focus on human rights violations perpetrated against Namibians by South African–appointed administrations overshadowed the larger issue of the lack of enforceable legal dispositions to protect Namibians' communal rights, including natural resources.[10]

THE UNIVERSAL AND THE PARTICULARS

Joining a minority in the field, I take as my objective to probe the universalistic claims of international law: the legal system that engendered colonialism.[11] My analysis focuses on the inadequacies of international law, in particular its incompatibility with the desire of the colonized to achieve sovereignty and self-determination. The Namibian case exposes such weaknesses and contradictions. It demonstrates the subjective nature of international law and its vulnerability to politics, especially to the self-interest of hegemonic powers. I explore two important factors that undermine the universality of international law: the dependence of its norms on Western culture; and the dependence of the rules and processes of the law, as well as the structure of the discourse of international politics, on various phases of Western imperialism.

Regarding the first factor, international law has been contingent upon the resources and limits of the Western culture of which it is a product. The right to self-determination, like other rights claimed by the colonized, derives from particular conceptions of community and politics that are specific to Western culture. Dating from the tumultuous era spanning the twelfth through the sixteenth centuries, the prevailing characteristic of this culture has been an endless quest for material well-being and a reliance on violence to achieve political ends. The political thinking that resulted from this era has been marked by concerns with rights, property, and political representation that derive from a distinction between the political and the juridical spheres that is nonexistent in many other cultures.[12]

The so-called discovery of the New World in 1492 added an international dimension to the European phenomenon of complacent oblivion to the violent processes by which empires were constructed. This erasure of the manner of conquest from the discourses of law and international relations enabled the imperialist powers to claim rights and privileges within exclusively Western institutional contexts that would otherwise be considered illegitimate.[13] In sum, whatever the immediate objects of the norms of international politics, they have been marked by the obsession and the capacity of the West to dominate non-Europeans in a variety of hierarchical orders.

In chapter 1, I examine those elements of Western culture and systems of thought that provided the political means and legal justifications for the construction of empires. Also discussed are European perceptions of Africans from the late fifteenth through the nineteenth centuries. It is my contention that these perceptions were crucial to legitimizing European expansion. Emphasis is placed on the role of various agents (the Catholic Church, European adventurers, explorers, humanists, and social scientists) in formulating the authoritative image of Africa: that of man-in-nature in need of European guidance. I propose that these images of Africans as subhuman, uncivilized, or less intellectually endowed have been central to the dominant Western theories regarding Africa and Africans, from Hume, Locke, and Montesquieu to the present. They have guided Europe's relations with Africa during the period under consideration.

In chapter 2, I explore the structures of international politics and law in conjunction with the colonial discourse through various phases of Western imperialism. The emergence in Western jurisprudence of a discursive tradition that denies subjectivity (or humanity) to non-Europeans is also examined. This erasure of non-Europeans' subjectivity originated in the papal bulls of Alexander VI and continued in the writings of Hugo Grotius, Seraphin de Freitas, James Lorimer, and other founders of modern international law. The discursive obliteration of Africans' humanity effectively eliminated the possibility of their participation in the formulation of the rules of international law and politics.

The ultimate aim of this chapter is to uncover the link between the colonial discourse and international law. The colonial discourse, as indicated by Talal Asad, is the product of specific texts generated by philosophers, scientists, decision makers, humanists, and theologians directly involved in or supportive of an expansionist process.[14] It does not, however, encompass all Western discourses; Western elites and learned communities have not been unified and uniform in regard to Africa. Rather, they have been consistently heterogeneous and in disagreement. From antislavers to abolitionists and philanthropists and, more recently, anarchists, socialists, communists, feminists, and ecologists, segments of Western society have vigorously opposed European imperialism. In sum, the texts used in considering the colonial discourse do not necessarily represent the majority view of their time. Nor are they the most empirically credible. They are, however, authoritative texts,[15] and, as such, served as the foundation of international law and relations.

The colonial discourse in this study may be traced to the ideas and theories of specific Western philosophers from Hume, Locke, and Montesquieu to the present; the speeches and writings of statesmen like Gerig Benjamin, Leon Bourgeois, Georges Clemenceau, Geoffrey de Courcel, Charles Faure, J. du Fief, Lloyd George, Riccardo Pierantoni, Charles Robert, Jan Smuts, and Woodrow Wilson; and the essays of legal scholars and theorists like Edouard P. Engelhardt, Seraphin de Freitas, Francis Galton, Hugo Grotius, H. Duncan Hall, and James Lorimer. The work and careers of these figures contributed to a body of knowledge that "invented" Africa solely as a geographic space to be exploited. In pursuit of this objective, they effectively suppressed "radically opposed utterances," be they European or other.[16]

Whether embodied by international law or theories of international politics, the colonial discourse has its own economy: its generative rules, naming systems, preconditions, and implications. Throughout the book, I have deliberately appropriated referents derived from

the colonial discourse and its processes of ordering and homogeniza-
tion whose primary objects were control and domination. In other
words, although the metaphysical fictions of "Europe," "European,"
"Western," "Africa," "African," "Indian," "colonial," "colonized,"
"colonizer," "New World," and "Third World" are historical products with shifting meanings, they all result from the same textual
processes. The meanings of the referents "non-European" and "other"
are particularly interesting as a result of the change in European attitudes that occurred after the "discovery."[17]

RHETORIC OF CONTROL

The remainder of the book is a critique of the bodies of rules, procedures, and concepts that prevailed during colonization and decolonization. My central concern is not how the colonial discourse reconciled the right of colonial peoples to self-determination with the
need of the colonialists to retain their hegemonic positions. Rather,
I seek to demonstrate that the dependence of international politics
on the European-dominated political economy and its legal apparatus resulted in two of the most significant paradoxes of decolonization. The first is that only the rights sanctioned by the former colonialists were accorded to the colonized, regardless of the needs and
demands of the latter. That the will of the colonial powers was so
central to the implementation of self-determination was not considered an aberration in international law. The deliberate marginalization of postcolonial societies is also evident in statutes and judicial
opinions that have sought to preserve by legal and economic means
the privileges that the former colonial powers would have had to
forfeit after genuine self-determination.

The second paradox is that the rules and procedures of decolonization were determined and controlled by the former colonial powers to effect specific outcomes. This is a paradox because the right to
self-determination is generally understood to mean the absolute political authority to create rights and obligations for oneself, or the authority to legally bind the self.[18] The rules and processes of decolonization
not only denied African communities the right to the protection
of the law, they failed to recognize Africans' need for such protection.

As in the colonial discourse, international law has generated a multitude of meanings for political autonomy, sovereignty, and self-determination that have taken into account geography, culture, and race.

The differentiation of rights and needs according to geographical distance has been one way to justify the colonial order. Geography has also been used to explain the cultural, political, and economic dissimilarities between Europe and non-European communities.[19]

Such has not always been the case. Prior to the fifteenth century, Christians and non-Christians interacted in a world system that was centered around several distinct geographic units, some of which were nonetheless connected. Despite the violent confrontations that marred intercommunal relations, these geographic entities generally acknowledged the religious and cultural dissimilarities of other regional units as differences, but not the kind that the West later felt compelled to suppress.[20] Western Christians regarded non-Europeans of the "Old World," in particular Tartars, Asians, and Arabs, as radically different human communities or political entities, capable of having their own, albeit inferior, cultures and religions.[21] Throughout this era, Christians' only disposition toward non-Christians was the Christians' belief that it was their duty to convert, and thereby save, non-Christians.

The relationship changed in the aftermath of the "discovery," when Western conquerers began to use images of witches, wild men, and animals — all intolerable aspects of the European self — to characterize the peoples they subordinated, dominated, exploited, or simply marginalized.[22] This led to the modern alterity that, more than geography, has provided the structure of the colonial discourse.[23] In this alterity, the "other" is the product of a textuality that, through intellectual assumptions and methods, has transformed mere cultural and historical variations into essential distances.

REGIMES OF EXPLOITATION

The "discovery" of a "New World" marked a turning point in alterity and the ordering of the universe. In 1492, according to Eric Cheyfitz, European Jews, Africans, and peoples indigenous to the Caribbean were brought into a common history — one of textual appropriation and material expropriation — through a "conjection of European violence."[24] The "naked inhabitants of the New World," henceforth homogenized as "Indian," were denied sovereign rights simultaneously with the expulsion of the Jews from the Christian kingdom of Spain. That same year, Spain defeated the African Moors. These perceived Christian successes, as well as European navigational and technological achievements, emboldened European scientists, jurists, and theologians to claim the rest of the world for Europe.[25]

Beginning in 1493, Western Christendom promised spiritual salvation and material comfort to the whole world under a European-dominated "universal" order. Initially, the pope, through the Iberian monarchies of Spain and Portugal, promised redemption to "Indians," Africans, and other non-Europeans by means of conversion to Christianity. The pontiff and the Spanish and Portuguese monarchs also imposed European spiritual guidance, political domination, and unrestricted access to the others' territories and resources as necessary requirements of their mission.[26]

The Christian-inspired "universe" was justified, then ordered into specific forms of knowledge within a totalizing ecclesiastical system that established hierarchical and exploitative relations between its Christian subjects and the other. This system appropriated the post-discovery Indian, Jew, African — or, more generally, the other — as mere objects of discourse to be "settled down,"[27] stripped of essential communal rights within the European-dominated international order. In particular, the fifteenth-century papal bulls and related norms of intercommunal relations allowed Christian missionaries, pirates, and adventurers to exploit Indians, Africans, and other non-Christians. According to Kirkpatrick Sale, Spanish, Portuguese, and other Christian entities derived the desired material gains from the relationship, including new foods, medicines, and treasures. Despite their promises, the Christians failed to uplift the other.[28] In fact, they brought both misery and ruin.

The structural basis of this fifteenth-century ecclesiastic system, that is, the configuration of power within Western Christendom, changed over time. During the sixteenth century, for instance, the Protestant Reformation rejected papal authority, leading to the emergence of new churches and political entities in Europe. These events in turn altered that continent's balance of power. Yet, the emerging authorities adhered to the existing hierarchies between Christians and the other. They maintained the ordering mechanisms of the preceding ecclesiastical system, as well as appropriated the established *teleos* of intercommunal relations within a European-dominated international order.

Indeed, the Christian-inspired "universe" has continued to provide the philosophical foundation for the totalizing cultural, political, economic, and legal systems of knowledge that have sustained Western hegemony. The particular articulations of Western hegemonic systems, including the norms of international law and relations, have reflected specific historical situations and objects of intercommunal relations. For instance, at its inception, modern international law reflected political, social, and political transformations in Europe and the global order. In the aftermath of the Protestant Reformation and related social and economic changes, international relations were dominated by political and military competition among the new European powers. During this time, the fruits of overseas plunder failed to satisfy Europe's growing demands for agricultural products and other precious materials. As a result, Christian rulers authorized their nationals to secure political influence over and control of geographical spaces belonging to the other. This process facilitated a more intensive exploitation. Under the new norms and principles of intercommunal relations, European adventurers, merchants, and colonists received the protection of domestic laws and governments in their new endeavors. Later, interested imperialist powers turned to settlement, slavery, and other forms of human bondage in order to achieve their objectives.[29]

Further variations in international relations have been represented by specific international systems and organizations, as well as distinct juridico-political norms and principles. The historic combinations of institutions, norms, and principles have formed the bases of various international regimes. Although these juridico-political regimes result from mutations in the metaphysical processes of totalizing systems, they preclude material and discursive practices that contradict the basic propositions of the totalizing systems of the international order. These propositions include the necessity of Western hegemony and leadership within a hierarchically integrated global order and political economy.

Western systems incorporated Africa into the global order and placed it at the bottom of the European-inspired universe. Four juridico-political regimes have defined Africa's position in this international order, which in turn has determined Africans' relations to the West. The first regime, which originated in the 1493 papal bulls of Alexander VI, spanned the period of the Holy Roman Empire, the years of the trans-Atlantic slave trade, and the era of informal empires. The second began with the 1884–85 Berlin Conference and the imposition of the German protectorate in Namibia. The 1919 Paris Peace Conference marks the start of the third regime. Under this regime, the League of Nations introduced the mandate system, a colonial device for the collective exploitation of the colonies of the defeated powers under one administration. The fourth and current regime, that of the United Nations, established both trusteeship and political independence in place of the mandate and formal colonial rule.

METHODOLOGY

My analysis draws on official documents (charters and resolutions) as well as speeches of participants in critical international forums (the Berlin Conference, the Paris Peace Conference and Geneva Congress, the UN San Francisco Conference) that laid out the structures, rules, and procedures of each international system and regime. The reading of these texts is complemented by a discussion of the ideologies, rhetoric, and systems of thought formulated by lawyers and politicians connected with the implementation of Western policies. Besides its emphasis upon the historical, cultural, and ideological contexts of specific political and legal texts, this study draws on works pertaining to the political economy of imperialism in Africa in general, and in Namibia in particular.

There is no single identifiable method to this study because, as Peter Mason has stated, "writing about otherness is ... writing otherwise."[30] Just as the colonialists founded their discourse of the other upon a blend of juridical, theological, sociological, ethnological, anthropological, and economic knowledge, so too does this study in international law and international relations draw from a broad range of disciplines in the social sciences and the humanities, regardless of traditional boundaries. The aim of this study is indeed to write otherwise in order to write about the pathos of a tradition of Western discursive practices.

Genesis, Order, and Hierarchy

In recent years, natural-law theorists, realists, and other liberal critics of postivism and formalism have jettisoned the argument that Western powers and their dominant classes held their imperial rights by virtue of nature or reason. They have acknowledged the fallacy of imperialist claims to the right of occupancy. The liberal critics, according to Johannes Fabian, have recognized the purported philanthropic and altruistic thrusts of such claims for what they are: "a monstrous lie perpetuated for the benefit of one part of humanity, for a few societies of that part, and, in the end, for one part of those societies, its dominant classes."[1]

Liberal scholars have also condemned Western colonial policies and, in particular, have acknowledged that such international institutions as the mandate and trusteeship systems were manipulated by colonial powers for their own ends.[2] In this regard, they denounced South Africa's violation of the terms of its international mandate in Namibia. They decried the perceived inconsistency of the United Nations Security Council and the International Court of Justice in their reluctance to take decisive action against the white minority government in Pretoria.[3]

Although they disagree with positivists and formalists concerning the nature of international law, liberal critics continue to be gripped by a mythical view of the present international legal system and its related international order. A plurality of liberals, in particular scholars of international law and relations, remains under the spell of the "mendacious fiction" that current international legal norms reflect collective or universal values and that the present system promotes the welfare of all. Accordingly, they consider the postcolonial order to be truly multilateral.[4]

In *An Introduction to the History of the Law of Nations in the East Indies,* for instance, C. H. Alexandrowicz emphatically asserts the historic universality of international law by contending that it was tainted by Eurocentrism only in the nineteenth century. Responding to the growing postcolonial disenchantment with the international order, he writes that international law is an identifiable body of norms that can be found in all geographic areas throughout history and that all nations, including non-Europeans, helped to develop it.[5] He insists in another book, *The European-African Confrontation,* that prior to nineteenth-century Eurocentrism, the law of nations was essentially based on equal rights and opportunities for all communities and nations. As evidence for this position, he maintains that the majority of Europeans respected the dictates of natural law in their interactions with non-Europeans. He also argues that the Asian and African partners of Europeans were familiar with the norms and processes of natural law with regard to treaty-making.[6]

A self-proclaimed Grotian, or natural-rights advocate, Alexandrowicz also contends that it was during the nineteenth century that non-Europeans were left "outside the confines of civilization" and international law shrank to regional European dimensions.[7] This claim regarding the impact of nineteenth-century Western imperialism on international law is shared by critical realists, in particular empiricists. The latter also blame contemporary positivists and politicians for selectively using the dictates of the law in order to create privileges for a minority of states or racial groups within them.

Writing on the subject of the law of nations in *The Law of the Land,* Henry Reynolds contends that two hundred years prior to the nineteenth-century expropriations of indigenous peoples, Europeans had recognized their rights.[8] Reynolds uses historical accounts to shed light on the selective application of European laws by colonial settlers in Australia. In the tradition of critical realists, he attempts to demonstrate that legal doctrines are neutral and that it was forces independent of the law (for instance, policy makers and settlers) that interpreted the law to narrow self-interested ends.[9] In this regard, he singles out Australian jurisprudence for its "truly amazing achievement," the dispossession and oppression of Aborigines.[10]

Critical realists like Reynolds hold that the universal norms prevalent in natural law can be restored by ridding positive law of its latent instrumentality. Richard A. Falk takes this position in *The Status of Law in International Society*.[11] Falk maintains that the authority of international law (which resides in its universality) ultimately depends on the legitimacy of its processes. Accordingly, the norms of the present international system would be more authoritative if the decision-making organs of the United Nations included the perspectives of postcolonial nations in determining the common good or purpose. Likewise, he suggests that the international institutions of adjudication would render more legitimate decisions if they took into account the ideological and moral inclinations of the culturally distinct non-Western nations.[12]

The attempt to change the course of international law, to depart from its unjust legacy, has been problematic. Positivists, emboldened by the actions of the majority of Western nations, have taken any critical reading of international law as an ideological attack on the past by misguided activists and scholars.[13] L. C. Green is among the scholars who have reacted defensively to criticism of the international legal system. In his article "Claims to Territory in Colonial America," Green charges that the past imbalance in power relations between Europeans and non-Europeans has been exaggerated. He acknowledges that pre-nineteenth-century Christians' agreements with indigenous populations might have contained flaws, but insists that such defects were consistent with contemporary international practice and customs.[14] Accordingly, most Christian rulers and colonists acted in good faith and justly: "there is little doubt that they believed themselves to be acting in accordance with existing law."[15] Finally, Green's defense of past European practices relies on the interpretations of pre-nineteenth-century North American colonial jurists. He stresses that colonial jurisprudence must be analyzed according to standards prevalent during the fifteenth to eighteenth centuries. Challenging his critics, he accuses recent innovators of basing their arguments on political ideology and concepts such as self-determination, which he considers to be irrelevant to the analysis of past actions.[16]

The innovators include critical legal theorists of opposing intellectual traditions: Marxists, literary critics, poststructuralists, and others. While liberals aspire to restore the presumed universality of the law, these radical critics maintain that such a condition never existed.[17] The radical critics are joined by another group of innovators, mostly composed of postcolonial scholars and activists. In *International Law and Colonialism in Africa*, for instance, Umozurike O. Umozurike notes that international law not only validated imperialism and colonial practices but also has, since its inception, been "directed toward the promotion of European interests."[18] Umozurike and Third World innovators also point out the inadequacies of the international law system, particularly its failure to restore rights and dignity to postcolonial societies.

Consistent with their own analysis of the nature of the law, Third World innovators also agree with radical critics that the crisis of legitimacy suffered by the international legal system is multidimensional. Likewise, the problems of the international order, in particular the causes of international tensions and conflicts, require practical if ad hoc legal interventions. Umozurike and others from the former colonies disagree, however, with the assumption that the present international system and Western jurisprudence offer adequate bases for meaningful solutions and reform. Umozurike criticizes the majority of Western politicians, scholars, and publicists for their failure to consider the imposition of slavery, colonialism, and other forms of oppression of non-Europeans to be contrary either to the law of nature or to that of nations.[19]

The minority, composed of cultural and institutional critics, reject liberal modes of interpretation, whether for the purpose of justifying the norms of international law or of exposing the flaw of the legal system. These few critical theorists warn against current reliance on Western jurisprudence, in particular its idioms, as a basis for redress or reform within the domestic and international order. It is their view that the cultural and political trappings of any such dependence cannot be overcome by incorporating divergent non-Western views into the law.[20]

I support the contention of the latter group. This book begins with a critique of two erroneous assumptions born of current theoretical dependence on Western jurisprudence and the related legal culture as resources to practical solutions and reform of the present international system. The first dubious contention emanates from the positivist view that Western jurisprudence is the outcome of a rational process and that rights created by international law have reflected the wishes of concerned nations. The other basic inaccuracy, originating from natural-law advocates and critical realists, is that there exist certain atemporal universal rights, applicable to all, that were only temporarily suppressed during nineteenth-century European imperialism.

The positivist view that international law is the outcome of a rational process and that rights, including universal ones, are derived from legislation and legal precedent takes as its context a crucial theoretical distinction. This distinction is that the formation of the norms of international relations and their given meanings differ from the constitution of their operations: international politics. This process is said also to differ from the gradual changes that led to their inception, or legal history. This approach presupposes that: (a) the rules, processes, principles, and doctrines of the law provide the groundwork for a universal order; and (b) colonial jurisprudence (a term many positivists would dispute) is the result of anomalous policies inconsistent with the natural order. Unfortunately, these assumptions are neither historically accurate nor ideologically neutral.

The special body of rules that applied to European relations with non-Europeans emerged long before their full implementation by Western powers and colonial settlers during nineteenth-century Western imperialism. The legal thinking that propelled the processes of Western Imperialism changed dramatically then as a result of the object of Europe's relation to the non-European world. It follows that these special norms were the result of ideologically driven doctrinal interpretations and judicial applications of communal rights that came into existence during the era of conquest. Finally, the execution of treaty, property, and other rights in the Americas, Africa, Asia, and elsewhere was ultimately a political question. Indeed, the different phases of international law — legislation, interpretation, and execution — satisfied different requirements of imperialism.

In contesting the "naturalness" and universality of the law of nations, I will approach international law as an ordering language rather than a set of neutral and unconnected principles and doctrines. The law, as I see it, is arbitrary and doubtless "more confused, more obscure, and probably less easy" than is suggested by the interpretative modes discussed here.[21] My purpose is to analyze the historical affirmation of Western hegemony in the international order and the legal, political, and ideological conditions of sovereignty and self-determination in the postcolonial era. The hegemonic dimensions of international law cannot be explored without stressing their modes of operation (perceptions, philosophic interpretations, values) and functions (the reproduction of the international order). It is my contention that European perceptions of the self and their metaphysical representations have been crucial to the structure of international law. They have enabled Western Christendom (and, later, the West) to create juridical instruments with which to maintain exploitative relations with other continents within presumed universal orders. In this context, sovereignty and self-determination have reflected the dominant European culture and functioned as a mediating ideology, reconciling the juridical means for attaining hegemony with the opposing need to project the rights and obligations created for the other as objectively derived from universal values.

GENESIS OF CHRISTIAN SOVEREIGNTY

I begin with the proposition that medieval Christianity and papal interpretations of the Scriptures have defined the modern international order, including its hierarchical system and various forms of unequal subjectivities (or sovereignties). These hierarchies and subjectivities in turn have delineated the realm of international law from the Renaissance through the Enlightenment to the present. My position substantiates three essential points made by Michel Foucault in *The Order of Things*.[22] The first is that the classical episteme, to which the Renaissance merely contributed a new configuration, created the hierarchies underlying international relations and its norms. Second, although international law did not emerge as a distinct discipline until the seventeenth century, it has depended upon the same original script as the classical episteme, genesis, to constitute its subjects and objects. Third, international law functions, like the classical episteme, through an allotment of signs to particular perceptions, thoughts, and desires that it represents as universal. While Foucault established the manner in which the classical age defined the realm of the Renaissance and natural history, he confined himself to describing epistemic transformations, leaving aside their purposes.[23] Building upon

Foucault's contribution, I propose to analyze the transformation of international law by focusing on the purposes of the alterations.

Right to *Imperium* and *Dominium*

The general issue of political authority (or *imperium*) and the "relationship that holds together persons, things, and actions" (*dominium*)[24] came to the attention of canonists and European jurists during the Middle Ages. During this era of prolonged European debate over Christian rights both within and outside of Europe, the Roman Catholic Church was among the first to take a firm position. It presumed that the church was not one of many institutions, but the ultimate sovereign power of humankind. This supposition was eroded by a number of historical changes, including transformations within the church and the struggle for political authority between temporal rulers and the papacy.

Before Pope Innocent III emphasized the primacy of the papacy and the church in the late twelfth century, the dispute between the pope and the European rulers had been temporarily settled by the Concordat of Worms (1122). This agreement between Pope Calixtus and Emperor Henry V brought about a new modus vivendi between the church and temporal rulers within the Holy Roman Empire. It was a compromise that allowed the church to remain the ultimate spiritual but also political power while relegating to temporal Christian rulers certain lesser rights and prerogatives over their subjects. The church would no longer stand between the rulers and their subjects in reference to earthly matters.

The proclamation by Innocent III of papal plenitude and the supremacy of ecclesiastical authority within the Holy Roman Empire was a response to growing internal pressure for reform. Indeed, during the later Middle Ages the primacy of papal authority was undercut by theoretical debates over the nature of political authority within Europe itself. Several European monarchs, including King Edward I of England (1272–1307) and Philippe IV of France (1285–1314), successfully challenged Pope Boniface VIII, Innocent's successor, concerning the universality of papal imperial powers. Their objections presaged the sixteenth-century Protestant Reformation, when the papacy lost ecclesiastical authority over a large part of Western Christendom.[25]

The opposition of European monarchs to the authority of the pope was first framed in terms of the agency of *imperium*, purposefully defined as lordship (and later sovereignty) and *dominium*, the sphere of political influence over peoples, policy, and property. These concepts were understood in religious, legal, and political terms to be articulated around the identity of the various communities. Each secular ruler (monarch) who represented a community claimed to possess the right to sovereignty. This right was exercised against any domestic rival claim, and also abroad against the external encroachment of the papacy.

The Concordat of Worms also constructed a political universe (res publica, or common order) in which the pope remained the *suprema protesta*: the only authority who acted independently of any external power but God. The pope was followed in this hierarchical universe by lesser European authorities (monarchs) who held their power by papal volition.[26] The rest of humankind, forming the base of the pyramid, was incorporated into this temporal hierarchy by successive papal bulls. In the new order, the pope remained at the pinnacle, followed by European kings and their subjects. "Old World Infidels" (Chinese, Indians, and Muslims) came next, above Africans and, after 1492, the "New World Infidels."[27]

Unam Sanctam: A Claim to Power

The question of non-European political authority, property rights, and freedom of faith also arose in this ecclesiastical consensus among Christians to impose their authority over non-Christians. Prior to this consensus, Western Europeans maintained an extended network of trade routes in all parts of Europe, including the farthest regions of Russia, the Middle East, the Orient, and Africa. These relations were based on collectively formulated mercantile and maritime rules that necessitated a shared vision of intercommunal relations as well as juridical principles pertaining to the rights of each community.[28]

During the early Middle Ages, Europeans and the others (mostly Turks, Arabs, Tartars, and Chinese) lived in competing but not antagonistic self-centered universes, each guided by a belief in the self as the center of the entire universe. During this era, the greater part of their intercommunal relations involved, although they were not limited to, exchanges based on mutual interests in an increasingly integrated international economy. According to Janet Abu-Lughod,

Europeans joined Arabs and Asians in a long-distance trade system that extended from the Mediterranean to the Red Sea and the Persian Gulf, linking these regions to the Indian Ocean through the Strait of Malacca and to China.[29] This relationship was essentially characterized by the absence of hegemonic power(s). Despite the many cultural and political differences among the communities involved in this eastern trade, each trading partner accepted the mutuality of interests.

This view of intercommunal relations changed when the papacy reconfigured its authority throughout the world. While in Europe the church was compelled to relinquish political power to temporal rulers, in other parts of the world it proclaimed its sovereignty. Beginning in 1302, Boniface VIII proclaimed that humankind (including non-Europeans and non-Christians) could be saved only through Christ, the Catholic Church, and its apostles. In *Unam Sanctam*, dated December 18 of that year, he declared that in the interest of salvation every human creature was subject to the Roman pontiff. Through this statement, the Catholic Church claimed sovereignty over the world, both Christian and non-Christian. From this date, the debate over the exact spheres of authority between the papacy and non-European spiritual and temporal rulers was theoretically resolved in favor of the church—and ultimately Europe.

INTER CAETERA AND OTHER PAPAL BULLS

Prior to the "discovery" of the New World in 1492, theologians and jurists accorded limited rights of *imperium* and *dominium* to "Old World" infidels. These "rational nonbelievers," identified ethnically as Turks and other Asians, or confessionally as Muslims, possessed a recognizable right to self-rule ownership of their lands. However, these communities lawfully retained political authority and land rights only as long as they did not wage war upon Christians or obstruct their right to free trade.[30] The 1492 discovery of previously unknown infidels brought about a new awareness of the universe and added new dimensions to European attitudes toward non-Europeans. As a result, Christian theologians altered the existing tripartite division of the universe (Europe, Africa, and India and China) to account for new peoples other than the descendants of Shem, Ham, and Japhet.[31] They also developed distinctive notions of political authority applicable solely to the new infidels. As "nonrational Infidels," devoid of any recognizable religion, they were not accorded the same rights as "Old World Infidels."[32]

Following the discovery, Pope Alexander VI seized upon the opportunity to reassert himself as the sovereign leader of the Holy Roman Empire and other Christian empires and kingdoms. The pope not only considered it his missionary duty to extend his leadership beyond his established European empire, he was willing to use the agency of European rulers to achieve these ends. Thus, on May 4, 1493, responding to Spain's appeal for papal legitimation of its acquisition of New World territories, he issued two bulls. The first *Inter Caetera* proclaimed that the newly discovered world was to be divided between the Christian kingdoms of Spain and Portugal.[33] The second *Inter Caetera* ordered that the "natives" be taught "the good customs of Christianity," but left the details of the implementation of the mission to the monarchs of Spain and Portugal.[34] Spain and Portugal were permitted to demarcate their respective spheres, which they did in the treaties of Tordesillas (1494) and Saragossa (1529). Later papal bulls reiterated the right of the Iberian monarchs "to navigate the ocean sea, seek out the islands [and] ports," as well as to forbid "under penalty of excommunication" other Christians from challenging the said Catholic rulers.[35]

The legitimacy of the pope's bulls was tenuous at best, given his waning authority in Europe. By the time these bulls took effect, only the monarchs who stood to benefit from them accepted their legitimacy. As a result, the validity of the Spanish and Portuguese claims could easily be contested. To correct this flaw, Spain took several steps, including the highly symbolic assumption of political authority and sovereignty in its possessions.[36]

Indeed, the Spanish and Portuguese claims to a divinely ordained mission resulted in contestations by other European powers. By the end of the sixteenth century, the Netherlands, England, and France had joined Portugal and Spain in the scramble for New World possessions. Their argument was not with the bulls' claims of Christian sovereignty over non-Christians but with the allocation of the New World territories exclusively to the Iberian powers. In the centuries that followed, the pontifical bulls and their predictions remained the metaphors for inter-European treaties pertaining to the other. They were also used as guides for the nascent relations between Christians and non-Christians.

DISCURSIVE CANONS

The Catholic Church initiated the philosophical formation of non-Christian otherness during the Middle Ages when the pope first claimed full sovereign authority over non-Europeans. By the sixteenth century, European jurists and other theorists had adopted the theological justifications of non-European otherness. This process of epistemic distinction between the self and the other climaxed in the seventeenth century, at the height of the Protestant Reformation and the Catholic Counter Reformation.[37] It was during this era that theorists reconciled nature and history through imagination. They established metaphysical relations between the natural order of things and perceived hierarchies among humans.[38] In general, their views promoted the notion of Christian/European superiority and championed Christian/European interests over those of the other.

This process of non-European alterity was represented in three genres of discourse that depended for their forms on three different historical periods. The first genre arose in the ecclesiastical context of the discovery of the New World in the fifteenth century. The second genre emerged during the era of the Enlightenment and owed its form to a hierarchy of peoples and civilizations. The third genre, also the colonial discourse, was a product of nineteenth-century natural history and imperialism.

Salvation through Submission

The events of 1492 and 1493 provided the theological atmosphere, as well as created the intellectual disposition, for the formulation of a body of knowledge in which the universe was unified under Western Christendom. They also facilitated the theoretical invention of a Christian subject and its non-Christian other (combining non-Europeans of the Old and New Worlds), separated by distance, culture, and faith, but united by providence under Christian guidance or responsibility. As a result, from the turn of the sixteenth century, the norms of intercommunal relations emerged as a recognizable language with identifiable discursive propositions along with its own tropes, metaphors, and vocabularies. The most significant proposition of this era was the Christian mission to bring salvation to heathens and other nonbelievers through conversion and subsequent incorporation into the Christian order.

The sixteenth-century Christian view of nonbelievers was that they were sinners who lived in spaces outside of Europe and in a different time frame, that is, before salvation.[39] Despite this common premise, the church and early missionaries played contradictory roles in the New World and elsewhere based on conflicting views of the nature of the infidels and of salvation. The majority of church leaders viewed salvation in secular terms involving domination and exploitation. A few, however, attempted to protect the natives from European greed and violence. Indeed, a significant minority, including the Dominican friar Antonio de Montesinos, engaged in moral struggles to free all humans, European settlers and native Americans alike, from sin, for the sake of salvation.[40] They believed that the end of the world was near and that it was the duty of the faithful to forgo possession of material goods in this life in order to prepare for heavenly rewards. Bartolome de Las Casas also viewed the teachings of Jesus and the New Testament as evidence that the struggle against injustice could not be separated from the quest for paradise.[41] From his perspective, and that of like-minded individuals, Christ and his apostles were hostile to the interests of the wealthy. Indeed, throughout European expansion, some theologians presented Christianity as protective of the powerless and the dispossessed.[42]

These exceptions notwithstanding, most missionaries took their guidance from Popes Boniface VIII and Alexander VI, who, despite conflicting theological views, formulated their position to conform to the political climate of European expansion and discovery.[43] From the outset, these popes expected Christian missionaries to combine their religious mission with political functions by encouraging them to teach the natives about the benefits of "legitimate trade."[44] Consequently, most missionaries helped to contain native hostility toward European dispossession and exploitation. Many Christian proselytizers backed secular humanists like Juan Gines de Sepulveda, who, unlike Las Casas, justified the brutal methods of conquest. In the same vein, the Dominican Francisco de Vitoria demanded church neutrality in regard to development in the Indies on the grounds that the conscience of Spanish monarchs was sufficient to guarantee that the rights of the "barbarians" would be protected.[45]

De Vitoria and other apologists of conquest called on native converts to accept their conditions,[46] on the grounds that the Bible exhorts Christians to be indifferent to their station in life.[47] These Christian proselytizers selectively used the teachings of the Old and New

Testaments to justify their actions against natives everywhere. While they quoted the New Testament to demand native submission to authority, they referred to the Old Testament to justify war as a means to achieving their own political ends.[48] Waging war was said to be sanctioned by the Bible if the result was the conversion of the multitudes. The conversion of the unfaithful, even through the use of force, was the moral obligation of the believer to the nonbeliever.

Christian Self-Centrism and Narcissism

The mid-sixteenth-century Protestant Reformation and Catholic Counter Reformation were followed by the seventeenth-century European scramble for global influence. The intra-Christian schism opposed various denominations that were identified with nationalist aspirations in different segments of Western Christendom. This coincidence of religious and communal identity brought about new discursive practices, but it did not alter the dominant Christian attitudes toward non-Christians. Where once the Catholic Church claimed true faith and its own chosenness, a multitude of Christian denominations now competed with one another for this position. Each breakaway church boasted a privileged mantle in the Kingdom of Heaven and claimed an indisputable universal authority.[49]

The seventeenth-century quest for influence that opposed different Christian denominations added a new dimension to European imperialism. Each denomination backed its own community, and subsequent alliances of European communities, in a competition with Rome aimed at representing the universal, the standard by which all others must be measured.[50] During this era, Catholic and Protestant entities continued to interpret intercommunal relations according to their own views of the Kingdom in which the chosen occupied a privileged place. Both groups used biblically derived images to promote national interests, as well as to justify extraterritorial adventures. They believed that it was their duty to provide salvation to the "fallen" other.[51]

Since the seventeenth century, Western theologians have taken their own cosmology for the universal and their values as the norm. Their myths of European chosenness and of the Christian mission subsequently entered humanist and juridical discourses. While the new discourses abandoned the theological foundation of European expansionism, they replaced it with a new, equally mythical one. For instance, expert publicists projected Columbus's voyage and similar

Christian achievements as an indication of European superiority.[52] Where the theological dichotomy of the chosen and the fallen emphasized spiritual and communal differences, the new discourses perceived "barbarians" and other strangers as a menace to legitimate commerce and development.[53]

This fixation on the self and on self-interest can be an obtrusive self-love (amour propre) or an abstruse yet recognizable self-love (amour de soi).[54] In the narcissistic moment between the Middle Ages and the Reformation, Christian theologians and other theorists posited the European ego as the sole locus of intercommunal relations. They exceeded both brands of self-love, posing the erasure of the other as requisite of self-interest. This Christian movement developed a pathos: an obsessive love for the self, a self-centeredness that required the subjection of the other. It virtually eliminated the possibility of coexistence and denied the validity of contending selves.[55]

The European obsession with the self resulted from specific beliefs (e.g., Christian chosenness) and to conquest and other choices that projected the interests of Western Christendom as the sole source and primary cause of all intercommunal relations. Significantly, this narcissism also allowed for the denial of the other as a bearer of interests. It also enabled Christian theorists to subsume the other selves into their own in order to posit their desires and values as universal. As a result, Christian theorists constructed their own communal identities in conjunction with the erasure of the other, the infidels, from the political cosmology.

AN AUTHORITATIVE DISCOURSE

From the time of the discovery to the eighteenth century, few reputable Christian missionaries or theologians, not even Las Casas, questioned the basic claim of Christian sovereignty over natives. Most Christians believed in the unity of the realm, the Kingdom, or the universe.[56] In this view, the universe and its history were united in the Word. The universal "designated the whole world at all times."[57] Initially, the overriding concern of the church was to incorporate the fallen back into the realm, the Christian universe. In this regard, the overall Christian attitude toward non-Europeans remained ambiguous; both the ecclesiastic views of the other and church attitudes toward the natives varied according to historical periods and the biblical views of individual clerics. This ambiguity in turn caused contradictory sentiments concerning the "nature and place of the natives."[58]

During the time when the church oversaw European expansion, Christian missionaries never adopted a unified position on the nature of their relationship with the fallen souls they went to save. The most enlightened Christian proselytizers, according to D. W. T. Shropshire, were puzzled but relieved that the native was skillful and "apparently rational in many of his quite ordinary, everyday avocations."[59] Most missionaries, however, held the opposite view. Their arguments were grounded in speculations regarding the nature of what they perceived to be fallen souls. These missionaries, and some theologians, maintained that the natives were generally possessed by the devil. A few even moved beyond the contestation of native nakedness and lack of social structures to justify native bondage, including slavery, as moral.

Despite these contradictory views and perspectives, it can be said with certitude that the Western discourse concerning the other has remained grounded in certain myths.[60] The rendition and articulation of these myths has been part of a systematic body of knowledge that constituted a particular genre of European discourse on the other. This second genre was actualized, during the era of the Enlightenment, by scholarly and professional pronouncements on the presumed characters of native Americans, Africans, and other non-Europeans. Besides supporting the theses of their authors in other respects, these commentaries subsequently constituted an authoritative discourse on the other. This discourse owed its form to contemporary discursive classifications of peoples and cultures into distinct species and civilizations. It justified European domination of the world by claiming European cultural supremacy and a presumed racial superiority.[61] By elevating racial characteristics to new heights, the Enlightenment provided nineteenth-century explorers, merchants, and social scientists with the theoretical basis of a third genre. I shall discuss the third genre, the colonial discourse, in the last section of this chapter.

Origins of the Authoritative Discourse

The ecclesiastic interpretation of the universe, universal history, and the mission changed during the eighteenth century, when Christian history was transmuted into natural history. During this Enlightenment era, an assortment of theorists, publicists, adventurers, and politicians began to construe universalism and universal history in an entirely new light. While they freed Europe from the tyranny of the existing discursive traditions, the dominant protagonists of the Enlightenment retained the received Christian perceptions and attitudes toward non-Christians.[62] In particular, they preserved the classical medieval Christian mission and its representation of the Christian self and the non-Christian other.

Certainly, the movement that propelled Europe to new heights during the eighteenth century was not monolithic. Nor did the participant humanists and theorists share the same views with respect to the other. A significant minority made commentaries on non-Europeans in their treatises on the problems caused by the ongoing social transformations in Europe. Writing during the dramatic unfolding of the Enlightenment, Locke, Hume, Montesquieu, Hegel, Kant, and other participant philosophers and learned elites proposed the sanctity of rights and liberties as central pillars of civil society. In the process, they made assertions concerning the other that appeared to be, in the words of H. L. Malchow, "rambling asides" to otherwise critical essays on civilization, social formation, political legitimacy, and other compelling contemporary issues.[63] Indeed, the majority of Enlightenment utterances concerning the other were limited to citations or brief references to the existence of native Americans, Africans, and others in a state of nature similar to that of Europe in its immemorial past. Although they were unsubstantiated, these isolated remarks were critical to the general perceptions of the European self and of the other. They also served as the basis for justification of ongoing Western imperialism.

First, the Enlightenment utterances concerning the other confirmed the European individual and polity to be the sole bearer of culture. They did so by antithetically pointing to the absence elsewhere of civil society, or what they termed civilization. According to Peter Mason, in an age when Europe was defining itself anew, the defenders of European culture defined themselves "in a way resembling that of a photographic negative." They created an image of themselves by portraying everything that they were not, or thought themselves not to be.[64]

Having created their own image and its opposites, the dominant protagonists of the Enlightenment then used these images to provide solutions to the most burning sociopolitical questions of their time.[65] Often, they provided cures to European ills through manipulation of existing images of the other, or by instigating fear of the unknown.[66] In their analyses of the political turbulence caused by eighteenth-century social transformations, social scientists and humanists perceived similarities between the rebellious European masses and their anarchic ways on the one hand, and the "naked multitudes" in the Americas and elsewhere on the other.[67] As a result, they stressed the need to preserve the self (the domestic social order) and its superior institutions (civil society, constitutional government, and legitimate trade) against corrupting influences. They also cautioned the masses against the anarchy that might result from their agitations by pointing to countermodels of civil society in Africa and the Americas.

The Enlightenment also reaffirmed Europe as the central locus of intercommunal relations by drawing on the medieval Christian view concerning the other.[68] Enlightenment humanists and theorists drew on this medieval view concerning the other when they discursively transformed the formerly Christian mission into destiny, willed by God and historical circumstances.[69] They promoted Europeans' advances, then limited to weaponry and the navigational capacity to travel beyond the oceans, as evidence of Western superiority.[70] They not only assumed that Europe was destined to be the predominant force in history, they claimed that the destiny of the human race lay in its hands.[71] Accordingly, they propagated the notion that Europe conquered the world in order to lead it to civilization.[72]

Significantly, these Enlightenment "rambling asides" concerning the other generated a systematic body of knowledge that invented non-European spaces, including Africa, and their inhabitants as objects of Western discourse. Contributing to this knowledge, European theorists ranging from natural historians in Britain to social contractarians, rationalists, romantics, and empirists cited both presumed lived experiences and unsubstantiated accounts to support their claims that native Americans, Africans, and others lacked civil society and the corresponding concepts of property and lordship. These authoritative views of the other have formed what Talal Asad has termed the authoritative discourse. This discourse has had two principal features. First, it has been based on a combination of facts and hearsay, history and legend. Second, the authoritative discourse has consistently eliminated the possibility of any radically opposed utterances or perspectives.[73] Its primary function has been to define the role and place of concerned non-European communities in the global order.[74]

The State of Nature in British Thought

The rapid development of natural history in seventeenth-century Britain was partly due to the decline of the influence of religious thinking in politics. During the Restoration, scientific knowledge and natural history had overthrown reliance on religious thought. Religious zealots were replaced in public life by philosophers of moderation who relied chiefly on rationalism and empiricism as their sources of knowledge. However, the new philosophies never abandoned Christian values and their symbols.[75] Nor did they abandon the inherited view of Africans and native Americans as wild men-in-nature, unattached to their lands and incapable of contractual relations.

John Locke's contribution to this philosophy included, but was not limited to, a general consideration of individualism and property and a theory of contract as the basis of social formation. In Locke's theory, there was a direct relation between property and contract. Property was natural to the individual in the same way that the color of eyes and skin and mental capacity were to the body. It was also created by improvement through labor. Once obtained, property was exchanged through contract. The contract was the cause of all rights and obligations among individuals. It was the basis of exchange of property as well as the initial convergence of wills. As such, the contract allowed individuals to join their property and form social entities, the basis of the civil polity.[76]

The contract was for Locke the metaphor of origin. It made it possible for rational individuals to transcend the original state of nature, to bind others, and to accept obligations to them. But not all individuals or peoples were capable of contracting. This capacity was the domain only of peoples endowed with natural reason. Only such individuals could trust one another to honor their mutual obligations. In contrast, peoples living in the state of nature could not trust, nor should they be trusted. Locke cited the barbarians of the Americas as an example of nonrational people who lagged behind Europe in mental maturity. Citing the works of Josephus

Acosta, a Jesuit missionary who spent time in the Americas, Locke claimed that the "men" in the wilderness of Brazil lived in nature, subject to no laws:

> There are great and apparent conjectures, says he, that these men, speaking of Peru, for a long time had neither Kings nor Commonwealths, but lived in troops, as they do to this day in Florida, the Cheriquanas, those of Bresil, and many other nations, which have no certain kings, but as occasions offered in peace or war, they chose their captains as they pleased.[77]

When rapid transformations in technology and the political repercussions of revolutionary changes in France and elsewhere affected the cultural and economic conditions that had provided the context for social contractarians like John Locke, new philosophers emerged on the European scene. Within the new intellectual environment, philosophy and political thought assumed new dimensions. The preeminence of production and output, a consequence of industrialization, introduced political economy into the body of knowledge. In this new climate, the "achievements of white men" served once again as evidence of Western superiority and the rationale for imperialism.

A precursor to this trend, David Hume prepared the blow against the theories of social contract, both in England (John Locke) and on the Continent (Jean-Jacques Rousseau in France). Hume rigorously applied empiricism to ethical and political questions only to validate the fiction of exotic foreign peoples living in a state of nature.[78] In explaining the relevance of customs to political beliefs and institutions, he argued that there were sets of beliefs that allowed humans to "establish harmony between the course of nature and the succession of ideas." As a system, custom effected a correspondence between resemblance and contiguity on the one hand, and the force of ideas on the other. The principles embedded in customs were "so necessary to the subsistence of our species, and the regulation of our conduct" that they were indispensable to the understanding of human nature.[79]

The subsistence of the species depended in part on the interrelations between customs and the "notion of rights." In this context, Hume justified European imperialism, the transatlantic slave trade, and colonialism by offering an explanation based on achievements: "I am apt to suspect," Hume wrote, "the Negroes and in general all the other species of men to be naturally inferior to the Whites. There never was a civilized nation of any other complexion than White, nor even any individual eminent either in action or speculation."[80]

French Troglodytes

Beginning in the sixteenth century, the contribution of French theorists to the development of political and legal thought bore the imprint of René Descartes and other prominent French philosophers. Descartes made his mark by capturing his generation's discomfort with the heightened authority of traditionalists in French philosophy. His greatest influence rested in his destruction of traditional and religion-inspired "absolutes" as well as the secularization of the religious notion of natural law. He also introduced experimentation and rationality as method. His assaults on tradition as the foundation of philosophy and ideology made him a spokesperson for those who rejected dependence on established scientific methods. His advocacy of the good sense of the scientist as an observer appealed to other scientists.[81] It is Descartes's departure from tradition that laid the foundation for the "enlightenment movement." As a consequence of his posture toward authority and tradition, the Enlightenment philosophers and literary figures focused mostly on the relationship between human nature and an unspecifiable universal reality.[82]

In the eighteenth century, Enlightenment philosophers, who self-consciously criticized religious absolutes and traditions, failed to extend their criticisms to imperialism. At a time when French involvement overseas became a dominant reality, they seldom condemned slavery and other forms of oppression of non-Europeans, also the result of absolutism and the abuse of the "natural rights" of indigenous peoples. Instead, many Enlightenment philosophers condoned various forms of imperialism. For instance, Charles-Louis de Secondat, better known as Montesquieu, skillfully combined rational philosophy and law to further disenfranchise non-Europeans. In justifying his position in *The Spirit of the Law,* Montesquieu argued that all human beings shared the transcendental and universal impulse (or a tendency) to regulate their relations among themselves as individuals, as well as with society and their creator. The impulse that guided humans in their relation to a creator was a certain natural tendency equally shared by all. Thus, it was a foregone conclusion that in "the state of nature," the state in which the creator made the world, "men" were born equal.[83]

According to Montesquieu, humans evolved from the state of nature at a differing pace, depending on their mastery of reason. As a result, societies could not remain equal because they were not equally endowed.[84] In *Persian Letters,* where he illustrated the causes of social and cultural differentiation, the lifestyle of the good troglodytes served as an analogy of the state where virtue and nature were identical.[85] Montesquieu maintained that the natural impulses of the troglodytes had been lost to ambition and the desire for wealth and luxury in the state of war and contention—his analogy for modern society. Once lost to human ambition and desires, the state of nature could not be regained. The only solution, according to him, was to recover it through regulation, that is, positive law.[86]

Montesquieu assigned to positive laws a role different from that of the law of the natural order of things. The purpose of positive law was to maintain harmony, then justice. The justice promoted by positive law was justifiably an unequal justice. Montesquieu properly identified this brand of justice as legal justice, which he opposed to equal justice. It is in this connection that he justified the subordination of the wife to the husband and the subjection of the peoples he perceived as subhumans (native Americans and Africans) to Europeans.

Montesquieu's contribution to the understanding of governments and their diversity is also indicative of his view of non-Europeans. He attributed the different forms of government to climatic, geographical, and cultural differences among the peoples and nations of the world. This relativism seems anti-imperialist on the surface, but he was a consistent relativist only as far as European and a limited number of foreign cultures were concerned. Thus, referring to Africans in the context of colonial conquest, Montesquieu denied them any humanity: "It is impossible that we suppose that these peoples are humans; because, if we suppose that they are humans, we would start thinking that we are not Christians ourselves."[87]

Although extreme, Montesquieu's posture was not unusual. The decline in prestige of the clergy and nobility and the rise of the bourgeois elements from the Third Estate to positions of power and influence had affected popular perceptions of French colonies and their inhabitants.[88] Before the overthrow of the clergy and the nobility, the Third Estate was made up of merchants, artisans, peasants, clerks, and the like. With the advances of the bourgeoisie and the spread of mercantilism, the Third Estate disintegrated, giving rise to a strong and politically powerful class distinct from the remaining poor segment of the population. Merchants, artisans, and shopkeepers, all members of the new capitalist class, considered themselves above members of society who remained in poverty.[89]

French intellectuals and writers who emerged from this situation posited themselves as the depositary of the knowledge of moral standards for French society and others as well. The "philosophes" worked comfortably with the new division of society of which they were products. They began to attribute to wealth a social prestige that they linked to the virtues of hard work and intelligence.[90] In the eyes of the *hommes de lettres*, literacy, like wealth, indicated the level of reasonableness. The mind responsible for a genial work or literary proficiency was superior to those of peoples who had remained in poverty. Reason was therefore attributed to mental capacity materialized in writing skills and entrepreneurship.[91] In this light, the majority of philosophers viewed the bourgeois class as the conscience of society and humanity.

Faith in the reasonable individual combined with lack of confidence in the "crowd" (populace) motivated the philosopher to request that the people be enlightened (educated) about the desirable values of society. It was believed that with education there would be more reasonable people and a decrease in the number of irrational members of society. Even egalitarians like Rousseau and Condorcet, who distrusted philosophers more than they did the people, viewed in education a means to elevate the people to a position equal to that of the enlightened bourgeoisie.[92]

The view of the nonliterate as irrational was transposed to the relations between Europeans and non-Europeans. Jurists and philosophers almost unanimously perceived in the rule of reason and commerce the means by which the benefits of civilization would be brought to the "noncivilized" world. Because reason was an endowment of the enlightened Europeans, it was appropriate for the wealthy and educated of Europe to be the agents of civilization overseas, and to determine the ways in which their mission should be accomplished.

The turbulent revolutionary years did not alter the imperialist mentality of the French bourgeoisie in the nineteenth century. Instead, after the defeat of Napoleon, French expansion was actively supported and promoted as a way of recovering national pride. Heavy reliance on the state to promote commerce in post-Napoleonic France testified to the fact that the French bourgeoisie's belief in free enterprise and individual freedoms did not conflict with the quest for markets even if this increased the role of the state overseas. Thus colonial conquest was in perfect accord with the rationalism of the paternalist state.

Rational Imperialism in Germany

In Germany, philosophical speculation was invigorated by the sixteenth-century split within the church. This intellectual movement was reinforced by the political role assumed by that country toward the end of the eighteenth century. The emerging German role itself was due to the technological innovations that occurred in Prussia. These impressive intellectual and technological advances produced a generation of rationalists and romantics whose ideas justified German imperialism.

Martin Luther's departure from Catholic orthodoxy and the Reformation that followed was one of many assaults on absolutism and despotism during the sixteenth century. Initially, the assault was limited to the prejudices of orthodoxy against reform (and later) secularism. The effects of Luther's movement and the ensuing religious persecutions led romantics and rationalists to place their trust in freedom of thought, both religious and secular. They hoped that freedom of thought would generate not only consensus but also the rule of reason among the people.[93]

After Luther, however, freedom of thought became "the corollary of the faith in reason,"[94] when the proponents of the new "religions" developed a political agenda. This agenda consisted of creating the foundations for a political formation acceptable to all Germans. The new political formation would be the result of a consensus guided by reason. Reason, they thought, was the best intellectual tool available to humans in the management of their affairs. It was, however, the modernization that put Germany in a dominant position among the industrializing European states that determined the final outlook of the rationalists and romantics. As a result, the actual formulation of the political system occurred in the later stages of this philosophical movement.

Gotthold Ephraim Lessing first provided the general frame for its conception. In *Dialogues for Freemasons,* Lessing argued that whatever consensus might guide German polity must be the result of rational thinking. All Germans should be able to live in unity under one state, whose role would be reduced to giving way to the rule of reason.[95] While Lessing speculated on the role of the state, he left out the identity of the reasonable citizen, the purveyor of consensus.

As happened in France, the belief that reason belonged to the educated led theorists, including Immanuel Kant, to separate reason from the general customs and manners of the people.[96] Contrary to reason, which is universal and not subject to variation, the argument went, manners and customs differ greatly according to geography and climate and the degree of instruction. By implication, if the variations in the customs of the people in themselves did not create hierarchies, geography, climate, and instruction brought out the universal element—that is, reason—in some individuals more than they did in others. Those individuals, in particular the urban educated elite, were urged to assume leadership positions within the state.

With Kant, it became theoretically tenable to posit that only the enlightened elements of society possessed the eternal and universal reason.[97] The elite were held to possess all "those elements shared by all men," and embodied by reason, through which society reaches out to the laws of nature. Kant believed that the laws of universal reason were inseparable from the mind that constructed them. In other words, even though they are inherent in nature, the laws of universal reason were constructions of the mind.[98] According to his reasoning, truth is ontologically relative, but only the trained minds of the elite can lead to its discovery.

The division of citizens into nonenlightened and enlightened created a precedent for German perception of and attitudes toward non-Europeans. In the nineteenth century, when Germany took an interest in the colonial scramble in Africa, its colonial elite followed in the footsteps of their French and British counterparts in perpetuating the belief that the salvation of Africa depended entirely on its subordination to Europe."

Thus, in considering its duties toward German colonialists, the state assumed a political role equal to that of any major European power. Beginning with Bismarck, it was officially maintained that the duties of the German state toward its citizens extended beyond its national boundaries. This new perception of the role of the state was embraced by German political theorists, who based justifications of extraterritorial and colonial interventions on three factors: economic necessity, military readiness (especially after the Thirty Years' War), and social stability.[99] The benefit of colonial intervention was therefore linked to the German standard of living.[100]

From Colonial Notebooks to Science

The authoritative discourse was grounded neither in the most empirically credible evidence nor in the majority view. As demonstrated in Locke's case, for instance, the post-Reformation theoretical abandonment of the biblical and mythical images of Africans and others did not result in methodological (empirical) rigor. Locke fulfilled the requirement of evidence on a question so crucial to his theory — the existence of a state of nature — by quoting from one speculative source: Josephus Acosta. A self-proclaimed empiricist and a rationalist, Locke neither visited the concerned communities nor verified the accuracy of his source, nor even checked his information against competing views. In fact, Acosta's account was contradicted by those of more credible contemporary missionaries, among them Antonio Montesinos and Las Casas.[101]

That Locke's "man-in-nature," constructed from myths, has been so frequently incorporated in theory is indicative of the fact that in his day the discursive norms regarding non-Europeans depended upon the blurring of facts and legends. The majority of those who offered authoritative views on American Indians and Africa often relied on travel reports. This dependence was doubly unfortunate because the majority of European conquerors, travelers, and explorers lacked the scientific training of latter-day social scientists (who prepared the ground for further study of African societies and planted the seeds of the discriminatory policies of the colonial era).

Hume's thinking was also heavily affected by evolutionary if not racist doctrines that were entirely inconsistent with his own methodology of induction and skepticism: "In Jamaica indeed they talk of one negroe as a man of parts and learning; but 'tis likely he is admired for very slender accomplishments like a parrot who speaks a few words plainly."[102] Obviously, his thinking regarding slavery and imperialism was overdetermined by his sense of superiority and self-righteousness. This attitude resulted from the dominant British mentality, before and after Queen Victoria.[103] During this era, legal professionals and political theorists advocated free trade and civil rights at home and, simultaneously, European sovereignty over distant peoples. In response, European policy makers steadfastly held to negative ideas regarding the conquered in order to justify the means to conquest and, later, colonization.

An advocate of polygeny — the theory of the separate origins of the races — Hume held several political positions, including in the colonial office. As a result, his pronouncements regarding imperial matters carried some weight. One such pronouncement concerned the role of the state with respect to imperialism. Here, Hume emphasized both the role of established powers and the rule of laws in the civil polity. He then advocated a stronger state role in establishing civil laws throughout the empire to bring civility to those who lived by inferior ethical standards: anarchy and the rule of force.

Montesquieu's *Persian Letters,* like Locke's and Hume's treatises, formed an authoritative discourse that provided the methodological and ideological model for analyzing events and facts concerning the other.[104] The power of their discourse rested in its ability to represent myths as historical impression or evidence and then to posit them as a guide to the present. As noted by Eric Cheyfitz in *The Poetics of Imperialism,* that European present included domestic political turmoil as well as the pressure to pacify unsubmissive natives.[105] It was only convenient, therefore, for theorists and politicians to establish discursive order between these two phenomena. In the process, they duplicated their (negative) myths regarding the undesirable masses and their (positive) images of the noble and entrepreneurial classes and applied both sets of perceptions to the imperial context.[106]

Other interested Europeans "inherited a view of foreign peoples which was part-fantasy and part-hearsay, little more than an exotic fiction."[107] Their view not only exposed the venality of European life, it also served to justify religious conquests and economic exploitation.[108] Above all, theorists and publicists reached their conclusions on the basis of methods that found European "reason" to be the universal component of thought, thus present in all humans.

Then they advocated conquest as a means to its redemption among those other peoples. More importantly, the authoritative myth that portrayed non-Europeans as needy found its way back to colonial representations of Africans and others.

AUTHORITATIVE MYTHS

During the nineteenth century, colonialists and their allies in the scientific community interpreted the Darwinian postulate that human nature is uniform and universal to support the racist theories that justified colonialism.[109] They did so over the objections of prominent scientists, including Darwin himself, who disavowed the racist abuses of science by colonial apologists. Despite these credible dissents and objections, the interested parties upheld the most simplistic and malicious views of the other. Moreover, although by this time a great deal was known about other continents and peoples, the new colonial adventurers and explorers aptly reinforced past racist stereotypes and epithets in the collective mind.

In the new formulation, racial and cultural diversities were flaunted as evidence of the other's inferiority. By the nineteenth century, for instance, the British thought themselves to be at the top of a racial and cultural hierarchy. These Victorians, according to Ronald Robinson, placed "the Americans and other 'striving, go-ahead' Anglo-Saxons" next in line.[110] In this succession,

> Latin peoples were thought to come next, though far behind. Much lower still stood the vast Oriental communities of Asia and North Africa where progress appeared unfortunately to have been crushed for centuries by military despotisms and smothered under passive religions. Lowest of all stood the "aborigines" whom it was thought had never learned enough social discipline to pass from the family and tribe to the making of the state.[111]

In short, the presumption of uniformity in the evolution of universal history led the proponents of imperial conquest to conclude that the cultural variations observed elsewhere and the physical traits of the other were caused by some internal (mental capacity) and external (environmental) defects.

White Legend: Dark Continent

Explorers, adventurers, scientists, and colonial authorities effectively constructed the myth of the "Dark Continent" by deliberate rein-

forcement of erroneous information. The idea that Africans lived in
darkness, needing models or light, was created between the beginning of the slave trade and colonial settlement. This myth originated in philosophical concepts and deliberate manipulation of scientific knowledge in conjunction with the intensification of colonial
conquest. As a result, it was unaffected by the weight that empirical
evidence carried in scientific research; it reached the level of fantasy
among fervent imperialists between the Enlightenment and the industrial revolution.[112]

The myth of the Dark Continent was finally popularized during
the nineteenth century by various media, including travel reports.
Once, religious travels were the means of fulfilling the mission of
the church. The ethos of travel was to explore and prepare the Christian missionary to deal with unknown, evil-minded savages. Exploration was considered by the church to be a voyage inside the wan-
dering souls to be saved. These attitudes changed in the nineteenth
century with the completion of conquest and the need for colonies
and resources. The new trend was toward legend that justified occupation and expropriation. Explorers and adventurers wrote accounts and tales of supposed and actual encounters with Africans
in lengthy and stereotype-ridden notebooks, diaries, and reports.[113]
The result was a host of tales, mostly fictional, that provided the
public psyche with caricatures of Africans that bolstered the racial
prejudices left over from the days of the slave trade.[114] The objective of such tales was to condition the domestic European mood to
accept the crimes committed against Africans during conquest.[115]

During this era, the new view of human development was conveniently derived from the episteme of a scientific knowledge that
asserted a hierarchy among the species in the guise of enhancing
European "understanding" of the other. In this context, ethnology,
sociology, and anthropology provided scientific support to the notion that Africa had no history, thus lending legitimacy to the myth
of the Dark Continent.[116] The authoritative anthropological and ethnological views offered images of witches, wild men, and animals.[117]
Africa was also said to be inhabited by "subhumans with tails,"
"idolators and cannibals," or worse.[118] Africans were "little better
than brutes," with deficient mental powers or in a state of infancy.
This supposed mental immaturity of the natives provided the ratio-

nale for European paternalism: protecting them from the bad influences to which they could easily succumb.

Even European critics of imperialism did not transcend the notion that Africa was in need of "light." The nineteenth-century abolitionists who advocated the end of slavery also favored the threefold policy of commerce, Christianity, and emancipation. Many of them believed that Africans were in the main technically barbaric, at a preliterary stage of sociological development.[119] In fact, the abolitionists of the antislavery movement and other philanthropists insisted on a European trusteeship for Africans. They provided the necessary guidelines for such a system at the nineteenth-century Berlin African Conference.[120]

From Science to Imperial Advocacy

Most nineteenth-century social scientists combined science and politics to facilitate imperial pursuits by joining private or public groups with interests in the colonies.[121] The most committed to this end provided opportunistic conclusions to their sponsors to meet burning needs. Among those who ventured into Africa, description of local groups depended upon the particular designs of the moment. Predictably, the "more enlightened" of the natives, those in danger of being overpowered by "more brutish" ones, were the allies of the conquerors. Many such groups had entered into treaties or agreements with Europeans. As it often happened, the colonialists always intervened to "protect" the "defenseless" communities. Then they claimed their actions to be consistent with keeping the peace, in accordance with the mission of civilization.[122]

Francis Galton was among the scientist explorers who made the trip to Africa. He was an "inventor or innovator in the fields of statistics, meteorology, geography, heredity and eugenics, and criminology." A zealous scientist, he counted Darwin, Grove, Hooker, Broderick, and Spencer among his friends. Most important of all, Galton was an astute politician who knew that sophisticated knowledge was required in order to impose power. In his case, this knowledge involved the natives' character and customs.[123] In 1885, thanks to his travel and work among the natives of Egypt, Syria, and South West Africa, Galton assumed the presidency of the Royal Anthropological Institute.[124]

Galton's trip to South West Africa, in 1851, was sponsored by the Royal Geographical Society and the British colonial secretary.[125] When he and other British explorers arrived in the region, the Herero and Nama were engaged in territorial wars. Typically, Galton viewed in this local struggle an opportunity for Great Britain to broker the peace it desired in order to establish itself in the region. He therefore set out to find the "natives most susceptible to European values." When he found the first group, he wrote in his diary:

> A row of seven dirty squalid natives came to meet us.... They had Hottentot features, but were of a darker colour, and most ill-looking appearance: some had trousers, some coats of skins, and they clicked, and howled, and chattered, and behaved like baboons. This was my first impression, and that of all of us; but as the time came when, by force of comparison, I looked on these same fellows as a sort of link to civilization.[126]

Galton's diary exposes a familiar duplicity whose only purpose was to transform the "savages" into imperial subjects. He also understood his role to be a provider of tools of conquest to the merchants and future British investors. He was careful to anticipate the utility of involvement in local power struggles and sided with local groups in accordance with perceived imperial and personal interests. He was careful to rationalize his behavior by reiterating existing ethnic and racial stereotypes. The following diary entry is typical in this regard:

> This is exactly what I should conceive of the Ovampo; they evidently have strong local and personal attachments; they are also very nationalist, and proud of their country. I should feel but little compassion if I saw all the Damaras under the hands of a slave owner, for they could hardly become more wretched than they now are, and might be made much less mischievous; but it would be a crying shame to enslave the Ovampo.[127]

Although he expressed dismay at the level of social and political sophistication of the "Ovampo," it is obvious that he intended to maintain distance between Europe and Africa. He had also determined that the British should side with this African group in the event of conflict. Finally, Galton engaged in deliberate deceit in order to manipulate local conflicts and to pressure "collaborators" into "treaties of protection." Such treaties, we shall see, amounted to a transfer of sovereignty. In the end, Galton bullied Africans into submission through a code of laws called Pax Galtoniana.[128]

While Pax Galtoniana gave British colonialists the access they needed in the region, it was not sufficient to explain the exclusive privileges they claimed. In order to justify the exclusion of rival powers, Galton and other British reporters made unflattering commentaries about other Europeans as well. Thus, the British criticized the German attitude toward Africans and professed to be better suited to protect African interests. The French joined the British in their objections to the unfair treatment of Africans by the Germans and the Boers—Europeans of Dutch or French Huguenot descent. The British claimed that the behavior of their German and Boer rivals had a negative impact in the region, in particular in regard to Africans' perception of their "masters." Although British and French commentators often viewed German and Boer explorers and settlers in the same light, the Dutch settlers suffered the most negative reports:

> The Boers do not behave well to these tribes who were independent before the Boers intended on their domains, in consequence of which they have had continually to struggle with one tribe or the other in war. These natives are compelled to work. Some are paid and some are not. They buy the children of some natives and in war take as many as they can, and [the captives] generally [remain] till they die in a state of slavery.[129]

SUMMARY

The structure of the modern authoritative discourse regarding political authority in the international order originated in the Middle Ages. It has since been essentially Eurocentric. This Western disposition was not altered by the Reformation's rejection of Catholic traditions and absolutism. Neither did the intellectual movements that followed depart from this trend. Likewise, the post-Enlightenment interest in evolution did not correct Western perceptions of the other as inferior, but only caused a transmutation of the original ecclesiastical dichotomy of savior/fallen into one of civilized/noncivilized.

In the ideological instance, the Christian mission was replaced by the duty of the strong (also the "chosen") to attend the weak (the "fallen") and "needy" for the salvation/benefit of the latter. Later, the duty to assist transmuted into trusteeship in the name of civilization. In the following chapter I shall demonstrate that this ideology has been central to the structure of international law, which has depended upon various forms of three essential assumptions. The first has been the right of Christians (later the West) to sovereignty by virtue of faith, reason, and self-interest. The second assumption has been the Western duty to create and maintain (an international) order by all means (including force and political bribery) in the universal interest. Finally, it has been assumed that non-European communities have the obligation to adhere to the norms of the present order as a result of their emergence from the distant (Western) past where they have so far existed. In a very subtle way, the West is still assumed to possess intellect, reason, science, and wisdom. In contrast, it is still feared or suspected that the immature, unreformed other(s) may act through instinct and confusion. In short, the others may still need guidance, even against their own volition. Then as now, however, the aim of international law has been to justify or facilitate Western hegemony and its power to exploit the other(s).[130]

2

Partial Recognition to the Barbarous

The majority of international legal theorists have agreed that sixteenth- and seventeenth-century European religious and political struggles greatly influenced political theory and law. They have also claimed that these events helped to determine modern praxis. Specifically, they have maintained that the juridical notion of sovereignty has its origin in those European struggles, and that the Treaty of Westphalia, which ended the Thirty Years' War in 1648, established it as an essential principle of international politics. There is less accord, however, on the extent of the application of the principle of sovereignty outside of Europe. In particular, theorists have disagreed about whether European powers did, or were bound to, recognize their non-European partners as sovereigns in the course of their interactions.

The theoretical disagreement over the extent of non-European sovereignty has been grounded in distorted views of both the character of international law and the evolution of international relations within the Western-dominated international order. In this chapter I contend that the modern law of nations has been proposed by a select group of nations, not as the ethical basis of a universal order, but as a means to hegemony. As a result, international law has been composed of morally deficient and unrelated, albeit complementary, principles and norms. The legal provisions that have applied to non-Europeans have been culturally specific, enabling

Europe to undermine the other's subjectivity and sovereignty in the international order.

EPISTEMIC STRUCTURES

The debate over non-European sovereignty has been central to modern international law. Since medieval popes declared the universe unified under their authority, canonists and secularists, natural rights advocates and positivists have discussed the extent and appropriateness of Western attitudes toward the political authority of non-Europeans. While their arguments have varied in their perspectives and conclusions, most have omitted the importance of non-European alterity to the structures and hierarchies of international law. From the mid–sixteenth century onward, the relationship between European powers and non-Europeans was constructed upon the twin principles of either denying or suppressing the subjectivity of the latter. These principles manifested themselves in two related developments: the diminution of the juridical capacity of the other, a necessary condition for Western hegemony; and the institution of extraterritoriality, that is, the application of Western laws outside of Europe.

Jurisprudential Flaws

Most jurists have approached the question of sovereignty in the international order by examining the texts of the agreements entered into by Europeans and non-Europeans during the eras of conquest, informal empire, and formal colonial rule. The majority have relied on jurisprudential interpretations of the relevant juridical norms, legal principles, and doctrines.[1] Although they have maintained that this approach is the most dependable, their general conclusion has been that it is at best problematic. They have identified three interpretative difficulties that mandate analytical prudence: ethical, cultural, and ideological. The first arises with the comparison of past juridical norms and current ones. Green, in particular, argues that all juridical norms must be understood as they were perceived by the parties at the time of their interactions.[2] His argument coincides with Alexandrowicz's insistence that contemporary international law differs greatly from that of the past with regard to the forms and procedures of treaty making, the capacity of the parties involved, and the principles applicable to those parties.[3]

In general, twentieth-century European courts, tribunals, and other institutions of adjudication have upheld as legitimate the rights acquired by settlers, trading companies, and colonial states in the former empires prior to this century. One of the most celebrated precedents is a 1928 decision by the Permanent Court of Arbitration, a panel created by the 1899 Hague Convention for the pacific resolution of disputes. In this case between the Netherlands and the United States concerning sovereignty over the Island of Palmas (Miangas), the Swiss judge, Max Huber, found in favor of the Dutch that the island formed an integral part of the Netherlands. Judge Huber claimed that if the seventeenth-century agreements invoked by the Netherlands concerning the island did not constitute actual titles according to current international norms, they were "nonetheless facts which the law must in certain circumstances take into account."[4]

Regarding the second and third interpretative difficulties, defenders of the Palmas and similar rulings warn against the ideological and cultural baggage that often color the interpretation of historically specific legal expressions. In this case, Judge Huber professed strict jurisprudential interpretation and a reluctance to apply current rules of treaty making to past situations. Accordingly, he construed the relationship between Dutch nationals and representative Palmas natives to imply an acceptable power relationship. He also held that the treaties and other agreements between these two parties had effect because the parties were as equal as then permitted by international custom.[5] Judge Huber's opinion was that the conditions under which the Dutch obtained their rights over the islands were governed by the proper international norms of the time, and that those norms must be respected by contemporary theorists and practitioners.

Alexandrowicz is among the theorists who adhere to the dominant Western interpretations of past international agreements typified by the Palmas ruling. He contends that, prior to the nineteenth century, there existed a contractual equality between Europeans and native peoples based on a cultural parity among the major regions of the world. He premises his argument on the fact that, prior to the nineteenth century, the African and Asian trading partners of European merchants were fully autonomous, that is, sovereign in their own lands, and that they had independently developed comprehensive juridical norms. Specifically, he points out that Asians and other non-Europeans governed themselves according to their own centuries' old legal systems and commercial codes. These legal systems and commercial codes were founded on distinct ethical norms different from those of contemporary Europeans.[6]

Indeed, several regions of the world had contained autonomous and semiautonomous international political and economic systems. Asia, the object of inter-European competition until the nineteenth century, was characterized by a well-integrated political economy, complete with major trade routes, ports, and commercial instruments. The region surrounding the port of Malacca is a case in point. Until the fifteenth century, the port of Malacca played a central role in Asian commercial activities as well as in the development of commercial instruments pertaining to international trade.[7] During this era, four harbormasters handled incoming and outgoing boats. Each collected duties on the merchandise emanating from an assigned region: Europe, China, and other parts of Asia. They also provided godowns (warehouses and landing docks) for the storage of goods, as well as lodging for the owners.[8]

The state of affairs in Malacca changed drastically when the Portuguese captured the port in 1511.[9] In this case, and in others like it, Alexandrowicz fails to account for the shifts in the balance of power that began to occur during the rise of Western hegemony. More importantly, he gives little notice to the erosion of the juridical and political foundations of regional autonomous and semiautonomous political economies following the discovery of the New World.

Furthermore, while Alexandrowicz recognizes different cultural contexts to agreements between Europeans and native peoples, he makes two erroneous assumptions about the circumstances of treaty making before the nineteenth century. The first is that Europeans and others had the same legal frame of reference. This assumption is undermined by the fact that most agreements made reference to juridical notions that were specifically Western. Moreover, they were written in languages inaccessible to the native populations. The second mistaken assumption is that European values and traditions are the norms of any judicial or extrajudicial interpretation. He insists that "it is possible to solve most of the problems of interpretation by reliance on the legal definitions employed by the classic writers" — for instance, Gentili, Vattel, Grotius, Wolff, and Vitoria.[10] He refers to Asian and African legal terms as foreign to the established norms of international law.[11]

Alexandrowicz is not alone in implying cultural parity and acceptable power relations between Europeans and native peoples. Other Western jurists from a range of theoretical perspectives have endorsed the basis of such rulings as the Palmas case, despite the fact that the supporting principles of sovereignty and national equality have meant whatever European powers intended them to mean. Green, for instance, notes that European powers diminished the rights of indigenous populations to full sovereignty, that is, to conduct their affairs as independent nations. He argues that the colonists acted as they did primarily out of necessity; they were pressured by the circumstances of discovery and motivated by their superior technology. He also insists that, in any case, the colonists' actions conformed to international custom. In this vein, he claims that the power of the original inhabitants of conquered territories "to dispose of the soil, at their own will, to whomsoever they pleased, was denied by the original fundamental principle, that discovery gave exclusive title to those who made it."[12] Green claims that the only nations relevant for the purposes of international law were European nations and native powers recognized by them.

Even according to the terms of international law, such claims are erroneous on several accounts. First, while European colonists formed their attitudes toward indigenous populations through daily contacts, they derived their views of native rights to sovereignty, dignity, and property from the general philosophic and cultural environment of papal proclamations and the Enlightenment movement. This Eurocentric movement shaped all contemporary discourses, including legal ones. For instance, the legal concept of entitlement by discovery of previously inhabited lands was and remains essential to a distinct Eurocentric juridical discourse. It is difficult to believe that native peoples shared the view that their land had to await discovery by Europeans in order to emerge as a legal entity. Second, the norms applied to conquest by European conquerors were neither customary on the continent of their origin nor reflective of globally accepted international norms. Finally, the extrajudicial techniques, particularly the legal instruments used by Europeans in their interactions with the other, only served to facilitate European hegemony.

The colonists applied their own domestic laws to the conquered, less through persuasion and negotiation than by deceit, coercion, and, more significantly, unilateral interpretation of so-called mutual agreements.

Enlightened Univocalism

I argued in chapter 1 that the discovery of the New World marked the beginning of new forms of alterity in the international order.[13] This process began when Pope Alexander VI incorporated New World entities into the Christian universe by placing them under the full political authority of kings anointed by the Vatican.[14] During the seventeenth century, European theorists and publicists rid the international order of its ecclesiastical premises in favor of competing theories of international relations, complete with their own ethos. According to the new theories, the Christian universe, symbolized by the Kingdom of Heaven, was succeeded by the modern international order, dominated by burgeoning European powers, independent of the church.[15] During the Enlightenment, European intellectuals began to construe universalism to mean, initially, a totality (i.e., the universal order) and, subsequently, the application of the European model to all instances.[16]

Modern international law emerged in this context as a distinct discipline, separate from political theory and canon law. No longer expressed in the classical mode of knowledge, it introduced systems analysis and probability into the study of international relations by breaking away from the comparison between the Kingdom of Heaven and the international order.[17] Yet the new science established its own hierarchies in international relations when it incorporated the other into a European-dominated order. It was aided by the Enlightenment-created metaphysical distance, based on geography and culture, between the European self/subject of the law and its object, the non-European other. Indeed, during their inception, the law of nations and its interpretative traditions reflected other Enlightenment metaphysical processes. They depended upon the myth that the Western *logos*, and its ethos, were not only the ultimate standard of reason, they were the universal standard. The Western view of intercommunal relations and its norms were said to be the sole standard applicable to all parts of the world.[18]

The emerging law reflected highly differentiated and unequal power relations among European powers on the one hand, and between Europe and other continents on the other. With regard to the other, these international legal norms not only represented, in the words of Edward Said, the "univocal authority of Europe," they constituted Europe as their sole subject and the rest of the world as their objects. To paraphrase Said, European publicists and practitioners intended the dispositions of the law of nations to be both intelligible and effective, to clearly define its hierarchies and to provide the appropriate instruments for realizing them.[19] The rules, principles, and doctrines of international law were specifically intended to facilitate European expansion.[20] According to Olive P. Dickason, the legal principles during the post-Reformation era were, in rank of importance, "those of freedom of the seas, and rights of discovery and trade, rather than those of universal justice."[21]

Finally, international law provided the ethical and philosophical justifications for European imperialism through an arbitrary association of its own signs.[22] We shall see, for instance, that European publicists and practitioners construed sovereignty to imply inter alia the bearer of full freedoms and liberties, but they attributed this status solely to Christians/Europeans. In contrast, theorists construed non-European subjectivity, or sovereignty, contextually in accordance with the specific needs of European powers and colonists.

In sum, the distance that presumably separated the various communities of the international order has underpinned the structures of international relations and law since the Enlightenment. These structures are typified by the gradation of status and dignity of participating member communities and the application of different sets of norms to them. The dominant European position was that non-Europeans were primitives or savages who, although incorporated into the international order, were not yet ready for full subjectivity or sovereignty.[23] Consequently, both theorists and practitioners linked non-European sovereignty, and later self-determination, to a specific stage of development on a progression toward the European model.[24]

Unequal Burden under *Jus Gentium*

The international legal norms applied by Europeans in the course of their relations with the other have not contained the systematically arranged body of rules followed by European nations or their courts when considering international relations within Europe. Nor have the principles involved in these rules been similar to those relating to the relations among Europeans outside their continent of origin. The norms applied to intra-European relations (interactions among European communities within the boundaries of Western Christendom) formed a body of law known as *jus gentium*. By design, this law differed from the rules and procedures applicable in inter-European relations (interactions among Christian merchants, settlers, and adventurers abroad). These two sets of laws bore no resemblance to yet a third, which governed the dynamics between Westerners and non-Europeans.

The guiding force in the creation of the third set of norms was a political consensus among Christian powers regarding non-Christians' rights to *imperium, dominium,* commerce, and trade. This consensus was formed in several stages, over a period of centuries. During the initial stage, in the Middle Ages, Christian raiders, and the rulers who commissioned them, began to reject the dispositions of canon law as the basis of their activities outside of Europe. Instead, for reasons of convenience, they preferred to act under papal guidance, which, unlike canon law, sanctioned their extracontinental actions. The Christian rulers who ordered European expeditions obtained papal sanction for them, as well as absolution of their sins. In 1434, for instance, a group of Portuguese sailors, acting on behalf of their prince, captured slaves when they rounded Cape Bejador on the west coast of Africa. Although delighted with the prize, the prince was also anxious to clear his conscience. He sent a special message to the pope asking for forgiveness of his sins and expressing a desire to engage in future raids, and even conquest, in Africa.[25] The pope not only welcomed the "crusade," he forgave in advance the sins of Christians who intended to pursue similar activities.[26]

Although initially isolated, papal interventions in earthly matters multiplied during the first two centuries after the discovery of the New World. By the time Christian powers had circumnavigated the globe and systematic conquest had replaced looting and raiding, canon law was no longer referred to as the basis of Christian involvement in overseas commerce and power struggles. Instead, papal proclamations provided the discursive structures for European conquest abroad.

During the second stage of the formation of the political consensus in Europe, from the seventeenth century onward, theologians and secularists built upon papal ordinances, envisioning a new hierarchy of cultures and civilizations. They presumed that vital and indelible differences separated Christians from so-called Mahomedians and heathens. European intellectuals supported the Christian conquests in the New World and elsewhere on the grounds that the perpetrators and their rulers were bringing the True Faith to the native populations. They claimed that the actions of the colonists were guided by a certain natural reason that resided only in Christianity. In contrast to Europeans, indigenous populations were believed to possess inferior religions, social habits, moral sentiments, and political structures. In consequence, their communities were deemed to be without civil institutions and notions of rights. Conquest of these primitive societies was considered justifiable.

During this second phase, Christian publicists generally agreed that European sovereignty over the other was absolute. Consequently, the traditional distinction between natural and positive rights regarding the rights to property, the principles of reciprocity, and justice had no particular relevance outside Europe. European colonists supported their claims to non-Christian territories by amending canon and natural laws. While the latter maintained that natural reason concedes ownership to the first occupier, European colonists asserted that such owners must first possess reason, a capacity they denied to the native populations.[27] The Europeans argued that the native populations lacked either the necessary emotional attachment to the land or the proper social institutions to claim tenure—or both. Emerich de Vattel summarized the predominant view when he stated that the natives had no physical, legal, or emotional attachment to land or territory worthy of European respect.[28]

Extraterritoriality and Native Capitulation

By the sevententh century, according to J. Westlake, most European publicists and politicians doubted the capacity of non-Europeans to provide institutions or "government suited to the white man."[29] Because they assumed that native peoples lacked both reason and

appropriate civil institutions, European merchants and settlers unilaterally imposed the rules that governed both interactions among
themselves and between Europeans and indigenous populations. In
the case of inter-European relations, European symbols, formalities,
and rules created the material conditions for judging rival European
claims.[30] In this regard, each European power based its claims on
so-called lawful means that included capitulation, grant, usage, and
sufferance, by which European powers and their nationals wrested
political authority or sovereignty from the natives.

In the case of European-other relations, European symbols, formalities, and rules enabled the colonists to create rights, privileges,
and immunities for themselves and to impose nonreciprocal obligations on the natives within the natives' own jurisdictions.[31] The existence of juridical instruments such as capitulation treaties supported
the Europeans' contention that the native populations had agreed
either to relinquish partial sovereignty to the outsiders or to grant
them exclusive commercial rights, which also limited indigenous
sovereignty. For instance, a 1535 capitulation treaty between the
French Prince Francis and the Ottoman rulers guaranteed French
nationals and persons under French protection the privilege of free
trade in the Ottoman territory. The treaty also "allowed French con-
suls to have jurisdiction over their subjects" operating in Ottoman
territory.[32] This agreement was followed by others that simply extended French sovereignty to all territories that maintained exclusive
trade relations with France. In a similar case, England claimed that
it had by treaty obtained the right to forbid a Maratha ruler in India to establish external relations with other European powers without prior consultation with and consent of the English monarchy.[33]

European conquerors often deceived their local counterparts about
the implications of the agreements into which they entered. They also
manipulated indigenous power relations, forging local alliances in order to project their own power, and imposed punitive concessions under the guise of offering protection.[34] For instance, a 1788 agreement
between a group of British traders and a community in present-day
Sierra Leone noted that, in exchange for protection, the indigenous
people had agreed to surrender their rights to the land for the benefit
of the "free community of settlers," their heirs, and their successors.[35]
This and similar agreements were not only written in languages for-

eign to the natives, they were expressed in juridical idioms unfamiliar to them. As a result, the consenting local rulers, both legitimate and European-appointed proxies, lacked cultural and juridical frames of reference to express informed consent.

The unequal and nonreciprocal obligations to which the colonists committed the indigenous populations and their rulers were referred to juridically as burdens.[36] In general, Europeans imposed two types of burdens—permanent and transitory—on their partners in Asia, Africa, and elsewhere. Permanent burdens encroached on the sovereignty of the other and created effects that impaired the other's ability to act on its own behalf. Such burdens, designed to last in perpetuity, disallowed all future denunciations by the burdened party.[37] Transitory burdens, on the other hand, were limited in extent and duration.

The practice of imposing burdens emerged on the Indian subcontinent in the sixteenth century. At that time, the Portuguese, with the intent of thwarting the advance of Islam in the Asian hinterland, limited native self-rule. Under this arrangement, the native partners of the Portuguese temporarily deferred to the Europeans in their external affairs.[38] By the end of the eighteenth century, Portuguese colonists had replaced the more decentralized structures of Indians and other Asian empires with more centralized institutions under their own control. Likewise, the English and French by this time had promoted their appointed provincial governors in Asia to the formal rank of grand officer of empire, or comparable titles, reducing local rulers to nominal suzerains.[39]

Unequal Status and Dignity

In the post-Reformation era, most Western legal theorists did not accord equal status and dignity to non-Europeans.[40] Indeed, Gentili, Grotius, Wolff, and other founders of natural-law theory began their discussion of Christian rights by grounding subjectivity, or full membership in the community of nations, on a certain hierarchy of status.[41] Like his Catholic counterparts, the Protestant Alberico Gentili took the position that Christians were superior to infidels and heathens. With respect to intra-Christian relations, he urged Europeans to comply strictly with the terms of their engagements. In contrast, he advocated two types of attitudes in Christian interactions abroad.

The first concerned inter-Christian agreements between rival European powers during European expansion or conquest. The second related to European-other accords that were directed against the infidels, the heathens, or their interests.[42] According to Gentili, it was unlawful, even sinful, for Christians to undertake any engagement directed against the interests of their brethren, whether in conjunction with other European powers or colonists or in collaboration with non-Christians. In contrast, it was legitimate for Christians to collaborate against infidels and heathens. Gentili even urged Christians to force or coopt infidels in their promotion of Christian interests.[43]

Christian Wolff also established two kinds of equality as the basis for judging the commitments of political entities to one another. The first kind of equality, one of engagement, applied strictly to intra-Christian relations. According to Wolff, the engagements of Christian princes toward one another had equal juridical weight and obligated all parties involved in the same manner. This equality of engagement applied to inter-Christian relations outside Europe under limited circumstances. Thus, for instance, Christian princes were obligated to recognize the privileges accorded to a rival Christian by infidels. In inter-Christian relations, the origins of such privileges (expressed in capitulation treaties and other agreements) were subordinate to the status of the Christian sovereigns who were bound to uphold each others' rights and privileges.

The second kind of equality was one of status and dignity. This criterion applied to commitments made by a Christian prince to an infidel. Wolff maintained that Christianity and the strength and dignity of European powers conferred on Europeans a higher status than that conferred on the weaker heathen communities. Accordingly, because they possessed greater strength or status, Christian polities were justified in imposing unilateral burdens on weaker communities.[44]

REINTERPRETING THE HISTORY OF THE LAW OF NATIONS

The power dynamics that determined the content and form of intercommunal norms are not necessarily apparent in the constituent principles of the law of nations. As a result, international legal principles, and resulting doctrines, appear to be contradictory and indeterminate. Yet, these contradictions and indeterminacies have been outweighed by other internal consistencies and determinacies. The general principles of law are generally in conformity with both their assigned objects and their subjectively constituted *teleos*. Likewise, the constitutive norms of international relations may seem indeterminate, but European powers applied a determinate constellation of legal rules to specific regions and peoples.

The seventeenth-century conflicts between the Dutch and English, on the one hand, and the Portuguese and Spanish, on the other, initiated a legal and political tradition in inter-European relations: inter-Christian interactions outside of Europe. These power struggles also determined the norms of European-other rapports in modern international relations. With respect to inter-European relations, this power rivalry augured the eventual replacement of the papal-ordained international order of the Middle Ages with a secular one. Specifically, the Dutch and English criticism of the 1493 papal bulls precipitated the final demise of canon law. It also set the stage for the emergence of Enlightenment-inspired juridico-political principles based on civil law as the new norms of international relations.

A Eurocentric Process

The European power struggle provided the discursive structures that delineated the objects of modern intercommunal relations, including *dominium, imperium,* and commerce. It also determined the doctrinal formulation and, eventually, judicial interpretations of these legal objects, which established the basis of key principles of international law: communal sovereignty, freedom of trade, and guaranteed right to property. Finally, the related discursive structures provided the context for state practice, or custom, in regard to the norms of international relations.[45]

The conflicts that opposed the European powers arose when the Netherlands, and later England, emerged as the major sea powers, replacing Spain and Portugal in that position. Then, faced with Portuguese and Spanish claims to exclusive control over Asian trade, the Dutch and English contested both the authority of the power that granted those rights and, thus, the validity of the privileges themselves. Specifically, the Dutch and English rejected the legitimacy of papal ordinances that created exclusive privileges solely for the benefit of the kingdoms of Spain and Portugal. The larger issue was whether the Roman Catholic pope may grant exclusive control of trade and trade routes in regions not under papal jurisdiction to the exclusion of other Christian powers. The Dutch and English disputed the legal standing of papal bulls and ordinances. Yet, they supported papal proclamations concerning the natural right of Christian princes to govern within their own territories, as well as to impose their own rules on the infidels.[46]

The debate opposing Spain and Portugal to the Netherlands and England is therefore a logical starting point for the study of the structures of modern international law. This debate demonstrates two conflicting Western attitudes toward the other: first, Christian powers deliberately conceived of a law of nations that involved the other; and, second, they purposefully excluded the other from its formulation. To illustrate this point, I refer to the writings of two founders of natural-rights principles: the Protestant Dutch publicist Hugo de Groot, better known as Grotius, and the Portuguese law professor Seraphin de Freitas. Predictably, Grotius challenged the authority of the pope regarding the determination of the norms of international relations. In contrast, Freitas, who responded directly to Grotius's arguments against the Iberian privileges, defended the legitimacy of the ecclesiastically founded privileges acquired by Portugal and Spain.[47] Despite their disagreements, the two publicists upheld the notion that membership in the Christian community of nations was the basis for *imperium* and *dominium* in the international order.

Hugo Grotius: The Christian Right to Trade

In 1609 the Dutch were still technically at war with Spain, following their rebellion against Spanish domination. The northern provinces, which declared independence as the United Provinces, had emerged as a major contender for control of the principal sea lanes leading to Asia. Having already established themselves on the island of Mauritius, the Dutch now challenged Portuguese merchants in the Strait of Malacca. To bolster its case, the Dutch East India Company hired Grotius to prepare a statement on the law of prize, justifying the capture of a Portuguese galleon by a Dutch ship. The result was Grotius's renowned essay on the freedom of the seas, entitled *Mare Liberum,* and a monograph chapter on the law of prize.[48]

Grotius's justification of the Dutch East India Company's action involved the laws of nature as manifested in the mutual relations of states, the freedom of the seas, the right of self-defense, and the general modes of acquisition, including the right of booty. He rejected as unnatural the Spanish and Portuguese monopoly over trade in Asia. In particular, he objected to the notion that a single authority, with no global jurisdiction, could confer exclusive rights to overseas trade on any nation. "If the Pope has any power at all," he wrote, "he has it, as they say, in the spiritual realm only. Therefore, he has no authority over the infidel nations, for they do not belong to the Church."[49] Grotius extended this principle beyond the bounds of Asia. Indeed, he began his argument with a reference not to Asia, but to the New World.

Charging that the partition of the New World by Pope Alexander VI had been wrongly used by the Portuguese to justify their claims in the East Indies, Grotius set the stage to undermine their propositions:

> First, did the Pope merely desire to settle the disputes between the Portuguese and the Spaniards? Now if this be the case, seeing that the question concerns only the Portuguese and the Spaniards, the decision of the Pope will of course not affect the other peoples of the world. Second, did the Pope intend to give the two nations, each one third of the whole world? Even if the Pope had intended and had had the power to make such a gift, still it would not have made the Portuguese sovereigns of those places.[50]

After posing these rhetorical questions, Grotius argued that neither the Portuguese nor the Spanish had the standing to prohibit free access to the concerned territories. First, these lands were autonomous in their own right, that is, independent of papal authority. They had "their own kings, their own government, their own laws, and their own legal systems."[51] Second, even if the Portuguese and Spanish had been sovereign in Asia and the New World, they were bound by natural law to permit access to other nations. This obligation resulted from the reciprocal relations that lay at the base of natural law. Finally, Grotius asserted that the Iberian powers would be doing great injury to the Dutch by obstructing free access for the purposes of trade.[52] As a result, natural law permitted the United Provinces and their nationals to unilaterally appropriate the concerned Portuguese vessel. This action was consistent with the principle of self-defense, the natural right of a victim to retaliate for wrongful acts.[53]

Although Grotius's arguments were broad in scope, he did not apply the dispositions of natural rights and law to the other. Several of his arguments bore imprints of European Enlightenment attitudes. For instance, his defense of the relative autonomy of Asians was not a manifestation of his concern for their right to sovereignty. Rather, it was a springboard from which to reject the papal arbitration that had granted exclusive rights over portions of the globe to Spain and Portugal. Grotius's central concern was the immediate effects of the 1493 papal bulls on the emerging power of the Netherlands. Indeed, Spanish and Portuguese privileges stood in the way of the development of Dutch commerce and navigation.[54]

Like his Portuguese adversaries, Grotius granted only partial recognition to indigenous East Indian communities.[55] As conceived by Grotius, this recognition served both to support the right of Dutch merchants to unrestricted trade and to oppose the validity of Portuguese titles. The indigenous communities were free to enter into agreements with the Dutch similar to those upon which the Portuguese had founded their titles and privileges, he argued. They could conduct their affairs independently. However, they lacked the authority under natural law to grant exclusive trade to one Christian power, even one that claimed papal authorization. In short, Grotius's emphasis was on the natural rights of Christians/Europeans to free trade and navigation, not the rights of the other to sovereignty.

The necessary principles of inter-European relations, which included freedom of the seas and of trade, curtailed non-European political authority.[56] For instance, Grotius conceived of the right to unilateral appropriation to apply to extra-European contexts in which, he assumed, the indigenous populations had no clear title. Like most of his contemporaries, the Dutch publicist considered native peoples to have only limited sovereignty and, consequently, limited claims to their land.[57] Likewise, Grotius claimed that Europeans had the right to rescind their agreements in the event of war or other emergency. In considering the rights of native peoples in his doctrine of just war, he advocated Christians' right to wage war on non-Christians who did not open their door to trade and exploitation. According to Grotius, the Spanish would have been justified in making war on the Aztecs and other indigenous peoples "if they really were prevented from traveling or sojourning among those peoples, and were denied the right to share in those things which by the Law of Nations or by Custom are common to all, and finally if they were debarred from trade."[58] By implication, if they were denied free access, Europeans could unilaterally dispossess the native populations.

Freitas: The Christian Right to Remedy

Grotius's quest for free access to non-European territories for all European/Christian nations was strongly resisted by Spanish and Portuguese colonial classes. Seraphin de Freitas in particular devoted his career to attacking Grotius's position in order to defend the rights and privileges of Spain and Portugal against Dutch "agitation." Like Grotius, Freitas framed his defense of Portuguese rights in the discursive modes of the Enlightenment. Thus, he relied on the right of discovery, natural rights, the validity of acquired rights, and the autonomy of European partners in Asia and elsewhere in his justification of the Iberian privileges.[59]

Dismissing Grotius as a "heretic and anonymous Dutchman," Freitas challenged his interpretation of international law. In particular, he disputed Grotius's judgment concerning Dutch actions in the Strait of Malacca.[60] In his monograph *De Justo Imperio Lusitanorum Asiatico* (1625), which he dedicated to the Spanish king, Philip IV, Freitas argued that Portugal had legitimate claims to overseas territories and that these claims were valid with or without papal sanction. He insisted that Portugal had acquired its privileges through the right of discovery, and that many of its discoveries had predated the papal bull that divided the non-Christian world between Spain and Portugal.[61] Thus, Freitas concluded, discovery rather than papal authority was the foundation of Portuguese claims.

Freitas began his counterattack by rejecting Grotius's distinction between norms that applied to all, including native peoples, and rules that applied solely to Christians. In the monograph's first section, "Is Navigation Free Among all Peoples According to the Law of Nations?," Freitas argued that there was only one law of nations, with one end, the well-being of humankind, and one origin, natural reason. He asserted that all human beings held this common purpose and were united under a kind of republic of reason, led by one prince.[62] The Christian Prince, who was divinely guided by the True Faith, was uniquely endowed with pure, uncorrupted natural reason. Although non-Europeans possessed reason, it had been corrupted by idolatry and savagery. As a result, Freitas maintained, the well-being of humanity required that those not-so-fortunate heathens, barbarians, and infidels be guided by a Christian prince. This prince could only be Catholic. Protestants, like the Dutch, could never be entrusted with universal leadership because their faith was heretical. "Unrepentant Protestantism" eventually corrupted True Christianity, that is, Roman Catholicism.[63]

Not only did Freitas refute Grotius's logic, he also faulted his methodology, pointing to inconsistencies in *Mare Liberum*. Grotius's argument, as reconstructed by Freitas, was that communal privileges and obligations, whether mere political authority or full sovereignty, constituted natural rights. These natural rights resulted either from the prescriptions of natural law or from mutual agreements between consenting parties that permitted them.[64] Freitas argued that, if indeed natural rights could be granted by mutual agreement, then Grotius could not justifiably reject the validity of privileges granted by autonomous infidels to Christian nations.

The Portuguese professor maintained that, by granting special and exclusive privileges to the Portuguese, the natives were exercising a right they possessed under the same natural law recognized by Grotius. The native populations of a discovered territory could therefore prohibit commerce with another nation, as long as they did so in agreement with a Christian nation that granted them protection. It did not make sense, on the one hand, to claim that the rights of the primitive were grounded in immutable and indispensable precepts of natural rights and, on the other, to reject the notion that those same people could use their rights to bar any nation from trading with them. According to Freitas, the right to trade was granted as a favor by one nation to another. While the native populations could not deny all Christians the right to free trade, it was in their exclusive domain to choose the nations with which they would establish trade relations.[65]

Finally, Freitas objected to Grotius's formulation of the law of war, especially his stipulation of the conditions under which Europeans could declare war on native populations. Unlike Grotius, Freitas denied the justice of declaring war on a non-Christian prince who refused to open his door to European trade. Waging war against infidels was justified only when they illegally denounced existing agreements with Christian nations. On these grounds, Portuguese wars in Asia were justifiable, Freitas claimed, "because once [we were] admitted by treaties, and having established friendship with the peoples, [natives] sought to expel us through fraud, trickery and trappings; thus we avenged ourselves of such injustices and murders committed against us after we were betrayed."[66] Hence, Freitas implicitly argued that while European nations were not bound to respect inter-European agreements that threatened their self-interest, non-Europeans were obliged to abide by all agreements with Europeans, regardless of the consequences.

Political Imperatives and Expediency

The conflict between the United Provinces and Portugal ended with the decline of Portugal and the rise of the Netherlands as the power broker in inter-European relations. This balance of power resulted in new political imperatives that affected the practical, legal, and philosophical concerns of the formerly antagonistic parties. During the early phase of Dutch hegemony, Grotius built on the right of booty, unilateral appropriation, self-defense, and retribution to develop specific rules that protected Dutch interests and encouraged Christians to engage in mutually beneficial relationships. In his writings, he demonstrated his inclination for inter-European accommodation and dialogue, which would benefit the Netherlands as an emerging power. His effort in this respect culminated in the 1625 article entitled "The Rights of War and Peace." Writing toward the end of the Thirty Years' War, Grotius dedicated his essay to the "Most Christian King Louis XIII of France." In it, he advised that, in their relations with one another, Christians were obliged to keep their promises, to restore unjust gains, and to make reparation for wrongful acts.[67]

Freitas was also affected by the declining power of Portugal. He responded by defending Portugal's vested interests while appearing to accommodate to the new reality. For instance, Freitas agreed with Grotius that the promotion of open and free trade was in the interest of all nations. He insisted, however, that trade be conducted in an orderly manner and be based on clearly defined criteria. He argued that there should be an inter-Christian agreement setting the parameters of access and commerce as a prerequisite to Portugal's allowing other Christians to enter the foreign lands under its influence.[68] He insisted that prior to the establishment of such an agreement, the Iberian power was justified in unilaterally determining the terms of travel by other European nationals in its zones of influence.

Indeed, existing treaties between Portuguese nationals and native rulers had provided the juridical grounds upon which Portugal excluded other colonial powers. As we noted, during the era of conquest, Portuguese proselytizers and colonists had protected their possessions against the advances of other European/Christian nations by obtaining various kinds of treaties or accords. The majority of these Luso-native accords granted exclusive privileges to Portugal, to the detriment of rival powers.[69]

Again claiming to support the principle of open and free trade, Freitas insisted that other Christian powers were obliged to allow free access to Portugal, on the basis of that nation's adherence to the True Faith and its papal-ordained mission. He argued that Portugal had an interest in thwarting the spread of Islam in regions where the "Mohammedians were advancing their religion." As a result, it had the right to intervene and participate in trade in the said lands, even if they were under the influence of another European power.[70]

By the mid–seventeenth century, after the United Provinces had established supremacy in maritime navigation and overseas trade, Dutch jurists and politicians retreated from their past accommodationist attitude. Adapting their discourse on international relations to conform to their hegemonic position, they defended Dutch gains, and only when necessary sought consensus with rival powers over the key objects of international relations. They also undermined the capacity of noncontending powers (and the other) to achieve parity. The English and French acted in the same manner when they emerged as contending powers in the scramble for control of the Asian trade and, later, colonial rule around the globe.

DISCURSIVE STRUCTURES

It is evident from what precedes that the structures of international law and Western jurisprudence have produced specific sets of intercommunal relations. These interactions have been grounded in a determinate image of the world, the Western-dominated international order. The power relations embedded in the law can be recovered by opposing legal referents, metaphors, and symbols to international praxis. This discursive emphasis provides the means to uncover the process whereby legal symbols mutate into determinate signs of exclusion that produce their own referents. It is my contention that although the West has proclaimed the universality of the principles of international law (e.g., liberty, free trade, and property rights), Western praxis has excluded the other from equal participation in the international order. This praxis has also generated a jurisprudence, that is, legal doctrines and juridical idioms. The formulation of these doctrines and the determination of these idioms have mirrored historical sensitivities and the ethos of their times.[71] Modern Western jurisprudence has endorsed or condoned, but in either case perpetuated, the violent exclusion of the other.

Juridical Idioms and Referents

The relationship between the European self and the non-European other has been characterized primarily by confrontation arising from European expansion and the ensuing exploitation of the other. This exploitative interaction has been organized around a set of values, an ideology, whose philosophic system, or episteme, emerged during the Enlightenment to guide Western praxis.[72] Indeed, the Grotius-Freitas debate demonstrates that international law did not emerge from abstract natural rights, independent of historical situations. The general principles of international law appeared individually or in association, under specific circumstances reflecting actual power relations that indelibly influenced the content of the law.

Consistent with the circumstances of the emergence of international law, its application has not been neutral, absolute, or uniform. European hegemonic powers applied different combinations of legal norms to different peoples and regions, for the purposes of political domination and economic exploitation.[73] Far from being neutral, the juridical postulates offered as a means to resolving the other's "ills" (i.e., heathenness, backwardness) have been propositions for intervention and domination. In addition, the constellation of principles and rules that applied to non-Europeans was part of a generative process dependent upon a tradition of alterity and erasure, of silencing the rights, claims, and interests of non-Western communities.

Likewise, the doctrines and idioms of Western jurisprudence have reflected a subjectively constituted *teleos*. While some European courts have departed from the established jurisprudence, either by creatively applying the law or by rejecting given juridical principles as unconstitutional, they have not altered the overall effects of European state practice; nor have they negated the exploitation of the other. The majority of Western institutions of adjudication have followed legal precedents, that is, past judicial interpretations, as well as conformed to extrajudicial proceedings. These processes have traditionally included presumably universal Western expert opinion and state practice, the latter constituting custom. As a result, the jurisprudence has mirrored the hegemonic powers' representations of the object of the law.[74]

Finally, Western juridical idioms have also been deployed to fulfill strategic functions in the imperial order, including the destruction of discordant or foreign legal precepts. Specifically, the historic imposition of Western idioms of property, possession, and ownership on non-European cultures in discussions of land use, sovereignty, and political authority was intended to cause the physical collapse of the conquered cultures. It was also hoped that it would cause the discursive disappearance of local sign systems, including domestic laws, and their referents.[75]

In general, these cultures differed fundamentally from those of the West. Prior to European conquest, Asians (for instance, Chinese and Indians), Africans (from Egypt to Mali), and native Americans (the Mayas and Incas) had independently established successful civilizations and empires. These societies deliberately constructed notions and idioms of possession, property, and ownership intended to (re)produce specific communal relations. As Eric Cheyfitz noted, these legal instruments were meant to enable the various peoples who entered into agreements to think of crucial social roles, obligations, and strategic relationships according to predictable discursive patterns.[76]

The obliteration of indigenous legal systems resulted from discursive processes that cannot be understood through formal analyses of the supposedly universal international legal order. The indigenous legal notions and juridical idioms were destroyed when the conquering imperial powers imposed new ones in their place. The new notions and idioms were based on juridical principles and doctrines that guaranteed the Western hegemonic position. The purported constitutionality of private property and contractual obligations, for instance, effectively concealed the fact that the legal doctrines—themselves expressed in a specific Western political idiom—reflected the interests and needs of specific communities, namely, the colonizers.[77] This process of replacing one set of notions and idioms with another (exploitative) one produced grave epistemic repercussions for international legal discourse, as well as sociopolitical disturbances that affected intercommunal attitudes.

Law, Culture, and Ideology

As a constituent element of Western culture, the law of nations has been integral to a discourse of inclusion and exclusion. In this regard, international law has formed its subject and objects through an arbitrary system of signs. As a rhetoric of identity, it has depended upon metaphysical associations grounded in religious, cultural, or racial similarities and differences.[78] The legal subject, for the most part, has been composed of a Christian/European self. In contrast, the European founders of the law of nations created an opposite image of the self (the other) as a legal object. They realized this legal objectification of non-Europeans through a process of alterity. The other has comprised, at once, non-European communities that Europe has accepted as its mirror image and those it has considered to be either languishing in a developmental stage long since surpassed by Europe or moving in historical progression toward the model provided by the European self.

This discursive process of simultaneous inclusion and exclusion began long before the seventeenth-century emergence of modern international law. It has since been irreversible, unperturbed by occasional reconstitution of the European balance of power and divergent philosophical movements. Beginning with the Enlightenment, European theorists and practitioners established metaphysical relations (based on similarities or differences) between the self and a cluster of nonselves. These relations have formed the basis of specific juridical norms and legal doctrines. These, in turn, have provided the means by which Europe maintained exploitative relations with the other within the international order.

In this regard, the modern law of nations has functioned as an ideology within the presumed universal order.[79] In particular, specific legal constructs have mediated between two conflicting desires. The first has been the European expansionist urge and the related need for effective instruments for the exploitation of non-

Europeans. In contrast, there has been the opposing European need to project the international legal system, upon which expansion and exploitation are grounded, as objectively derived from universal values.

As an ideology, the law of nations has played a "manipulative" role in the Western approach to intercommunal relations.[80] The metaphysical processes of inclusion and exclusion in international law have allowed Western theorists and practitioners to accept as legitimate two contradictory thrusts. The coexistence of these drives has enabled the West to profess one ethos but act according to a different one. The first, morally consistent with Western self-perceptions, is a principled opposition to bondage and servitude. This thrust was embodied in the Enlightenment revolt against its European traditions of bondage and the concurrent proclamation of individual and communal rights and liberties as the basis of civil and public institutions. This impulse against tyranny has been typified by such axioms as "all men are created equal [and] endowed by their Creator with certain unalienable Rights."[81]

The other Western drive has been morally deficient, contrary to the antiservitude ethic. This thrust, the urge to control and dominate, has prevented the dominant classes of the West from envisioning (or imagining) any approach to intercommunal relations other than to exploit the other for their own psychological and material well-being.[82] This impulse to exploit has formed the basis of a constellation of norms that has justified and legitimized slavery, colonialism, and other forms of human exploitation.

The Res Publica and Its International Regimes

As we have seen, the norms of the international order that legitimized and facilitated conquest and colonization resulted from a political consensus among learned Europeans—initially, clergy, theologians, royal courts, and publicists. This consensus manifested itself through three discursive genres: ecclesiastical, Enlightenment, and colonial. Each genre of representation emerged during a specific historical phase: the Middle Ages for the ecclesiastical mode; the sixteenth-century Reformation and its aftermath for the Enlightenment equivalent; and the nineteenth-century new imperialism for the colonial version. These genres also reflected a unique configuration of power and ethos that, during each historical phase, provided the foundations for heterogenous juridical processes and multidimensional interactions among the various units of the international order. For the sake of analysis, these juridical processes and the related norms of intercommunal interactions may be organized according to time, geography, and the objects of international relations into international juridico-political regimes. Historically, these regimes have been implemented in order to obtain stability and predictable outcomes in intercommunal relations.[83]

The position of Africa within the Christian-inspired universal or international order has been determined by four successive international regimes. The first was inspired by the 1493 papal bulls that proclaimed the authority of the Roman Catholic pope and, by extension, his anointed Christian rulers over all humankind. The Enlightenment movement divested this regime of its ecclesiastic foundation but maintained its basic tenets throughout the transatlantic slave trade and the era of informal empire.[84] This first regime was replaced with one that formalized colonial rule in Africa during the 1884–85 Berlin Conference. This colonial regime was perpetuated by the 1919 Versailles Peace Conference and the 1920 Geneva Congress following World War I. In 1945, folllowing the San Francisco United Nations Conference, the colonial regime gave way to a fourth, postcolonial, regime.

Under the first regime, the right of Christians to sovereignty over non-Christians was said to be derived from natural reason, itself a reflection of the True Faith. This regime united humankind in a res publica (common order) under the authority of the Roman Catholic Church. During this era, the relationship between Western Christendom and Africa was guided by a presumed necessity to convert heathens to Christianity. This interaction changed with the advent of the slave trade, when Europeans added a racial dimension to their treatment of Africans. Missionaries and slave traders alike emphasized the whiteness of the messiah and God the Father as an illustration of white superiority.

This first regime climaxed during the Enlightenment with the emergence of modern international law and European domination of the global economy. In the epistemological instance, Europeans formed new ideas concerning the character of Africa and its sociopolitical institutions, cultures, and economies. European powers acted on the premise that Africa was ruled by barbarous and cruel individuals.

The cooptation, or pacification and removal, of such rulers was said to be necessary for the establishment of legitimate institutions. Europeans allowed some native leaders to retain limited authority over their own peoples, but they were bound to submit to European norms and to practice "legitimate trade" under European guidance.[85]

The end of the slave trade coincided with philosophical and scientific transformations that further affected the European-African relationship. During the transitional period leading to abolition, pseudoscientific racism defined the context of future European policies toward Africa. In order to bring civilization and light to a continent now characterized as dark, theorists and politicians urged alternative forms of control.[86] The new rationalization for the domination of non-Europeans was the supposedly scientific evidence of their racial inferiority.[87] In actuality, racism was simply one more instrument used to manipulate science and other categories of knowledge to political and economic ends.

In the transformation of the initial Christian and Enlightenment mission of salvation into one of colonial control, the desire to exploit and the availability of the means of conquest played an even greater role than the scientific rationale. Superior weaponry, medicine, and other technologies enabled Europeans to establish, and later to incorporate, their spheres of influence into the global economic system. The juridical instruments developed during the conquest of the New World and Asia offered colonial powers the means to meet the new requirements of imperialism in Africa. For instance, during the sixteenth-century conquest of the New World, European rulers proclaimed lordship over non-Christians and delegated their authority first to missionaries and then to fortune seekers and adventurers. This phenomenon recurred during the age of mercantilism at the end of the eighteenth century, when private European agents, settlers, and commercial companies were granted quasi-sovereign authority. Finally, in the nineteenth century, private agents, commercial companies, and colonial officers were bestowed with quasi-sovereign and sovereign powers in Africa, signaling the beginning of formal colonial rule.

In their efforts to establish a vast European-dominated empire, European powers created chartered commercial and trading companies endowed with powers that extended beyond their economic functions. Holding a dual juridical capacity, they engaged in political as well as economic activities. Specifically, they were granted exceptional or quasi-sovereign powers that included the active and passive right of legation and the right to conclude treaties with Africans and other non-Europeans. In addition, many chartered companies were vested with the authority to acquire territories and, when necessary, to wage war against those who resisted their advances.[88] Aided by military and other technologies, they established zones of influence through conquest, annexation, cession, and other forms of concession.[89] In these empire-building efforts, they also received extraterritorial protection from their home countries. This legal status enabled them to secure the protection of national armies (or similarly constituted security forces) in the event of conflicts with rival European powers, chartered companies, or indigenous peoples.[90] By the end of the nineteenth century, European powers had reconstituted trade in Africa on the basis of such informal empires, which gave them access to the resources necessary to support the burgeoning industrial revolution.[91]

THE LAW AS COLONIAL DISCOURSE

The second Western regime in Africa, formal colonial rule, was instituted in the aftermath of the 1884–85 Berlin Conference. Sustained by the precepts of natural history and pseudoscientific racism, the Berlin regime reasserted Western superiority and facilitated the conquest and exploitation of Africans. It effected Africa's marginality and subordination to Europe by articulating African otherness in a new system of signs that posited African disorders in the cultural and political spheres as a key justification for European political control. The formal colonization of Africa was construed as the means to African spiritual and political salvation, economic regeneration, and civilization.[92]

Once again, the new regime was replete with ethical ambiguities, but it was held together by the Western will to dominate. Like the one it replaced, the Berlin regime fulfilled two contradictory but equally significant programmatic purposes, exclusion and inclusion. First, because the Berlin powers excluded Africans from the proceedings of the conference, they were able to establish exclusively Western institutions to regulate trade and coordinate colonial policies. The

International Congo Commission, to be explored in chapter 3, typified the new regime, in particular its structures of subordination and exploitation. Second, the Berlin regime continued to retain Africa as an integral element of the universal order, albeit the most "backward." Claiming to bear the white man's burden, the colonial powers justified their new African regime on the grounds of philanthropy. This supposed altruism and guidance helped to legitimize European philosophical claims to universalism.

Ethnology in International Law

The international legal norms that, under the Berlin regime, applied to Africans were integral to the epistemic apparatus of colonial discourse. Like political philosophy, these juridical norms were shaped by natural history, in particular pseudoscientific racism.[93] Specifically, the ordering idioms of the law, including zones of influence and protectorates, reflected the naming system of the colonial discourse. This system depended upon such symbols as "dark continent" and "primitivism." In short, international law helped to invent Africa for imperial Europe, as well as to provide the means for political control and the acquisition of natural resources.

Nineteenth-century positivists assumed that international legal norms reflected natural phenomena. Sharing the imperialist aim of the colonial discourse, they drew on the scientific notions of racial hierarchy in their "discovery" of the properties of the natural phenomena reflected by the law. James Lorimer was among the pioneers who used the materials furnished by racial scholarship as a guide to the essential "ethical elements" of the principles of international relations.[94] In a book begun while he was chair of the British Institute of International Law, Lorimer acknowledged the influence of Orientalism on his approach to international law and relations. He claimed that "no modern contribution to science seems destined to influence international politics and jurisprudence to so great an extent as that of ethnology, or the science of the races."[95] In this text, which he proposed to "the exceptionally advanced and cultivated class of students," Lorimer advised his readers to incorporate "ethnical differences" in the study of international law:

> The international law question is, whether, in the presence of ethnical differences which for jural purposes we must regard as indelible,

we are entitled to confine recognition to those branches of alien races which consent to separate themselves from the rest, and ostensibly or professedly, to accept our political conceptions.[96]

Indeed, anthropology and ethnology provided Lorimer and many of his contemporaries with the foundation from which they developed legal categories that applied solely to non-European communities.

In his quest for such legal constructs, Lorimer first defined the status of the different "ethnical communities" that composed the international order. Specifically, he determined that humanity was divided "into three concentric zones or spheres—that of civilized humanity, that of barbarous humanity, and that of savage human-ity."[97] Lorimer argued that Britain's interests would best be served if it granted varying degrees of juridico-political recognition to each branch of humanity commensurate with its position in the hierarchy. The highest degree of juridical recognition was plenary, and it applied to nations that ethnically resembled the British—that is, white and presumably civilized nations—though it did not imply national equal-ity. Lorimer envisioned that the claim of recognition to which states are entitled would be proportionate to their power, for "even within the sphere of plenary political recognition, States are no more equal to each other, in the absolute sense, than their citizens are equal."[98]

While plenary recognition was itself hierarchical, it accorded more rights than any other form of recognition and applied only to so-called progressive races. Lorimer argued against "extending the rights of civilization" to so-called nonprogressive races. These other races, according to him, lacked reason and science and, indeed, had not produced "one single individual who has been distinguished in any intellectual pursuit."[99] They were also incapable of performing their duties under plenary recognition, that is, according to civilized stan-dards.[100] As a result, they deserved lesser rights.[101]

The degree of recognition granted to non-European communities depended upon the sphere of humanity to which they were assigned. In this regard, Lorimer claimed that natural law and reason accorded Britain (and other civilized nations) the authority to make such assig-nations. Similarly, it was up to them to determine the degree of recog-nition they would grant to the noncivilized. In exchange for this priv-ilege, civilized nations were bound to exercise judgment on a scientific basis. By means of scientific inquiry, Britain was to establish the degree of political and cultural maturity of the communities in question.[102] Indications of such maturity included the ability of peoples to govern themselves "by means of representation."

Among non-European communities, Lorimer claimed, the Old World infidels of Asia were culturally mature, but politically barbarous. They trailed behind civilized Europe in their degree of social and political organization. As a result, they deserved only partial recognition:

> The sphere of partial political recognition extends to Turkey in Europe and Asia, and to the old historical States of Asia which have not become European dependencies — viz, to Persia and the other separate States of central Asia, to China, Siam, and Japan.[103]

The vast majority of non-Europeans, whom Lorimer termed the "residue of humanity," belonged at the bottom of the hierarchy. They were supposed to be both culturally and politically immature. Lorimer presumed this residue to include Africans, Australian Aborigines, the native populations of the Americas, and so on. According to Lorimer, these savages had not achieved the degree of social and political organization of other communities. This majority was thus unfit for any political or juridical recognition. To grant recognition to the savages would be contrary to natural law. Not only would it be futile, it was not up to Britain to attempt to "advance or retard the progress of human life" by fiat of recognition.[104] Although political and juridical recognition was not in order, the reality of European contact with savage communities necessitated some form of recognition: natural, or mere human recognition.[105]

Lorimer's views were not unusual. Like his contemporaries, Lorimer claimed objectivity, but his desire to separate facts from values was belied by the instrumentality of his theory on international relations and law. For instance, he condoned European expansion by insisting on the benefit of imperialism for the barbarous and the savages. He believed that the attainment of civilization by these nonprogressive peoples entailed granting to Europeans unrestricted trade and free access to natural resources. He advocated the achievement of this end by any means necessary, including force.[106] Finally, Lorimer considered the right of European nations to conquer others to be integral to the idea of liberty.[107] Accordingly, European conquest of "weaker nations" was an expression of natural law, "measured by the power which God has bestowed on the aggressor, or permitted him to develop."[108]

Discrimination under Positive Law

Like that of most of his contemporaries, Lorimer's perspective on communal rights reflected the juridico-philosophical transition from natural to positive law. This theoretical conversion also coincided with the progression of capitalism and the related integration of colonial economies into the European-dominated global economy.[109] Indeed, the transition from natural rights to positively defined individual and communal rights coincided with the mid-nineteenth-century European shift from prestigious adventures and petty trade to the radical exploitation of the material and human resources of future colonies. In this context, the theoretical proclamation of the sanctity of individual liberties and property rights served as a cover for the juridical expropriation of native populations.

Unlike their predecessors, nineteenth-century positivists recognized that Africans and others had physical relations to their lands. As a result, they rejected the old axiom that non-European territories were without lord or owner. However, Western metaphysics once again stripped Africans of the attributes of subjectivity and impaired their rights in order to establish the right of Europeans to dispose freely of African territories. Indeed, during this era of informal empire, European theorists and practitioners acted on the assumption that Africans maintained an imperfect relation to their environment, including land and its natural resources.

Positivists replaced existing juridical idioms and rights with new ones, through metaphysical processes that entitled European claimants to political authority, land, and resources. The new processes were intended to provide guidance to rival European powers, chartered companies, and settlers. The presence of a foreign state or its nationals in any African territory was said to signify the desire of the concerned party to establish political influence or control. Just as occupation under civil law was the first step toward possession and title, foreign presence symbolized extraterritorial sovereignty, or initiation of it.

In this atmosphere of conquest, European powers imposed Western idioms of property and property relations as the basis of social relations. African territories were acquired through conquest, annexation, or other forms of outside administration. Documentation also became a necessary component of agreements between the conquerors and non-European societies. As a result, the emerging colonial powers supported their claims by obtaining protection treaties and other concessionary agreements with the native populations. Finally, European powers could freely exchange their protectorates or colonies through mutually agreed upon accords of cession.[110]

When the end of Western imperialism shifted from the acquisition of special privileges to the assumption of political power, jurists and politicians insisted on the strict enforcement of procedural rules of evidence and entitlements. The new rules of procedure served to determine the status of private property. They were also central to the colonial discourse. Specifically, they were deliberately intended to annul prior ownership (by Africans and others) and establish new property relations under new structures. For instance, the new requirements, rules, and procedures united the right to a thing and the possession of that thing in a title.[111] The title was not only proclaimed to be the source and de facto antecedent of property right, it was signified by a written document.[112] This written document, also title, was introduced as evidence of property despite the fact that most communities were unfamiliar with such documents. The implementation of the rules of entitlement left the colonized without the means to protect their rights, both tangible and intangible.

By the turn of the twentieth century, European powers had successfully established total control over their African possessions. They now needed new legal systems that enabled them to maintain their imperial holdings. The new legal environment was constructed around images provided by contractual principles and related doctrines. These doctrines rejected both the fairness of exchange and inherent justice (the legal basis of early mercantilism everywhere) as the foundations of contractual and other forms of obligations.[113] Under formal colonialism, European powers began to place the emphasis on the wrongs of unilateral abrogation by Africans of past agreements, enunciated by the terms of surrender to conquest and of punitive capitulations to the militarily powerful as well as those of concessions and protection treaties. Subsequently, the colonial powers insisted on the duty of their African partners to compensate them for damages resulting from breach of contracts. In fact, they enforced African compliance through coercive political, economic, and military means.

Perpetual Metaphysics

Throughout the colonial period, Western powers adapted the formalist view of the role of the law in societal development: that the contract was the primary implement of social interactions and the primary means of transfer or alteration of property. As the primary tools of colonial relations, however, contractual agreements resulted from unequal power relations and depended upon foreign idioms. Whether written or not, European-African accords generally imposed unilateral burdens on the indigenous populations. These unilateral obligations resulted from both informed consent and deceit. As in the case of Namibia, colonial powers and nationals introduced in the language of their agreements technical and obscure concepts that were foreign to African legal cultures with the clear intent of deceiving their native partners.

In contrast, European-African agreements lacked guarantees for African right to European performance. In this regard, virtually all protection treaties related to enforceable land transfers and seldom to African protection against foreign settlers. In other words, whereas colonial powers and settlers promised protection to their African partners, they actually expropriated native populations. They also claimed the right to wage war if necessary in order to establish free access to natural resources for the general welfare. Instead, they brought about misery, exploitation, and underdevelopment.

In their enforcement of the contractual obligations, colonial powers and courts also sided with settlers and other colonialists. The different administering authorities and colonial courts supported individual European claims to property against African demands for reciprocity. In these instances, they always sided with the propertied classes in the colonies and at home, that is, with industrialists, financiers, settlers, and their local allies.[114] They focused chiefly on the illegality of breach of contracts by Africans or on the monetary and other privations suffered by Europeans as a result.[115]

Western powers maintained the same attitude during decolonization. They insisted upon preindependence agreements that included the constitutional protection of selected rights and liberties.

In reality these conditions to national self-rule protected former colonialists against postcolonial deprivation of property and other material losses. In contrast, the former colonial powers and Western-dominated international institutions have not considered it morally or jurisprudentially necessary to compensate Africans for expropriations, damages, and losses suffered during colonial rule.[116]

Condoning this Western attitude, international legal scholars have rejected postcolonial demands for restitution and reparations on the grounds that it would require state or outside intervention in essentially interpersonal or contractual relations. This position reflects the prevalent formalist prejudice against state adjudication of individual rights and privileges. However, current theoretical opposition to this particular kind of state activism starkly contrasts with the legitimacy accorded to another form of intervention: that resulting from the idea that states are constitutionally bound to protect the interests of their nationals abroad, including settlers and other colonialists. Indeed, during their tenure, Western colonial powers legislated individual rights and liberties as well as the terms of societal interactions in their colonies. They determined the rights and liberties of various elements of colonial society (including Africans and European settlers and companies) in a manner consistent with the realization of the larger imperial rights.[117]

In the following chapters, I analyze colonial rule and decolonization in Africa (particularly Namibia) in light of the three international regimes and their corresponding legal systems. These juridico-political regimes have characterized Europe's relations to Africa. They were instituted by the 1884–85 Berlin Conference, the 1920 League Convention that followed World War I, and the 1945 United Nations Conference. My aim is to demonstrate that international law and specific juridical constructs have functioned in the dominant European culture as an ideology that has mediated between the expansionist desires of Europe, the juridical means to attaining hegemony, and the opposing need to project these juridical means as objectively derived from universal values. This process began with the inception of international law and continues in the postcolonial era. Its sole purpose has been to perpetuate Western hegemony and to erode non-European sovereignty and the other's capacity to overcome a subordinate position.

3

Natives' Right to Dispose of Themselves

The 1884–85 Berlin Conference ended the phase of non-Christian alterity when the right of the infidel to *dominium* and *imperium* was flatly rejected. It partially restored the status of Africans—they were promoted from humans without civil or sovereign rights (the dominant view throughout the slave trade) to individuals with limited political rights, including the right to dispose of themselves—but this exclusively European meeting formalized the division of Africa. The final accord, the General Act of Berlin, also signaled the absolute rule of positive law on that continent. It imposed perpetual burdens on Africans by compelling its peoples to surrender full political authority to colonial powers.[1] It restricted the right of indigenous peoples to dispose of themselves to a narrow choice between colonial masters. According to Belgian delegate Edouard P. Engelhardt, modern science had positively recognized the right of "indigenous tribes ... as independent states to sign treaties, to consent to the total or partial abandonment of their sovereignty, whether by definitive cession of their territories or by the stipulation of a protectorate."[2] In sum, Africans' role in the Berlin regime was limited to their juridical capacity to surrender other rights to European powers.

DISCURSIVE STRUCTURES I

The nineteenth-century debate over the direction of colonial engagements opposed two philosophies: paternal protection and radical exploitation. The first was advocated by philanthropists (mostly political progressives, scientists, and liberal Christians) who envisioned a postabolition paternal protection of Africans. In contrast, colonialists (generally private individuals, companies, and government officials and institutions) were primarily dedicated to the integration of African colonies into the global political economy. The Berlin Conference, dominated by conservatives and capitalists, resolved the debate in favor of the latter.[3]

The international regime established by the Berlin Conference had two principal objectives. One was to formalize colonial rule by determining the rules and procedures applicable to foreign administration. The other aim was to normalize the collective exploitation of the newly "discovered" Congo Basin. The participants accomplished their second objective by creating an international enterprise inappropriately named the Independent State of the Congo (or ISC). The ISC was then placed under the supervision of the International Congo Commission (ICC).

Philanthropist Thrusts

The ideological impulse that shaped the Berlin African Conference had its antecedents in the late-eighteenth-century British exploration movement and the contemporary philanthropic humanism in favor of African emancipation. The latter originated in the abolitionist movement, when mostly progressive antislavers criticized human bondage and proposed in its place the threefold policy of Christian humanism, commerce, and emancipation. With respect to Africa, philanthropist and abolitionist proponents of reform sought to replace coercive conquest with negotiated annexation or guardianship. They initially gained their strength from unrelated scientific and political developments. Specifically, they benefited from scientific pronouncements, and public acceptance of them, that Africans were inferior but still human.[4]

After abolition, many Western progressives categorically opposed any new forms of exploitation, yet the majority of abolitionists and philanthropists did not dispute the legitimacy of European rule in Africa. They simply lamented its excesses and demanded the restoration of a balance:

> How are we to frame a just estimate of the value of our civilization for the natives of Africa? Clearly, in order to do this, we must strike

a balance between that which it takes and what it gives in return. Thus, as takers, we exploit their land and their labor on terms highly advantageous to ourselves. As givers, then, can we be said to offer measure for measure?[5]

The transformation desired by the advocates of Africans' rights, emancipation, took on various configurations depending on whether its proponents referred to African slaves or people living on the African continent. With respect to Africans who lived on the continent, the equivalent of emancipation was rhetorically framed to mean the "well-being of the native populations." As stated in Article VI of the General Act of Berlin: "All the Powers exercising sovereign rights or influence in these territories pledge themselves to watch over the preservation of the native populations and the improvement of their moral and material conditions of existence, and to work together for the suppression of slavery and the slave trade."[6]

The emancipationists wished to free the slave within the "minimum decency which humanity required,"[7] but they insisted on European guardianship.[8] They considered Africans to be in a mental state of infancy and therefore incapable of standing by themselves. As a result, the primary political goal was the creation of societies that, in the words of French premier Georges Clemenceau, "compl[ied] with certain principles of government" to be determined by Europeans.[9]

Indeed, most humanists accepted the premise of "European guardianship" as a "sacred trust of civilization."[10] Some promoted "trusteeship" as a necessary guarantee to effective peace among the "barbaric tribes" of Africa: "local wars ceased wherever there was effective [European] authority ... [when c]onflicts and litigations among African states were subject to prior mediation."[11] Emile Banning, the philanthropist and Belgian delegate who made this assertion, also believed that "legitimate commerce" reduced tension and led to "legitimate government" and peace: "economic legislation would rest upon an identical base and their political rapports would depend upon deliberate transactions, sanctioned by the maritime powers of the two worlds [European and American]."[12]

Africans' Right to Dispose of Themselves

The emancipationists were also emboldened by the legal culture, particularly its firm endorsement of the right of communities to dispose of themselves. From its origin in the eighteenth century, Western theory had framed the right of peoples to dispose of themselves (later construed as self-determination) in opposition to foreign sovereignty (papal or monarchic). It was exercised against the right of any other power but that of the entity that claimed it.

The right of peoples to dispose of themselves depended upon free and unconstrained will of the self to determine its own political system and affiliation. In Europe, where it was first applied, this legal and political concept propelled the populace to the highest level of authority as the repository of sovereignty. There its application took several forms, including referenda, consultations, and plebiscites, all intended to determine the future of communities with ambigious political status or distinct identities. In sum, the *teleos* of self-disposition was autonomy, or itself. This right was considered void when and if its end were decided by any other self but that which sought it. Finally, to dispose of the self, a community was supposed to have the power and will to decide, fully cognizant of and prepared to accept the consequences of its action.[13]

Imbued in this legal tradition, the emancipationists insisted upon similar mechanisms of native consultation that would legitimize any transfer of power. Ironically, the rational basis of European paternalism remained the systematic belief in black inferiority. In this regard, the emancipationists shared the epistemology of the colonial discourse.[14] Whereas the right of peoples to dispose of themselves implies an active and independent role, Africans were expected to surrender their right to sovereignty and related privileges to a colonial power of their choice.

In the end, the General Act made explicit references to the much-publicized philanthropic sensitivity of the participants by endorsing the "right of the indigenous populations to dispose of themselves" as the cornerstone of colonial relations.[15] However, praxis endorsed by the 1885 Brussels Convention and comparable forums indicated that the *teleos* of Africans' right to dispose of themselves was to transfer their "hereditary" right to their "soil" and self-rule to foreign powers.[16] African rights were not absolute rights but privileges bestowed by colonial powers upon pacified native populations.

Certainly Western humanists (abolitionists and philanthropists) maintained their position on the preservation of the welfare of the native populations throughout the Berlin Conference. Their requirements included the eradication of internal slavery as well as the prohibition of the sale of alcohol. They also sought to curtail the sale of automatic weapons in order to prevent an arms buildup. As a result, the General Act committed the signatory powers to "watch over the preservation of the native populations and to supervise the improvement of the conditions of their moral and material well-being." It also made formal references to guardianship and protection.[17]

Although they were aesthetically cogent, the Berlin dispositions lacked enforcement instruments or measures, and in many ways were only a parody of the philanthropists' concerns. This situation also allowed for abuses. In fact, the impulse of the Berlin Conference was to implement colonial cooperation, hegemony, and African nonsubjectivity. With regard to the arms race, for instance, the General Act, the 1890 Brussels Treaty, and other comparable acts selectively banned several categories of firearms between the twentieth parallel north and the twenty-second parallel south. The selection of the area of enforcement, extending from the southern tip of the Sahara Desert to the area of the Limpopo River, allowed Europeans to maintain superiority over Africans throughout conquest.[18]

Nor did the Berlin Act and subsequent accords eliminate the practice of internal slavery by European explorers and private companies. Rather, this prohibition was selectively applied to non-Europeans as a means to eliminating more experienced competitors. For instance, the Berlin powers targeted Arab merchants and entrepreneurs for criticism and action under the interdiction clause. Although Arab traders internally enslaved Africans, the Berlin fiat only eliminated the more experienced Middle Eastern merchants (they had settled the eastern coast of central Africa long before Europeans) from competition in other areas.[19]

DISCURSIVE STRUCTURES II

From a strictly economic and political standpoint, the Berlin Conference can be traced directly to two events, both related to the industrial revolution and the mounting domestic need in Europe for natural resources and markets abroad. The first was the growing rivalry among colonial settlers in Africa and their demand for protection by their home governments. Indeed, the Berlin meeting occurred during a shift in the European balance of power in Africa. Specifically, Portugal, Spain, and the Netherlands were losing ground to Britain, France, and Germany in the territorial scramble. In the southern tip of Africa, for instance, Portugal already shared its influence with Britain and with whites of Dutch and French descent who no longer entirely depended on the Netherlands. This shifting balance of power was compounded by complementary changes in the economic strength and military capability of the competing nations.

The concurrent transition from competitive mercantilism to monopoly capitalism had also profoundly affected colonial interactions. Where once free mercantilist competition dominated inter-European relations, new explorers, merchants, and settlers now sought exclusive territorial control of trade and mineral prospects. This nascent demand for territory drew the opposition of both Africans and rival colonialists. As a result, the demand by new monopolistic societies for national protection and assistance grew ever louder. Meanwhile, each monopoly secured previously loosely defined zones of influence into exclusive domains, colonies, or protectorates.

The "discovery," in this context, of vast territories along the western coast of Africa and in the hinterland of central Africa confounded rival colonial powers, old and new. It aroused interest in Europe and the United States to define the rules or formalities for new occupations on the coast of Africa.[20] This opinion was conveyed by Frederick T. Frelinghuysen, then U.S. secretary of state, to the Senate:

> The development recently attained by the commerce of Western Africa has led the Governments of France and Germany to think that it would be for the interest of all nations engaged in that trade to regulate, in a spirit of mutual good will, the conditions that might secure its development, and prevent disputes and misunderstandings.[21]

The conference offered Spain, Germany, and France the opportunity to check excessive territorial or commercial ambitions in the central and southwestern region of Africa.[22] According to Geoffrey de Courcel, the French envoy, France was only interested in preserving its national domains against Anglo-Portuguese encroachments.[23] The French prime minister, in particular, was satisfied to adopt consensual rules on free trade on the "mouth of the Congo." Additionally, Jules Ferry desired an understanding on the extent of such rights for Western nations that had no colonies in Africa in order to prevent abuses.[24]

As newcomers to colonial conquest, Germany and Belgium sought the means to establish themselves as contenders for empire. They desired a European summit to ward off challenges from more experienced colonialists in the African "spheres of influence" of their own nationals. In particular, Germany feared that the monopoly of the Bremen merchants and missionaries in southwestern Africa and elsewhere would be broken by Dutch and British settlers. Bremen merchants and missionaries in the region had continuously complained of the "intrusion of Cape Colonial cattle traders from the south."[25]

The General Act of Berlin satisfied the conflicting desires of the participants and their citizens. It first sought to guarantee the freedom of trade and access proposed by the German chancellor, Prince Otto von Bismarck, King Leopold II of Belgium, and the U.S. government: "no power which exercises sovereign rights in the region [was] allowed to grant therein either monopoly or privilege of any kind in commercial matters."[26] Second, the Berlin Act created the International Commission of the Congo in Central and South Central Africa, around the mouths of the Congo River.[27]

Quasi-Sovereign Association

Among the propositions made by Western humanists (philanthropists and abolitionists and others), the conferees were most impressed by the notion of trusteeship (or guardianship) and its economic corollary of exploitation and development. This seemingly liberal position also supported the colonialist principle of gradual integration of colonial economies into the global colonial structures (an integral component of the European system), according to the degree of evolution of the natives.[28] The philanthropist thrust enabled the colonialists to present their mission in a new light. De Courcel summed up the new mission as "not only to exploit, but to civilize; two inseparable missions, because ... the conservation of the indigenous population and its participation in the development of these regions are indispensable to a lasting [European] prosperity."[29]

The Berlin forum was intended therefore to determine the appropriate juridical basis for colonial relations in Africa generally and, in particular, to coordinate trade along the Congo, its basin, and other territories not yet formally controlled by colonial powers. Prior to the Berlin meeting, the newly "penetrated" Congo Basin was the scene of competing claims by various colonial agencies and individuals. The key player, the Belguim-based International Association of the Congo, enlisted the services of Henry Morton Stanley to survey the region. During 1877–78, the British-born American explorer terrorized native chiefs into submission: "I skirmish in their streets, drive them pell-mell into the woods beyond, and level their Ivory temples."[30] Stanley returned to his Belgian employer "with no less than 450 alleged treaties." These treaties transferred African lands to the Belgian International Association.[31]

Stanley also met Belgian King Leopold of Belgium and advised him that the Congo was poised to be a profitable enterprise with the requisite development and investments. Leopold was advised by the International Association of the Congo that several British and French entrepreneurs were equally interested in such an enterprise. Fear of Belgium lost in an uncontrolled competition compelled King Leopold to propose the Berlin Conference. The governments of France and Germany, however, were first to propose that "the principles adopted by the Vienna Congress with a view to sanctioning free navigation on several international rivers [in particular the Danube] be applied to the Congo and the Niger."[32] The juridical principles involved concerned bodies of water (i.e., seas and rivers) adjacent to or flowing through more than one country. These norms granted equal access to the populations that depended upon the seas or rivers for their existence or activities.[33]

Oddly, the nations and populations represented by the Berlin powers were not situated on the banks of the Niger and Congo Rivers. Nor were these powers chosen by the populations thus situated to represent them. As a result, the European powers created a novel institutional framework to coordinate policy in the mouths and basin of the Congo. The so-called International Commission of the Congo (ICC) was uniquely designed to promote colonial rule by juridical means. The role of the ICC was to minimize confrontation by providing the political and economic impetus for cooperation to rival claimants. It did so by extending the customary principle of freedom of navigation and trade in Africa to all imperialist powers, including the United States and Turkey, which had no Sub-Saharan African possessions.[34] Finally, the ICC was the first juridical instrument specifically designed to ensure collective colonial exploitation by subordinating African subjectivity to European desire. The development of commerce in Africa, said Britain's Sir Edward Malet, gave rise to "the very legitimate desire to open up to civilization those territories that have hitherto remained unexplored and unoccupied."[35]

The ICC was conceived as a state unto itself, neutral and free of any national state,[36] but it was an entity with no ordinary features. Nothing was exact for the ICC; in the words of the Italian Riccardo Pierantoni, it "unite[d] within itself the double nature of a state and an international colony."[37] Indeed, the ICC was a subject of convenience, an institution endowed by legal fiction with the attributes of an autonomous state. The International Association of the Congo, a private enterprise, provided the embryo of its government.[38] This novel status for a private company presented practical difficulties, especially in the area of its being recognized by other states. With U.S. mediation,[39] this difficulty was resolved by attributing juridical sovereignty to King Leopold, who then deputized his authority to the ICC for practical purposes.[40]

Initially, the ICC was dominated by philanthropists and other liberals who positioned themselves as mediators of the complex relations between Africans and Europeans. Africans, who were conspicuously absent from the Berlin summit, were not represented in or by this body.[41] Predictably, the ICC soon succumbed to the ambitions of members who, as colonial officers, promoted the national policies of the five state members: Belgium, France, Great Britain, Germany, and the United States. The final blow came when King Leopold II replaced the ICC with the Congo Free State, thereby transforming the territory into a personal colonial estate.

The transformation of the ICC into an independent state responsive only to King Leopold initially triggered opposition among other colonial powers. The initial suspicion gave way to reluctant acceptance when it became apparent that the declaration of the Congo Free State did not violate the "Berlin spirit":[42] it did not totally preclude the free pursuit of commerce and the rights of other colonial powers to explore and exploit the Congo's natural resources.[43] King Leopold's action, however, further integrated the Congo and its inhabitants into a global economic system. African rights to property and *dominium* within the new state remained similar to what they had been under the international commission.

Protectorate and Other Submission Treaties

The Berlin Conference also provided the required legality to new and past colonial claims by legitimizing all forms of European authority in Africa: zones of influence, protectorates, and colonies. Under its terms, the primary evidence of any colonial claim was the effective control of the territory.[44] A claimant power was required only to demonstrate that it had established effective control by annexation or obtained protection or other concessionary agreements from the natives of a territory.[45] In practice, foreign control was often preceded by accords with the natives granting the colonial power exclusive rights of trade and dominion. The acquisition of exclusive trading rights and dominion was followed by the establishment of a "zone of influence," accompanied by the proclamation of a protectorate. The latter was a government by a protector, which differed only in degree from the absolute sovereignty bestowed by annexation or occupation.[46]

The Berlin discussants and other European publicists attributed the juridical forms of the zone of influence, the protectorate, and annexation to cultural precedents, namely, the theories of contract and representative government.[47] The advent of capitalism in Europe had freed the individual from previous forms of bondage, specifically serfdom and slavery. Citizens were presumed to be independent economic agents in the marketplace, where they were free to enter contractual agreements. The individual also played a critical role in legitimizing authority. Representative democracies gave form to individual participation in governments through election. The processes of individual participation and democratic representation affected the theoretical foundations upon which publicists and others built the legitimacy of public authority.

The widespread acceptance of individual consent as the source of obligations in both economic transactions and political affiliation compelled Europeans to redefine the epistemological foundation of colonial bondage. This intellectual disposition had political implications as well. As in contractual relations or political representation, the will of the indigenous populations became the sole source of their obligation to transfer their rights to property and sovereignty to colonial powers.

This contractual image of colonial relations belied the precepts of the colonial discourse as well as the power dynamics of most transactions, which opposed protector (or conquering) powers to protected (conquered) communities. The colonial discourse made an unambiguous distinction between the individual rights of Africans and their political rights as communities. As individuals, Africans had been emancipated from slavery and could engage in economic activities as agents—provided such relations occurred within the strict boundaries of colonial relations. In contrast, Africans' right to dispose of themselves conflicted with the outward limit of the political authority, which the colonial powers retained under the General Act. In this sense, the right of the conquered to dispose of themselves was *not* a full political right but a humanitarian gesture.[48] Neither was this right derivable from ordinary contractual relations. The object of the transactions (alienation of native rights) was not negotiable. Moreover, the natives did not have the juridical grounds to alter or reject the framework of the relationship. To paraphrase a British delegate, His Majesty's government, and others, allowed the sovereign right of the "inferior races" only if it was strictly limited to participation in the transfer of territories.[49]

The sole rational basis of the protectorate was the unwavering belief in African inferiority.[50] Ironically, the presumptions of mental immaturity and juridical incapacity did not undermine the contractual principle of good faith in colonial transactions. Nor did colonial coercion nullify native consent. In fact, the essential element of colonial transactions remained the legal title they conferred as material evidence of European influence.[51] Modern international law, according to American delegate Jason A. Kasson, "followed a path which [led] to the recognition of the rights of the indigenous races to voluntarily dispose of themselves and of their hereditary soil."[52] Finally, African right of consent remained valid only when the party concerned did not resist colonialism. The government of the U.S. supported any rule that, in Kasson's words, "sought the voluntary consent of the indigenous peoples whose country is transferred in instances where the concerned parties did not commit any belligerent acts."[53]

Kasson reflected the pivotal epistemological relation of the colonial discourse: European rights in Africa were linked to the inferiority of the natives.[54] The American minister in Germany and others believed that Africans did not possess equal rights and privileges. They were mere "tribesmen" or "savages" who happened to occupy specific geographical spaces that they could not legitimately claim as their own. Accordingly, African right of consent was secondary to the colonial right of control or access: "no foreign power … was disposed to subordinate a priori its distant conquests to native sovereignty."[55]

In general, the Berlin regime was predicated upon unilateral burdens, in particular a unidirectional transfer of rights from predetermined transferers to select Western recipients. Africans were expected to grant specific tangible property rights as well as intangible special privileges to public or private colonial agents through concessionary treaties or private agreements. In contrast, the European parties committed themselves only to unspecified general obligations (for example, attending to the welfare of subject populations.)

The legal norms applicable to these situations once again exceeded the *jus gentium*. For instance, the domestic legitimacy, or lack thereof, of an African party mattered only if its determination affected the positions of contending European parties. Only then did colonial powers consider the political status of the consenting party according to local laws and customs.[56] By the end of the nineteenth century, the political and military reality in Africa enabled European colonial authorities to interfere with local political processes and disputes. These power relations allowed for the rise to power of African rulers who owed their legitimacy to the backing of the outsiders. They needed and eventually relied on the protection of their foreign backers to ward off internal challenges as well as outside aggressions.[57]

THE GERMAN RIGHT OF INTERVENTION

By the time Germany's colonial ambitions materialized in the middle of the nineteenth century, both the colonial discourse and the art of intervention had been fully developed. Each occupier relied on military advantages and local agents or collaborators who identified with the ends of colonial rule to retain control. Lacking the advantage of experience in colonial involvement, the first German nationals to arrive in South West Africa soon discovered that their success depended on adherence to the rules of colonial engagements. These rules required that they obtain concessionary agreements from the populations or effective control through military and other means or both.

The Rhenish missionaries and Bremen merchants used all the available cultural, mental, and intellectual resources in securing the South West Africa protectorate, but they also benefited from the new cooperative climate of the Berlin regime. The protectorate, which guaranteed annexation and noninterference by other colonial powers, was one of the traditional tools of political control. The official German annexation took place years after Emperor Wilhelm I first agreed to extend the protection of the German empire to its nationals, merchants, and missionaries in the southwestern territory of Africa. Wilhelm's decision was followed by the raising of the German flag over German settlements in the territory and the institution of a local administration. These events occurred prior to the Berlin Conference, which preceded formal proclamation of annexation and protectorate yet confirmed German influence over the territory.[58]

In general, the circumstances of German control of the territory differed from those of its predecessors. In particular, the established rules and procedures did not apply to the German case, in part because the participants to the Berlin summit had placed the requirements of collective access and free trade above any other concern. As a result, the conference recognized German authority in South West Africa even before it obtained the required protection treaties or exercised effective control. German authority was solely in the legitimacy it had acquired from the trust that other colonial powers placed in it and its acceptance of the principle that its protectorate would be limited to administration, with no promotion of exclusive colonial privileges.

The post-Berlin protectorate reflected the two conflicting tendencies of colonialism during this period. On the one hand, national interests and capital in need of colonies promoted protectionism and monopoly. On the other hand, the colonial powers responded to the imperatives of competition to maintain freedom of trade. The protectorate provided Germany with the colony it needed, but it had to comply with the rules of competitive capitalism embodied in the cooperative spirit of Berlin.

The needs of colonial powers more than any other factor dictated the terms of each protectorate. These terms depended upon a host of political factors that did not necessarily relate to the actual occupation of a territory. According to Kader Asmal, the conference did not directly address territorial claims, even though the question of effective occupation was on its agenda. The majority of territorial claims were decided outside the conference, by bilateral or multilateral agreements. The conference was concerned with "the nature of colonial occupation and the definition of the political objectives towards people under colonial control which were to be imposed in the future on any power occupying any part of the coast of Africa."[59]

Colonial Collaboration and Complicity

The actual form of the German protectorate in South West Africa depended on colonial cooperation in securing occupation, the cohesiveness of goals, and the actions of colonialists in the face of African resistance to colonialism. In this case, the complicity of Britain and British settlers in the Cape Colony was essential to German successes in crushing resistance, establishing control, and thwarting the ambitions of the Portuguese settlers and Afrikaners. British cooperation was indispensable in taming the ambitions of Portugal and the Portuguese nationals and Afrikaners whose ambitions endangered the balance of colonial interests. Britain's recognition of German interests and its cooperation with the establishment of the German protectorate were motivated by British rivalries with Portugal and Afrikaners.

By 1884, for instance, a group of Transvaalers and Cape colonists had begun to create a colony north of their own, extending into what would become South West Africa. These Afrikaner farmers and British merchants, led by one Willem Jordaan, "bought" a vast land area north of German settlements and declared a republic. The site of the Afrikaner-dominated Republic of Upingtonia lay in a region that more or less corresponds with the present district of Grootfontein.[60] The mineral-rich territory was strategically located between the British and German zones of interest.

The existence of the Afrikaner republic posed a direct challenge to British hegemony in the southern tip of the continent and to German interest in establishing a protectorate in the region. Jordaan, the leader of the new republic, and his group of Trek-Boers had allied themselves with Portugal. The founders of the new republic sought authorization from Portugal to establish themselves north of the Kunene, somewhere near Humpata.[61] Jordaan also directly opposed British colonial designs. He was a rival of Cecil J. Rhodes and his agent Robert Lewis as well as William Coates Palgrave, the British governor of Cape Colony.[62] Great Britain could not tolerate the challenge posed by the existence of Upingtonia to its economic interests and its reputation as the leading colonial power. In its opposition to Upingtonia and Jordaan, Britain found an ally in Germany. They conspired together to destabilize the new nation. Upingtonia subsequently dissolved in 1886, following the assassination of its creator, Jordaan—allegedly by the Ovambo chief Nechale.[63]

Both Britain and Germany benefited from this collaboration. In return for the German promise not to challenge Britain's rights to the deep-water port of Walvis Bay and the surrounding area, British authorities assured Germany of their assistance in establishing the protectorate.[64] For instance, the governor of the Cape ignored a request by British settlers to extend the protection of the Crown to the populations of the region north of the colony largely because of his desire to cooperate with German settlers. Britain had previously acquiesced in Bismarck's decision to extend German protection to German citizens "in the manner and in the degree in which the empire generally allows."[65]

During their collaboration, Britain and Germany maintained similar reactions to private individuals whose behavior was either contrary to official policy or judged unbecoming to colonialism. Such was the case when Cecil Rhodes attempted to interfere with German control of South West Africa. In this endeavor Rhodes enlisted Robert Lewis to obtain concessions from Africans.[66] Once an interpreter and assistant to the governor of the Cape, Lewis had extensive knowledge of the territory and even some of African languages. A military strategist, he had also served as resident trader to many local chiefs, including Hendrik Witbooi, to whom he provided credit and ammunitions, among other things.[67]

Lewis confronted many German settlers, including Dr. Heinrich Göring, with whom he debated the legality of his activities. He rightly contended that Göring's claims to the territory were not founded on actual control. In addition, Lewis insisted that the German claims lacked the required internal legitimacy, the consent of the native populations to treaties of protection. When Germany proclaimed the annexation of South West Africa in 1890, it had only obtained the agreement of few African chiefs. According to an official British account, only two of the seven "independent, wealthy and powerful" chiefs who were related to the Kamaherero of Okahandja had entered into agreement with the German authorities by 1890. Likewise, three of twelve acting Nama leaders found the Bremen merchants worthy of their trust.[68] Eight other leaders followed the path of Hendrik Witbooi in rejecting German "protection."[69]

Even though Lewis's arguments were consistent with the rules of colonial engagements, he and Rhodes were forced to cease their activities because they conflicted with the official position. Göring was in accord with the official understanding, and as a result he received official support long before he was appointed imperial commissioner with the juridical capacity to engage the German Crown.[70]

Protectorate: Symbol of the New Regime

The protective sovereignty that Germany exercised in Africa was different from the European norm. It was a colonial ownership over a territory that was not ownerless and, therefore, required specific juridical arrangements. Typically, the African party was required to recognize the jurisdiction of the German emperor over German settlers, and to refer all disputes between natives and Europeans to the German authorities.[71] The natives were also expected to grant unrestricted trade rights, guarantee the security of settlers, and respect European property. Like formal colonial rule, the protectorate made African external relations dependent upon Germany. The settlers demanded grant concessions, but they also interdicted the natives from entering into treaties or "dispos[ing] of their land or the interests therein to any nation or the subjects thereof without the prior consent" of the settlers. Finally, African chiefs were required "in the event of disputes with other chiefs, to call in the German authorities as mediators."[72]

Significantly, the protectorate allowed Germany and other foreign powers to wield greater influence over internal political processes. Germany used its influence to create political discord among Africans in order to establish a political order it controlled.[73] In this process, the colonial power was aided by the virtual integration of the local colony into the global political economy. The colonial economy created social and economic differentiations that affected local power struggles and structures. Africans who collaborated with the colonial system had greater access to resources that were not locally available. The African collaborators received "the highest protection" of the German Crown, along with recognition and support of their jurisdiction and control over their own people. In addition, the settlers promised to "respect the laws, customs, and usages of the natives" and to pay the usual taxes to the African chief.[74] As a result, the collaborators emerged as a powerful economic and political force, strong enough to either oppose the old leadership or attempt to co-opt it into partnership. In the most extreme cases, the emerging socioeconomic class overthrew the existing structures of power in collaboration with German settlers.[75] Whatever the origins of intra-African conflicts, they weakened all the parties involved. The internal power struggle allowed German settlers to eliminate opposition to their own rule and establish control over the territories of the victors and vanquished. The settlers accomplished this control over a period of a decade as they persuaded or coerced African chiefs to accept "protection" under highly unfavorable conditions.[76] In practice, the treaty of protection was an instrument of expropriation without compensation. Such agreements contained no mechanism for the enforcement of German obligations. In contrast, when it suited their policy and designs, the settlers "did not hesitate to hold their part of the agreements binding on the natives, while absolving [themselves] from the liability to give protection as promised."[77]

Monopoly of Property Relations

The objective of the protectorate was first and foremost to ensure the protection of colonial settlers and their activities by imposition of political control and metropolitan laws on the presumed legal vacuum in Africa.[78] The subordination of inter-African relations to the prior approval of German settlers was particularly important in the transformation of property and economic relations and the imposition of capitalist norms in the region. The latter had drastic sociopolitical implications for the indigenous communities as well as for the individuals engaged in public and private transactions.

The distorting effects of German laws on African norms predated the formalization of the protectorate.[79] During the period preceding formal annexation, commercial transactions and other civil contracts between the Bremen merchants and Africans were scattered and not yet regulated by any body of law that Germany would recognize. Yet, during this period, the German merchants dictated the terms of trade as well as laid the foundation for later colonial transformations.

The successes of the settlers were due in part to the long history of British and Dutch and Portuguese colonial activities. Specifically, British settlers from the Cape and Afrikaners had made extensive contacts with the populations of South West Africa centuries before the arrival of the first German mission. Similarly, the Portuguese had made many trips to parts of the territory from their colony of Angola to the north. These contacts involved military confrontations and alliances that contributed to the weakening of African societies and institutions and, subsequently, their capacity to resist German domination.[80]

The contacts also involved trade relations governed by European terms and norms. Thus, the first transactions between Bremen merchants and Africans invoked European units of measurement even though it was not entirely evident that Africans understood those units. In May 1883, for instance, Frans Adolf Eduard Luderitz, a Bremen merchant, concluded a purchase contract with Josef Frederiks, chief of the Bethanie people, that transferred Angra Pequena and the adjacent area, within a radius of five miles, to the German merchant.[81] This agreement gave the German businessman his first land acquisition.

In August 1883, Luderitz obtained another agreement from Frederiks concerning a strip of land "twenty geographical miles wide."[82] According to the historian Horst Drechsler, the German merchant took advantage of Frederiks's ignorance to extend this land beyond what the Nama leader had expected. Frederiks signed the agreement, envisioning the mile to be 1.7 kilometers according to British units of measurement. Luderitz did not inform the chief of the existence of a German mile, the equivalent of 7.4 miles. It was not until the actual delineation of the land that Luderitz insisted on using the German mile, in effect taking from the chief a vast territory. Frederiks objected, to no avail. Luderitz enforced his understanding of the agreement against the chief's will because he possessed the coercive means to do so. It was on this land that the settler directed the first geological exploration, intended to determine the territory's riches.[83]

Besides enticement and deceit, extortion was a commonly used means of acquisition. In July 1885, Luderitz's agents obtained the agreement of another Nama leader, Cornelius Zwartbooi, for a land exchange. According to the accord, Luderitz would obtain a portion of the coastal area inhabited by Zwartbooi and his followers, which lay between Omaruru and Swakop, in exchange for two locations in the Okombahe and the Waterberg areas, which lay deep into Hereroland. Luderitz claimed that he had acquired rights to the two areas in a prior deal with the Herero. This claim was in fact false, and Luderitz deliberately intended to deceive the African chief. Since written titles were not common among Africans, Zwartbooi did not require documentary evidence. He relied on personal trust. When the Nama chief and his people moved to the Herero territory, a confrontation ensued as the Herero stood firmly against Luderitz's claims. Again, German influence was coupled with the coercive means to impose the outcome of transactions such as land exchanges.

Partnership between Capital and State

Before South West Africa was formally declared a protectorate, German agents—farmers, company owners, miners, and financiers—acted on their own, independently of the state and finance capital. Adolf Luderitz and his followers, for instance, acquired great tracts of land in the hope that discovery of minerals would raise the interest of finance capital and the German public in colonialism. Such an interest, the settlers hoped, would compel the government to grant them the power they needed to pursue their colonial expansion.

Indeed, the discovery of minerals in 1884 by a group of German experts ignited interest in colonialism among German capitalists.[84] This initial discovery was followed by many others that confirmed the existence of diamond, gold, and other minerals in the territory. As expected, the interest of the German business community in the territory grew stronger with each discovery, propelling the issue of territorial acquisition into the domestic political agenda. Many interested parties expressed their views in the guise of nationalism: German pride, Germany's rightful position as a European power.

The land areas covered by Luderitz's transactions provided the Bremen merchants with their first satellite in the region. On April 24, 1884, Luderitz hoisted the German flag for the first time over the area known as Angra Pequena.[85] The German chancellor approved of the action under pressure from local constituencies with interests in colonial expansion. He was also impressed by the announcement that a team of scientists and prospectors had concluded that the territory was rich in natural resources and minerals. That announcement itself had confirmed the belief of the settlers that the territory occupied by the Herero contained enormous natural resources, while that of the Nama had unlimited potential for agriculture.[86] More important than land transactions and commercial disputes, the need to establish a colony laid the groundwork for full-fledged German intervention. Indeed, Prince Otto von Bismarck had yielded to business interests in 1885 and endorsed the creation of the German South West Africa Company.[87]

When the formation of the company was announced on April 30, 1885, its primary purpose was to take over Luderitz's possessions.[88] One reason for this takeover was the fear that Luderitz could not meet his financial commitments and as a consequence could lose his interests to non-Germans. The move by German capital was clearly informed by both nationalist sentiments and economic interests. However, the request of capital to the Bundesrat (German parliament) to create the company did not mention the financial bailout of Luderitz's possessions. Rather, it stressed the role of Germany in a future world order dominated by colonial expansion. Also motivated by nationalism, the Bundesrat lent its support and protection to the colonialists' efforts and to the capitalists who financed them. In this way, the myth of German national interests in South West Africa was created and the interests of the company confused with those of the country.[89] As a result of this juxtaposition, the protection of the company abroad became a national priority even though at home it served only the interests of its owners.

Throughout, Bismarck insisted that the administration of the colony would not be a state matter. The chancellor was not convinced of the necessity of his personal involvement until he was presented with the advantages of chartered companies in promoting national colonial objectives. The proposition of pursuing colonialism at a low cost captured his attention; he was impressed by the organization of British royal charters.[90] In Bismarck's mind, the German South West Africa company was first and foremost to remain financially self-reliant. In this scheme, the cost of colonial administration to the public remained minimal.[91] However, the company was granted special powers, notably the juridical capacity to engage the authority of the German state. As a public agent, the company could therefore receive concessionary agreements from African sovereigns on behalf of the German Crown. The company's official mandate was that of a quasi-sovereign public institution. Its authority included the power to acquire territories and the right to engage in trade and administer and assume governmental and legislative powers over the inhabitants of such territories.[92]

Much to his displeasure, Bismarck's dream for orderly administration of the colony was shattered by subsequent events, in particular the financial difficulties of the company and African resistance to colonial rule. The chancellor was compelled by public interests in the colony and concerns for the security of the settlers to appoint a public administrator to the colony and to proclaim the territory a German protectorate. For the majority of the settlers, the official annexation of the territory revolutionized the initial mandate. To them the new status of the colony implied that "the native tribes would have to give up their lands on which they had previously grazed their stocks in order that the white man might have the land for the grazing of his stock."[93] They were comforted in this belief by the decision of the German government to impose a series of protective laws that retroactively applied to all previous engagements to which German nationals were a party.[94]

The proclamation of the protectorate was followed by the designation of the first imperial commissioner. The subsequent behavior of the commissioner drew Germany further into confrontation with Africans and the ensuing militarization of the territory.[95] The commissioner, Heinrich Göring, required the assistance of the German army for the first time in 1888, following a disagreement with the Kamaherero.[96] A still reluctant German chancellor initially replied that

it lay outside the adopted programme of German colonial policy to intervene for the purpose of restoring, on behalf of the State, organizations among uncivilized peoples; and by the use of military power to fight the opposition of native chiefs towards the not yet established business undertakings of German subjects in overseas countries.[97]

However, Bismarck was pressured by the business community into sending a number of German soldiers to the colony. The first contingent of twenty-one soldiers arrived in the territory in 1889 under the direction of the von François brothers.[98]

Under the umbrella of the first public command structure, colonialists of all nations participated in the exploitation of Africans. The German South West Africa Company was acquired by British capital in 1892, for instance, with the strict understanding that it remained under German protection. The new owners, represented by Dr. Julius Scharlach of Hamburg, founded the more prosperous South-West African Company, which subsequently passed into the hands of Cecil Rhodes' agents.[99] Other private European agents also assisted the Germans in establishing final control over the territory. The British syndicate Kharaskhoma, for instance, encouraged three African communities to accept German protection. In return the syndicate expected to obtain concessionary rights in the territory from the German Reich.[100]

By 1893, German industrial and financial interests exercised significant influence over the national colonial policy. The territory's mineral riches had increased the demands of these interest groups for land, thus making land acquisition the most rewarding colonial endeavor. These groups joined the settlers, who needed more grazing and arable lands, in exerting pressure on the German governor Theodor Leutwein to define the boundaries of the territory. This territorial delineation entailed on the one hand a definition of the boundaries between areas occupied by Africans and Germans and, on the other, distinction of the German colony from other European settlements.[101]

The actions of the new governor alienated more Africans as well as created political turmoil. In response, Leutwein committed more troops to preventing the rise to power of African leaders hostile to German interests. Their first assignment was to prevent a coalition between the Nama and the Herero. In effect, Nama chief Hendrik Witbooi and his Herero counterpart Samuel Maharero had decided to halt their long-standing hostility in order to deal with developments in their homeland.[102] One effect of the cessation of hostility and the unity agreement was to eliminate the need for German protection. The Germans interpreted the African action as an affront to their control. Captain Curt von François responded with a distress call to Count Caprivi, the German chancellor, for additional troops to protect the settlers. On March 16, 1893, the new forces arrived.[103] A month later, von François set out to break the unity between Nama and Herero by attacking Witbooi, who was most antagonistic to German interests. Von François demonstrated German power by launching a surprise attack against Witbooi. In the battle of Hornkranz, German soldiers inflicted heavy losses on Nama troops and civilians.[104]

THE GERMAN SOUTH WEST AFRICA PROTECTORATE

In the nineteenth century, European politics was still dominated by "great men": dynasts and monarchs. Sovereignty and political legitimacy were vested in kings, princes, and autocrats, yet Europe was striving to strike a balance between these rulers and democratic elements. While the trend toward greater democracy in Europe was initiated by the bourgeoisie, the colonialists in Africa operated on the feudal notion that central authority invested in a ruler was necessary to the existence of the polity. Their colonial control depended on treaties and other concessions from African rulers. The colonialists sought out central African figures with whom they engaged in comprehensive and lasting agreements. The colonialists acted, falsely or rightly, as representatives of their own kings and princes. The approach most widely used by German settlers was to offer the African party the "protection" of the Prussian Crown in exchange for acceptance of German authority and laws.[105]

The centrality of the ruler in the polity served colonialists who negated African sovereignty by reconciling African autonomy with the belief that non-Europeans were constitutionally inferior to Christians. The colonialists wanted to replace African institutions with subservient central authorities.[106] The search for subservient or sympathetic African rulers required greater colonial interference in African political processes, especially in such decentralized political cultures as South West Africa's was. In this case, the degree of decentralization partly explains the degree of German activism in trying to control political successions.

During the second half of the nineteenth century, the Rhenish mission sought full monopoly over the region inhabited by the Herero. Initially, the mission asked the elder Herero leader, the Kamaherero, to protect them against the wrath of native religious leaders who were angered by the arrival of the mission.[107] The missionaries were still negotiating the terms of their relations with the Herero when the Bremen merchants arrived in the 1880s. They too were pressed by competition from British traders in the south and therefore sought concessions from the Herero leader to expand beyond the area of Windhoek. In exchange, the two German communities promised that the Kamaherero would receive the protection of the Prussian king in intra-African conflicts, especially if other African leaders opposed the Kamaherero's cooperation with the European merchants and missionaries.

The Kamaherero was already committed by similar arrangement to Palgrave, the governor of the Cape. Palgrave had promised to protect the Herero against the Boers, who at the time were making incursions in the territory. Instead, Palgrave placed undue restrictions on the chief's authority. As a result of this experience, he welcomed the advances of the Germans with some hesitation.[108] Under the Kamaherero's conditions, the German settlers stayed in the territory and entertained a loose and undefined relationship with the peoples and other leaders. The Herero leader, like many in the region, remained tolerant of the German presence. His own son even converted to Christianity and was baptized as Samuel.

It was not long before the behavior of the Bremen merchants began to irritate the Africans. In spite of opposition, the merchants aggressively undertook the purchase of land. They made deals with individuals and leaders that involved communal and collectively owned lands. Many of the transactions were contrary to custom and were concluded with individuals who lacked the authority to engage the entire community. Respectful of the laws and customs of his people, the Kamaherero initially refused to alienate either the land or his right as sovereign. He rejected all related German proposals.[109] One contemporary observer maintained that the African leader "would not hear of such a thing as German protection, refusing to sell an iota of territory. He was not even prepared to concede mining rights to Herr Luderitz."[110]

The firmness of the Kamaherero's position frustrated Luderitz's effort. In response, Luderitz exhorted German authorities to put pressure on the natives and to bring the colonial question into German political debate. Luderitz used his respectability in German colonial quarters to appeal directly to the Prussian king. In one letter Luderitz complained that the Kamaherero's opposition to his proposals signified an opposition to German national interests.[111] Luderitz equated, for the first time, the interests of the Bremen merchants with German national interests.

This stalemate between Luderitz and the Kamaherero remained until the Kamaherero's death on October 27, 1890, which opened up the opportunity for the settlers to enter the succession process in order to manipulate the outcome. The settlers used their influence to subvert the procedure by which the Kamaherero's successor was chosen. Their choice was the eldest son of the late chief, Samuel Maharero, disregarding Herero customs. The successor would have been the Kamaherero's nephew, Nikodemus Kambahahiza Kavikunua, chief of the eastern Herero. In Herero custom, the Kamaherero's son Samuel was a younger brother to Nikodemus. The settlers who did not trust Nikodemus and his followers conspired with Samuel to bar his cousin from power, and a German military court subsequently tried Nikodemus and his supporters as rebels and condemned them to death. They were executed on June 12, 1896.[112]

Centralization of Power under German Rule

The colonialists methodically replaced decentralized, loosely regulated African societies with a highly centralized and authoritarian colonial state. One intermediary German objective was to centralize power in the hands of reliable and loyal individuals. In this case, the settlers preferred Samuel for various reasons, including his early conversion to Christianity. They doubted Nikodemus's reliability because, although he was a Christian, he was not a devotee of the church. Samuel, on the other hand, was not only persistent in his faith, he had also indicated a flexibility not seen in either the old Kamaherero or Nikodemus.[113] The settlers' choice of leader transcended personal sympathies. They wanted to strengthen the Kamaherero's position within the Herero power structure in order to increase their own position as colonizers. The adopted title for the Kamaherero in the German political lexicon was supreme chief—a reference the chief conveniently adopted.[114]

However, the German plan for a centralized political structure had greater political and cultural implications unparalleled in Herero traditions. The Herero had never acknowledged a paramount chief, in the sense of a ruler of all Hereroland. The Kamaherero held a central position within Herero power relations that did not translate into a centralized power. He was merely an overseer and guardian of the customs and laws of the land. He was not above the scrutiny of parallel authority bearers in the Herero power structure. In fact, this parallelism in the power structure explained the processes of succession. Under Herero rules, a legitimate successor to the paramount chief had to be one of the leaders serving under his umbrella.[115]

The transmutation of the authority of the Kamaherero was inconsistent with an otherwise highly decentralized power structure and as a consequence caused resentment toward the new chief. Herero elders initially opposed Samuel's leadership because of both his sympathies for the Germans and the position he occupied. The office of Kamaherero was as religious in character as it was political.

Opposition to Samuel's rule grew so violent that Captain Curt von François invoked German patronage to intervene militarily on behalf of Samuel.[116]

The personalization of political authority was essential to the colonialist plan to transform African political and cultural institutions into instruments of colonial expansion. Thus, following Samuel Maharero's assumption of power, the German settlers began the systematic subversion of local institutions, political and otherwise. In the words of one Dr. Felix Meyer, "the Colonial Administration created not only a new authority; but it also broke into the laws of succession and inheritance of the Herero."[117] The authority of the Kamaherero was extended to include a juridical capacity comparable to that of a sovereign. In his new capacity, Samuel Maharero was vested with the power to alienate land, along with all other tangible and nontangible things, as well as the privileges and rights attached to them.[118]

The kind of individual power that the colonialists helped to create dispensed with the Herero relations to their community, land, and cattle. The Kamaherero could unilaterally undertake actions that belonged to the domain of a council of chiefs or elders. In time, the new leader began to commit himself to a commodity exchange completely foreign to communal ways. The new chief, like many before him, began to promote the kind of individual entitlements proper to capitalism and colonial exploitation.[119]

Seeds of Confrontation and War

The German expectation that Samuel Maharero would be totally compliant was not fulfilled. During his brief collaboration with the Germans, Samuel realized that his compliance to foreign pressures and manipulations cost him his legitimacy and his own people's loyalty. Samuel decided on these practical political grounds to reconsider his own interests. His reversal brought first unease among his former allies and then the reprisal of the colonialists. The reprisal was led by a coalition of German interests that comprised capital, represented by Adolf Luderitz; the German state, symbolized by Commissioner Heinrich Göring and Captain Curt von François; and the clergy. This coalition set itself to undo Samuel's power and also that of other elders.[120]

NATIVES' RIGHT TO DISPOSE OF THEMSELVES · 103

In 1889, for instance, Captain Curt von François, chief of German colonial forces, requested that Samuel allow him to move his troops from the center of the settlement ceded to the South West Africa Company to a place where they could be better protected against rebel attacks. In order to comply with this request, Samuel was to surrender more land to the settlers. The chief considered the people he would alienate and denied the request. His refusal angered von François, who retorted that while Africans' ownership of the land and their freedom to do with it what they pleased could not be disputed by words, they might reconsider if "armed might" was applied.[121] In response, Samuel suggested that von François return to his homeland because, he said, "I gather from the way you act that you are at war with us rather than at peace."[122]

In the 1890s, German colonialists often clashed with Africans for similar reasons. African resistance was weakened, however, by the disintegration of communal relations and the debilitating effects of land rights and trade relations imposed from without.[123] As Europeans trekked back and forth throughout the territory, a number of African leaders, especially Nama and Herero, made impressive inroads in the new political economy. White traders from England and South Africa provided their native allies with the means of trade (extended credit) as well as the material means (guns and ammunition) to protect themselves or to conquer their neighbors. Such was the case of the legendary Hendrik Witbooi, the Nama leader who resisted German rule until his death on October 29, 1905. In effect, before the arrival of the Germans, Witbooi—like many other African leaders—operated in the new political economy through different networks. These blooming networks were disrupted by the arrival of the Germans and the pace at which they attempted to impose political control over the territory.[124]

German settlers disrupted the old trade patterns and networks and in their place created new ones for their own benefit. They were encouraged in this process by the cooperation of British settlers as well as the fact that African resistance was unorganized. Like Witbooi, each African leader was concerned with his own survival in resisting German intervention. In the particular case of Witbooi, the colonialists failed to co-opt or to defeat him directly through their military attacks. Instead, the settlers offered material advantage to other Nama leaders in exchange for their support in isolating their rival.[125]

African opposition to German rule grew even stronger as it became evident to many local leaders that the natives were dispensable to the European desire for political and economic control. In fact, no African leader could count on the loyalty of the German administration when territorial gains were involved. Governor Leutwein's strategy of control consisted of a combination of influence, coercion, and intimidation. Theodor Leutwein was also known for his inclination to resort to dubious means to extract African consent or cooperation in his designs. He set the tone of his style in 1894 when, before negotiating a protection treaty, Leutwein organized the arrest of Andreas Lambert, the Khauas leader. Lambert was captured in an armed confrontation and indicted for the murder of a German settler.[126] He was then brought to Leutwein to negotiate the terms of his release, including a proposal for grant concessions to German authority.[127] Lambert gave his initial approval to the protection plan while he was in captivity, but he expressed the desire to consult with his chief counselors upon his release, and he later retracted his agreement.[128] When Leutwein received word of Lambert's new position, he ordered the chief's arrest. The Khauas chief was charged with murder and executed on the night of his second arrest. This official murder opened up another opportunity for the colonialists to maneuver for control over succession.[129]

POLICING THE PROTECTORATE

The displeasure of Samuel Maharero, an early German sympathizer, with Leutwein's duplicity burst into open confrontation in 1895. In November of that year, Governor Leutwein began to impound Herero cattle under the supplementary clause to a border treaty that, Leutwein claimed, entitled him to the cattle. In contrast to the governor's interpretation, Herero custom and traditions proscribe the impoundment of cattle. The act was illegal, a more serious offense even than theft, because cattle had symbolic or religious meaning as well as material value.[130] The governor's decision to reduce all impounded cattle to merchandise to be exchanged for money was therefore an affront and a threat to the very survival of the Herero. Moreover, the clause cited by the governor restricted the land area available for the Herero's main economic activity, cattle raising.[131] These nomadic people viewed their confinement to small grazing areas as nothing less than a declaration of war.

The German governor was aware of the risks of confrontation. He sent a letter to all German missions to prepare them for the impending show of force against the Herero. The Herero and other Africans "would have to obey authority," he wrote. "They should respect other people's property; and withdraw from all areas where white settlers had established themselves; and they should not extend their cattle herd beyond measure."[132] Beginning with these orders, Leutwein undertook a "clear and deliberate infringement of African power structures, and [an] equally deliberate policy to reshape colonial and mission policy."[133] Legislation was an essential element of this drive for domination, for it defined the permissible as well as the prohibited.

In general, the laws enacted by the German administration allowed German authorities to control both the political and the economic sphere. The first category of colonial laws pertained to the attribution and transfer of jurisdiction for purposes of punishment and disciplinary control.[134] A second category regulated Africans' ability to move from one area of the country to another, particularly after the colonialists arbitrarily divided the territory among its inhabitants and themselves. These laws defined the terms under which the "natives" could "acquire land or an interest therein" and placed limits on the number of cattle that Africans could possess. German legislation also regulated the terms of the labor contract for all "natives" over fourteen years of age.[135] Finally, there were laws dealing with the control of population, childbirth registration, and "mixed population."[136] The third category of laws pertained to economic relations between Africans and Europeans, and they had the practical effect of restructuring the political economy of the territory in favor of the colonialists.

The Credit Ordinance

African resentment of European encroachment grew during the years between 1893 and 1903, when their lands and cattle were gradually transferred to European settlers. The toll on the Africans' herds was compounded during the last decade of the nineteenth century and the beginning of the twentieth by a plague that devastated what remained of their cattle and exposed most of the Africans to famine.

The colonialists, on the other hand, played on the vulnerability of hungry masses to press for greater control of the territory's resources. As in the past, the German administration combined legislation, adjudication, persuasion, and political and military pressure to bring Africans into submission to colonial demands.

At first the legislative approach seemed more appropriate. The colonial administration enacted many laws intended to shift economic power from Africans to Europeans. The most notable was the Credit Ordinance of 1903, which introduced cash as the medium of exchange in all legitimate commerce.[137] Prior to this ordinance, commercial transactions between Africans and Europeans were conducted on the basis of credit and sometimes barter. European merchants or Africans determined the value of the items involved. The ordinance authorized colonial settlers to collect their outstanding debts from Africans in anticipation of the monetarization of exchange. The 1903 ordinance added a time constraint as a means of pressure. European providers of credit who had a year to collect their claims from the natives had absolute power to determine the value of items they were to collect in exchange for their outstanding debts.[138] The colonial administration enacted the credit ordinance as a golden opportunity to dislocate African economic power.

The governor rightly assumed that the Africans would be unable to meet their engagements and debts at once and therefore would be forced to give up their cattle. The natives had no access to cash and therefore could not afford to owe German merchants large sums that they would be compelled by law to repay within a year. The governor was also prepared for African reactions, possibly confrontation. He knew that most African debtors would rid themselves of their possessions only to face the prospect of a life without any means of subsistence. Indeed, most Africans who lost their livelihood and possessions to cattle and legal plagues were willing to retaliate against the colonialists, and the desire to retaliate against the settlers was greatest among the pastoralists, the Herero.[139]

Genocide in the Omaheke Sand Veld

The massive expropriation of Herero cattle and land, following the promulgation of the 1903 Ordinance, created the greatest tension yet in the territory. This tension was exacerbated by the treatment of Africans during the construction of the Otavi railways. The hardship involved in the construction of the railways, compounded by previous experiences with the settlers, compelled Samuel Maharero to break his German ties and organize an armed resistance, which began in 1904.[140]

The initial purpose of Herero resistance was to convince the settlers to withdraw from the territory. It was orderly and directed personally by Maharero, who controlled its strategies. For instance, he instructed his men to limit their attacks to armed adult male settlers, especially German troops. In addition, the chief established a list of people and targets to be exempted from military actions. He had determined, for instance, that missionaries, regardless of their age and sex, were not responsible for the crimes committed by the administration and gave a strict order not to attack them. He successfully concentrated his ambushes and surprise attacks on German troops and military targets, but the Herero successes were short-lived because of the superior firepower of the colonialists.[141]

German troops and militia responded to Herero attacks by retaliating against children and the elderly, who were left behind in villages and hamlets by fleeing fighters.[142] The colonialists justified their actions by the support that Maha1rero enjoyed among all sections of Herero populations. In time, the settlers extended their retaliation to Herero women who, they rightly suspected, played a role in the anticolonialist struggle. The German response was brutal and extreme, in part because of long-standing degrading racial stereotypes of Africans. The settlers who had understood Africans to be inferior could not explain the number and effectiveness of Herero attacks. More importantly, German settlers estimated that Herero successes would demonstrate their own inability to control the protectorate. In short, racial fear and political insecurity combined to cause the Germans to resort to ruthless measures.

From the onset of the war, German soldiers were determined not to take any prisoners. Their decision was motivated by two considerations: they lacked the logistics to maintain large numbers of African prisoners, and they had received orders from their superiors not to surrender any land to the "rebels." German officials were determined to retain the colony at all costs. The German government instructed military officers and commanders to design foolproof strategies. In addition, the chancellor appointed Lieutenant General Lothar von Trotha to oversee the defense of the territory and the settlers.

Indeed, the military stakes were raised in June 1904, at the peak of the war, when the army officer took control of the colonial administration, replacing Leutwein, the civilian governor.

The military officer left Germany charged with putting down the uprising, which was becoming a political issue in the motherland. On his mission of pacification, von Trotha was armed not only with firepower but also with the racist assumption that Africans responded only to force:

> I know enough tribes in Africa. They all have the same mentality insofar as they yield only to force. It was and remains my policy to apply this force by unmitigated terrorism and even cruelty. I shall destroy the rebellious tribes by shedding rivers of blood and money.[143]

Von Trotha commanded a small colonial army, with fewer men than his Herero rival, but he possessed a far greater gun power. Thus, the German officer had to make, as he remarked, an effective use of his means. Upon his arrival, the zealous von Trotha studied Herero fighting strategies and their movements on the terrain. He learned that the arid desert, the sand veld of Omaheke, was consistently used by Herero fighters as a refuge after their attacks against the heavily armed Germans. To his delight, he discovered that his troops too could exploit the strategic assets of the Omaheke sand veld. He decided to turn the African sanctuary into an effective and efficient instrument of death.[144]

Trotha's plan called for simultaneous attacks on all Herero units, on all fronts, except in the direction that led to the desert. Von Trotha expected the Herero to seek refuge in the desert if they were attacked on all other fronts. When the Herero escaped to the desert, von Trotha would close off the route until the fighters and their families ran out of food. Then the Germans would kill the starving Africans as they attempted to get out of the trap.[145]

On August 4, 1904, two months after his arrival, von Trotha ordered the final assault on the Herero in the Waterberg area, alerting his troops that the Omaheke sand veld was the natural escape route for the Herero. He issued an order to exterminate all Herero who took refuge in the desert. The attack went as planned. As expected, the Herero fled to the desert for protection. Soon thereafter, all routes out of the desert were shut off and defended by heavily armed German soldiers. Herero men and women of all ages died a slow and painful death by starvation. By the end of the hostility, more than 80,000 of the nearly 100,000 Herero people—women and men, young and old—had died.[146]

The German war against the Herero was so excessive that it sparked some protest. In March 1904, despite von Trotha's objections, some German soldiers received minor reprimands for their involvement in the genocidal lynching of Africans during the Herero uprising.[147] Yet, von Trotha's actions were consistent with colonial practice. In effect, colonial wars of pacification were seldom subject to the same rules as European wars. This point was made by von Trotha when, at the end of the war, he refused to leave for the protectorate unless he was given assurances that the Geneva Convention, the rules on the treatment of civilians and enemy prisoners, did not apply to colonial wars.[148]

The genocide of the Herero received nearly total support at home. The lone dissenting voice in the Reichstag was that of the socialist August Bebel, who insisted that parliament inquire into some of the worst incidents of cruelty. Besides Bebel, some liberals, notably philanthropists, condemned their government's and von Trotha's behavior. Elsewhere in Europe, other colonial powers raised only lame criticisms, to which von Trotha replied:

> As yet I have only been accused of excessive inhumane treatment of the natives, which gives me the right to oppose such views. Peaceful natives must be treated humanely at all events. But to adopt the same approach towards rebellious natives is to be inhumane towards our own fellow countrymen."[149]

The Hunt for Morenga

It was not until the Germans had dislocated the Herero from their strongholds that they began to exert pressure on the Nama, south of Hereroland. In 1904, the Nama too rose up against German occupation. The uprising began during the first days of October, when native insurgents killed forty German settlers. The Nama, a much smaller ethnic group, were quickly outgunned and subjugated. In this case, except for the most notorious rebels, the captured were not executed. The Germans deported a number of fighters and their families to the German colonies of Togo and Cameroon. Many of the deportees died before reaching their final destination. Of those who survived the trip, many more succumbed to the abrupt change of diet and the harsh climate of their new environment.

Despite the mass deportation, the Germans maintained the remaining Nama under constant military pressure. Jacob Morenga, a rebellious leader who succeeded Hendrik Witbooi, continued to fight German domination.[150] Morenga, whose father was Herero, was hostile to German rule and as a result incurred German wrath. In December 1905, Morenga's fierce resistance to a German attack forced the colonialists into retreat. Then the Germans made the tactical decision to suspend hostilities against the Nama for the duration of the German-Herero war and a number of less significant confrontations.

In February 1906, as the German war of extermination against the Herero was winding down, colonial units opened hostilities against Morenga. The 1906 battle continued until Morenga's death at the hands of British authorities. Morenga had fled south to the Cape to seek British assistance against the Germans; the British, perhaps knowing that Morenga's rebellion threatened all colonial interests, arrested and executed him in May 1906.[151]

4

Behind the Veil of the Trust

During World War I, the Allies (Britain, France, Russia, Serbia, and Belgium) and associated powers (Greece, Italy, and Japan) determined to eradicate the sources of conflict by rethinking the norms and values of the international system. According to Woodrow Wilson's fourteen-point peace proposal, the primary agenda of the peace conference was to set by treaty the terms of German (and Turkish) surrender, including reparations to the victims of the war. The second agenda item was the creation of a concert of nations to preserve peace through a "partnership of opinion" that would define the conditions governing interstate relations and the status of European minorities as well as dependent peoples.[1] The second objective formed the basis of the League of Nations.[2]

The victors accomplished their objectives at the Versailles Peace Conference, intended to rid Europe of the causes of confrontation, and the Geneva League of Nations Congress, meant to define the structures of the postwar order. The participants in these two forums claimed to have created an international system based on several key principles, most notably self-determination and recognition of ethnic and national rights. These postwar principles were implemented within the dismantled frontiers of the Balkans and Central and Eastern Europe. In parts of Western Europe, too, the victorious powers organized popular consultations in order to settle international disputes.[3]

In contrast, there was little doubt in postwar Europe about the prerogative of the colonial powers (also among the principal Allies and associated powers) to allocate Turkish and German dependencies, that is, to appoint a successor administration in each territory. Few Western politicians and scholars mentioned popular sovereignty, autonomy, or self-determination in reference to the other colonies. The critics, who professed a renewed commitment to native welfare, included liberal and humanist groups. In principle, they did not oppose continuing Western rule over the so-called non-self-governing peoples. They insisted, however, that the European powers act as "colonialists with a conscience." They generally demanded that the colonial powers commit themselves to acting in the future not as "owners" of the colonies but as trustees for the natives and the international community. The trustees would therefore reconcile their obligation to assist their wards (now uniformly referred to as non-civilized) materially and morally with their commitment to open trade and exploitation for the benefit of the so-called civilized community.[4]

Although they easily overcame credible domestic opposition to their new plans, the colonial powers ran into growing anticolonial resistance abroad. Western powers were particularly irritated that representatives of non–self-governing peoples demanded national self-determination within an interdependent postwar order. In Africa, where Germany's defeat had placed the future of its colonies at the center of the postcolonial debate, there was pressure for self-determination, or at least greater political and economic autonomy. Members of the African diaspora, meeting in Paris for the First Pan-African Congress, also opposed the imposition of new forms of foreign control on the former German colonies.[5]

Arab nationalists too pressured the Versailles Peace Conference and the League Congress to restore their right to unmitigated national autonomy and self-government. A plurality objected to the division of the Middle East into foreign protectorates.[6] Reflecting the views of many Arab elites, E. A. Omar, president of the Egyptian Association in Great Britain, protested

> against the recognition by the republic of the United States of the illegal protectorate imposed by Great Britain on the undefended and unarmed nation of Egypt during the course of this war [because] this act is a complete violation of [the] well known principles of justice and fair play to the weak as well as to the strong nations.[7]

Western nations responded to the mounting anticolonial nationalism by proposing new cultural (trusteeship) and political (mandate system) devices that perpetuated their hegemony. Theoretically, the mandate system reconciled colonial peoples' demands for self-government with Western economic, military, and political needs.[8] In practice, it institutionalized collective exploitation of the colonies (without the burden of collective administration) and provided alternatives to global colonial conflicts. These concerns took precedence over the right of the colonized to autonomy and self-determination. In fact, the mandate system had little bearing on the welfare of the indigenous populations; nor was it motivated by an outburst of Western conscience. It was a simple manifestation of self-interest.

DISCURSIVE STRUCTURES I

When the Versailles Conference convened, it was clear to the participants that the anticolonial view of autonomy was far more extensive than they had predicted. Noting the postwar change, Woodrow Wilson remarked that in every part of the world, not excluding the United States, society had been shaken to its foundations, and people had been awakened to the wrongs that had been done to them.[9] Indeed, the postwar attitude of Africans, Asians, and other colonized peoples was affected by three war-related events. The first was their participation in a war that had been portrayed as a struggle for freedom; this appeal to notions of freedom bolstered African aspirations for postwar autonomy. The Bolshevik Revolution in Russia during the war and the initial anti-imperialist ideology of the Soviets provided a useful discursive paradigm to many anticolonial movements that sought to dispute the validity of the colonial order. Finally, the war weakened borders and loosened national allegiances in Europe, giving rise to new communal, ethnic, and national identities in the Balkans as well as in Central and Eastern Europe. The Western decision to recognize the new entities intensified the desire of the colonized for national self-determination.

"La Dette de Sang"

The debate over Africans' place in the global order had been dominated prior to the war by ideas that had their origins in the Enlightenment. Before 1914, the Africans who lived in Europe and the educated natives—the *evolués* (who had evolved toward civilized status through education) and notables who served in local administrations—demanded social equality from their colonial overlords on the basis of received Western notions of education and social status. In France, as elsewhere, middle classes from the "old colonies" (later, Overseas Departments) and select African communes demanded equality. This meant French citizenship for those living in France and treatment of the educated and notables equal to that of French citizens of similar social positions.[10]

The performance of African troops against rival European soldiers during the war added a new dimension to their demands. It not only brought back memories of the 1896 Ethiopian defeat of Italy, it revolutionized the African discourse.[11] The African elite ceased to request equal treatment on the basis of social status or European citizenship as a reward for good behavior. Veteran activists and intellectuals began to insist on racial equality for the African diaspora in Europe and national equality for colonial populations. For these Africans, the sacrifice of their lives during the war was a debt sealed in blood that could not be reneged. This blood sacrifice (*dette de sang*) was the basis of African demands: assimilation within the metropole (racial equality); national autonomy within vast geographic ensembles (political integration and economic interdependence); or self-rule as separate and distinct national units (national independence).[12]

In France, for instance, African, West Indian, and Indo-Chinese elites and war veterans exchanged ideas about the emerging new order. Although these groups and individuals originated from diverse intellectual, political, national, and ethnic backgrounds, they joined in metropolitan human rights organizations to promote their various causes. The participants from the African diaspora created their own media for the purpose of actively engaging Western elites in a discussion about the future of colonialism.[13] Indeed, the African demand for autonomy and self-rule was firmly grounded in the European promise of autonomy in exchange for colonial peoples' participation in the "war for freedom." It was discursively articulated around the Western notions of political legitimacy, obligation, and representation. In the political realm, the desire to "speak for the self" led to the establishment later of such organizations and associations as the Ligue universelle de defense de la race noire and the Union inter-coloniale.[14]

The postwar Pan-Africanist discussions of colonial and national questions was not limited to the French African diaspora. A similar debate occurred in Britain and the United States among British West Indian and African-American activists, including W. E. B. Du Bois. In January-February 1919, these intellectuals, activists, and artists of the African diaspora joined their African counterparts, including many parliamentarians, for the first Pan-African Congress. The fifty-six participants were influenced by such diverse ideologies as assimilationism, Garveyism, and African socialism. Nonetheless, they agreed on a set of goals and requests for the upcoming peace conference at Versailles. The Pan-African Congress was organized to coincide with the Versailles Peace Conference, whose conclusions on colonial matters the Congress was intended to influence.[15]

The Effects of Two Revolutions

The October 1917 Bolshevik Revolution also affected the postwar political mood. It occurred in one of the least industrialized nations of Europe—Russia—but the size of the new state, its political impulses, its overlap with the end of the war, and the commitment of the provisionary government to "peace without annexations" mandated a reexamination of foreign policy by all states.[16] Many European states feared that the Bolshevik state would challenge the existing order and even exploit the existing tensions within Europe and in the colonial empires. The Russian revolutionaries did not alleviate this fear. Adding to the symbolism of the revolution, the Bolsheviks directly challenged the existing notions of legitimacy within the modern state. The theorists of the new nation professed a novel ideology that gave new meanings to the relations between the state, civil society, and the various classes that composed it.[17]

Another aspect of the revolution that was not lost on the colonial powers was the effect of the new revolutionary rhetoric on the mood of the colonized. The Bolsheviks, who had inherited an empire from their czarist predecessors, were compelled to deal with a question of particular relevance to all colonial and dependent peoples: the right of dependent communities within colonial and semi-colonial situations. Lenin's approach to the question of the non-Russian nations within the czarist empire was distinct from traditional dependent relationships under colonial rule.[18] He advocated the emancipation of non-Russian nations into equal partnership within a Union of Soviet Socialist Republics (USSR).

Abroad, Lenin countered the narrow Eurocentrist point of view that confined the question of national liberation and the right of the colonized to self-determination to outstanding national European interests. The Soviet leader claimed that the desire for national self-determination was a worldwide phenomenon that European imperialists attempted to suppress.[19] He and other Soviet leaders promoted the right of the colonized to self-determination as a central pillar of the "historical movement to overthrow the imperialist order."[20]

The initial decision of Soviet officials to support African self-determination was brought about, however, by fear that the colonies constituted a reserve from which Western powers would recruit armed troops for a war to destabilize the Soviet Union. Soviet officials decided to preempt Western destabilization plans by undermining the colonial empires. Thus, they targeted disgruntled African war veterans for indoctrination. African soldiers who participated in the most decisive moments of the war and marched to victory alongside troops of all nationalities were disappointed at Western reluctance to fulfill prewar promises of autonomy and racial equality.

Nor did educated veterans appreciate the decision of the victorious powers to occupy German colonies and positions in Africa. According to intelligence reports from the French Service de controle et d'assistance des indigènes, the agency that monitored colonial activists in France, many veterans who harbored grievances also had romantic views of the Bolsheviks.[21] After 1920, the Soviet Union sealed its sponsorship of anticolonial movements by providing financial support to a number of organizations in Europe.[22] Indeed, many nationalists who hoped to rid themselves of foreign domination looked to the Soviet revolution and its ideals as new referents. They pointed to the integration of non-Russian nations within the new state to illustrate their visions of a postcolonial order. Most notably, militants from the Ottoman dependencies and Indochina demanded a greater role for colonial populations in determining the terms of peace—specifically, their own emancipation from foreign domination. Although most of the nationalists did not share the ideals of the Bolsheviks, they viewed the revolutionary theories and ideals as new intellectual tools with which to challenge the foundations of existing regimes.[23]

The second event that affected public attitudes toward the post-war order was the collapse of imperial orders and the reconstitution of boundaries in Europe. The emergence of new national entities undermined the psychological foundations and ideological justifications of allegiance and legitimacy within European empires and states. Specifically, the reconstitution of Central European and Balkan states ended the role of dynastic allegiances as a legitimizing factor within the modern state.

The changes in Central Europe and in the Balkans brought about an existential crisis of legitimacy for the imperialist state and as a result undermined the theoretical and ideological foundations of the capitalist state. Likewise, the constitution of the Balkan states eroded the capacity of intellectuals to mediate between the hegemony of liberalism, imperialism (colonialism), and the rising tide of nationalism (self-determination).

In response to this crisis, a new breed of politicians and theorists began to rethink the basis of the hegemony of the state over civil society as well as the role of the imperialist state in securing European hegemony within the international order. Woodrow Wilson was such an intellectual. His fourteen-point peace proposal was inspired by both the United States' desire to impose itself as a world leader and concern over global upheaval:

> What does not seem to me realized in this blessed country of ours is the fact that the world is in revolution. I do not mean in active revolution. I do not mean that it is in a state of mind that will bring about the dissolution of governments. I do mean that it is in a state of mind that may bring about the dissolution of governments if we do not enter into a world settlement which will really in fact and in power establish justice and right.[24]

Wilson and other Western statesmen and intellectuals introduced into the political and legal discourse the notion that the state derived its legitimacy from the fulfillment of predetermined obligations to the home citizenry and the colonized. Hence the validation of the theory of obligations in the discourse of the modern state.

The existence, in this context, of an imperial state at home and abroad posed many dilemmas for politicians and theorists. At home, political and legal theorists easily faced the dilemmas of finding new justifications for the state in view of its deepening crisis in

Europe. Traditionally, Western philosophers who stressed state sovereignty and loyalty to the state based their claims on the axiom that the state deserved loyalty from its citizens because it freed them from bondage. In the new thinking, theorists emphasized that sovereignty in a democratic state was derived from the fulfillment of obligations to its citizens. The new trend also stressed the obligation of the state to provide for the security and general welfare of its people. Harold Laski, a socialist member of the British parliament, summarized this last point as follows:

> The liberal state, though it represented a definite gain in social freedom upon any previous social order was in fact no more than the exchange of one privileged class for another.... [It] began in a condition of society in which the few were rich and the many poor, it ended in a condition in which the few were rich and the many poor. Its explanations of this situation were hardly satisfactory."[25]

In the colonial context, the imperial powers discursively translated their new obligation to their nationals as extraterritoriality, applied as well to colonialists, settlers, and administrators. The colonial powers' need to reassert their leading role, however, was inconsistent with the dominant discourse on state legitimacy and self-determination. The inconsistency was more distressing because the anticolonial revolt against postwar imperialism was grounded in the ideals of democracy and representation. This anticolonialist challenge raised theoretical, conceptual, political, and ideological dilemmas for the ideologues, theorists, and politicians of the new order.

DISCURSIVE STRUCTURES II

Since Germany had lost the war and its colonies, it was fitting that the fate of its colonies (like that of the former Turkish dependencies) should set the background for Western discussion of the rights of colonial peoples. Once again, this postwar debate encompassed two distinct European desires and political outlooks. In the first category, according to Edith Sandhaus, there was the humanitarian aspiration of individuals (liberals, socialists, radicals) and groups (including labor unions, Fabian societies, and socialist and philanthropist movements) who wished to settle colonial matters according to the criteria of justice. The anticolonialist sentiments, mostly from left-leaning intellectuals and humanists, tilted the Western consensus toward greater autonomy for the colonies as they clashed with the opposing imperialist desires, backed by governments, to integrate the dependencies into the structures of the emerging "Open Door" policy, or free access to territories and natural resources.[26]

The Dawn of a New Era?

The views of the critics of colonial practices were colored by their disappointment in the failures of the Berlin Conference to honor its humanitarian thrusts. A number attributed the war itself to the imperialism augured by the conference: "the scramble for colonies, concessions, and markets where political sovereignty meant a differential advantage for the traders, manufacturers, and bankers of the country concerned."[27] Yet, although a few would have granted freedom to the German colonies, most postwar humanists wished to correct the course charted at Berlin by implementing a more sincere trusteeship: "service by the strong, and not the exploitation of the weak."[28] The new trust of civilization, according to Englishman John Harris, meant "the right of 'backward races' to rise in the civic, industrial, and political spheres to the full stature of a free manhood. It [meant] that no 'barriers' founded solely upon race, or creed, or colour may be erected against any race which is working out its own salvation."[29]

Both humanist camps feared that a future conference might repeat past errors by authorizing the outright annexation of German colonies by other colonial powers. This sentiment ran strongest among the American, British, and other opponents of a related French initiative who desired due appreciation of the interests of other nations. The British Congress of Trade Unions, for instance, feared that such a transfer of territory would transform German Africa into either new spheres of influence for the benefit of national capitalists or armed zones intended to advance the militaristic ends of rival governments.[30]

The British prime minister Lloyd George and foreign secretary A. J. Balfour responded to the sentiments of the Congress of Trade Unions by proposing an "appropriate" administrative formula for German colonies. This formula, tailored first and foremost to meet perceived British national interests, included the establishment of an international authority, or legislative body, based on principles such as the wishes of the natives; protecting them against exploitation and abuses; and native disarmament.[31]

The new liberal consensus on the "sacred trust of civilization" was based on a distinct perception of the order of rights and obligations in the emerging international system. The new humanism emphasized European obligation (the duty of the civilized) as the basis of any new form or measure of political (or administrative) control (or supervision) of the German territories.[32] It also grounded the proposed international authority in a humanitarian impulse: European conscience and duty.[33] It presumed that the "conscientious administrator" would "take care to make the proportion just ... for here is where the line is drawn between natural development in the interest of the natives on the one hand and exploitation on the other."[34] Finally, the humanist critics of the Berlin system provided the rationale for revoking German colonial privileges: it had mistreated "its" natives. In this regard, Great Britain and others cited German atrocities against the Herero.

While they reached a rhetorical consensus, Western humanists remained politically divided. A plurality rejected the suggestions put forth by "wild idealists" for native self-determination. These "realists" considered a complete transformation of the international system (including native autonomy) to be impractical at best.[35] Instead, Bishop Charles Gore of Oxford and others supported the proposals of "practical statesmen" like Woodrow Wilson, Lloyd George, and A. J. Balfour.[36] Indeed, these men rhetorically endorsed the liberal position that opposed territorial annexation, but "the nations that assumed ... the role of educators were less concerned to fulfill the mission of sacred trust of civilization than [with] their ordinary spirit of conquest and annexation and [obeying] the selfish plots of their leaders."[37]

Racial Sentiments

Political and racial sentiments tainted Wilson's and others' crusade for colonial reform, in particular colonial self-determination.[38] Wilson's position was based on domestic political considerations, notably congressional reactions related to the ratification of the League treaty. In conjunction with this, the American president associated colonial peoples' struggle for national equality with the African-American quest for racial equality. He was concerned that development on the racial front in Europe would have repercussions at home, particularly among black veterans. Specifically, he criticized France for sending integrated troops to the war front, putting blacks on "an equality with white men." Wartime integration, he feared, "had gone to the heads" of segregated U.S. black troops.[39]

Wilson viewed with suspicion any suggestion of racial or national equality, even when the equality proposed was limited to the imperialist powers. He vetoed a measure sponsored by the Japanese stating the "equality of nations" in response to the "anti-Orientalist" policies of Australia. This action in effect placed the United States on the side of Australia in keeping its territories "white."[40] Later, Wilson opposed any mention of racial equality in the League Covenant.[41]

In short, Wilson was not immune to the racism and evolutionist premises of his contemporaries. These ideas formed the basis of his proposed new trusteeship over the German colonies. In his mind, Africans, Arabs, and Pacific Islanders were in need of the protection and guidance of civilized European powers. The idea was to place "safeguards ... around the naked fellows in the jungles of Africa ... [and] around those poor peoples almost ready to assume the full right of self-government in some parts of the Turkish Empire: for instance Armenia."[42]

The postwar trusteeship had its ideological origins in Western legal instruments for the protection of minors and the tutelage of children.[43] By analogy, Western powers acted according to a mandate of civilization to advise and guide "peoples not yet able to stand by themselves under the strenuous conditions of the modern world."[44] As self-appointed advisers and guardians, Western powers entrusted a number of countries to assume responsibility for the trust territories. In Wilson's words:

> We will put you in charge of this, that, and the other piece of territory, and you will make an annual report to us. We will deprive you of your trusteeship whenever you administer it in a way which is not approved by our judgment, and we will put upon you this primary limitation, that you shall do nothing that is to the detriment of the people who live in that territory.[45]

Balance of Power

The events that led to the constitution of the postwar trusteeship "will hardly convince one that the idea of sacred trust was more dominant than that of annexation and division of the spoils of war."[46] Those who singled out Germany for the revocation of colonial privileges did so on two faulty counts. The first was that Germany alone, with its "Prussian sternness" endangered the lives and safety of the natives. Although the German war on the Herero had been grossly vicious, it did not significantly surpass Belgian atrocities in the Congo. France did not spare the Touaregs of Niger and Chad.

The second argument against German colonial claims, that Germany was naturally militaristic and imperialistic, was equally misleading.[47] In fact, the measures taken by the Allies and associated powers against Germany were equally driven by strategic concerns. The victorious powers were also strategically driven when they compelled Turkey, under the terms of the Treaty of Lausanne, to surrender its right over the former Ottoman Arab dependencies.[48] Great Britain, France, and the United States orchestrated the final demise of the Ottoman Empire for the sole purpose of preempting German gains in the weak Turkish Empire.[49] Wilson summed up the relationship between Germany and the Ottoman Empire:

> Turn your thoughts back to what it was that Germany proposed. The formula of Pan-Germanism was Bremen to Bagdad. What is the line from Bremen to Bagdad? It leads through partitioned Poland, through prostrated Roumania, through subjugated Slavia down through disordered Turkey, and on into distressed Persia, and every foot of the line is a political weakness.[50]

The Versailles Peace Conference and the Geneva League of Nations Congress privileged strategic issues, particularly the emerging balance of power. The Versailles Conference, begun on January 18, 1919, brought together representatives of the Allies, other nations formerly at war, "recognized states," and national minorities. The general armistice formalizing the peace was followed in 1920 by the Geneva Congress, which established the League of Nations. The objective of the new organization, according to Wilson, was to make it certain that

> the combined power of free nations will check every invasion of right, and serve to make peace and justice the more secure by affording a definite tribunal of opinion to which all must submit, and by which every international readjustment that cannot be amicably agreed upon by the peoples directly concerned shall be sanctioned.[51]

The Geneva Congress included the Versailles conferees and a number of African, Asian, and Latin American countries, but it was dominated by a core of colonial powers—notably Great Britain, France, Italy, and Japan. As permanent members of the League Council, these countries virtually controlled the direction of the new order.[52] Although they were aided by nonpermanent, or rotating, members, control over the Council by states with vested imperial or strategic interests prejudiced the settlement of colonial matters.

The distribution of power and regional representation within the second organ of the League of Nations bolstered the influence of the imperial powers in the emerging order.[53] The Assembly was formed by select nations from all continents. It seated Nicaragua, Panama, Brazil, Bolivia, and other Latin American countries along with the new nations of Central Europe. Japan, China, Persia, Hedjaz, Liberia, and Ethiopia were also admitted. But of the forty-one nations attending the first session, the majority came from Europe. The other members were mostly dominions and semiautonomous entities dependent upon rival imperial powers. Five members of the League Assembly—Australia, Canada, India, New Zealand, and South Africa—were British dominions, giving Britain six votes. This was an unwarranted presence for a strong imperial power, according to U.S. legislators who opposed the League of Nations.[54]

The United States also pushed for the admission of Cuba, Panama, and Nicaragua to the League for reasons similar to Britain's. Wilson clarified his position in response to numbers of Congress who objected to the undue influence of Britain and France within the the League:

> We ourselves were champions of giving vote to Panama and of giving vote to Cuba. I ask you in debating the affairs of mankind, would it have been fair to give Panama a vote, as she will have, Cuba a vote, both of them under the influence of the United States, and not to give a vote to the Dominion of Canada?[55]

Wilson also insisted that the League endorse the Monroe Doctrine, which applied to U.S. foreign policy in South and Central America, as a "doctrine of the world."[56] Article 21 of the League Covenant satisfied this demand by stating that "nothing in this covenant shall be deemed to affect the validity of international engagements, such as treaties of arbitration or regional understandings like the Monroe doctrine, for securing the maintenance of peace."[57]

Western powers had other juridical means at their disposal that allowed them to exert influence within the Assembly. Although the

Covenant attributed equal numbers of tasks to the Assembly and the Council, the resolutions of the Assembly required the affirmative vote of every member of the Council. Under Article V of the Covenant, the validity of the Assembly's decisions depended upon the unanimous vote of Council members along with the majority of other members. When the majority vote did not include all the Council members, the decision of the Assembly was considered a mere opinion. As a result, the participation of Council members in Assembly debates was sufficient to guarantee that the latter adopted no decisions that were prejudicial to Western interests. Non-Council members too were aware that the survival of the Assembly as a significant international organ depended upon their cooperation with the Council. As a result, the Assembly was rarely critical of Council resolutions and seldom opposed its decisions — especially those pertaining to colonial interests.

In general, the Council possessed powers denied to the Assembly.[58] The one exception was the authority of the Assembly to admit new members to the League by a two-thirds majority, but even then the Council could challenge the Assembly. In the case of the admissibility of Armenia, for instance, the opposition of the Council resulted in a public confrontation with other member states and subsequently the rejection of the membership proposal.[59]

Non-Self-Governing and Other People

The respective objectives of the colonial powers with regard to the non-self-governing territories (German colonies, Turkish and disputed dependencies) differed markedly. There was no divergence of opinion, however, about the prerogative of the principal Allies and associated powers to appoint a successor administration in each of the non-self-governing territories.[60] The nature and form of this political control was determined during another Versailles meeting of the Supreme War Council, on May 7, 1919, when the participants decided to establish a trust of civilization, or mandate. This trust was the basis of Article 22 of the League Covenant:

> To those colonies and territories which as a consequence of the late war ceased to be under the sovereignty of the States which formerly governed them and which are inhabited by peoples not yet able to stand by themselves under the strenuous conditions of the modern world, there should be applied the principle that the well-being and

development of such peoples form a sacred trust of civilisation, and that securities for the performance of this trust should be embodied in this Covenant.[61]

This meeting not only made the final adjustment of colonial claims, it called on the Council to "determine the measures to be taken to ensure the observance of Article 22 and to apply the mandatory system."[62]

The special monitoring agency of the Council, the international mandate commission, finalized the allocation of the non-self-governing territories during its August 5, 1920, meeting in San Sebastián.[63] According to Paul Hymans, its rapporteur, the San Sebastián meeting envisioned the mandate as a binding trust and the mandatory powers as trustees of the League of Nations, especially its Council. Trusteeship over these presumed vacant (no longer virgin) territories was assigned to administering authorities on the basis of an agreement between the mandatory power and the Council.[64] This mandate agreement defined the character of the trusteeship, the manner in which the mandatory powers intended to administer their new dependencies, and the obligations of the mandatory toward the natives and other interested powers. This last element of the agreement stressed the economic relations between the mandatory and nonmandatory powers.[65]

As juridical instruments, both the mandate system and the mandate agreement presented operational flaws. Besides the fact that the constitution of the mandate itself was a unilateral decision by foreign powers, subject populations could not enforce its dispositions, nor did they have any legal guarantees that the mandatory powers would fulfill their obligations.[66] Theoretically, the right of local populations to petition the Permanent Mandate Commission protected them against abuses by the mandatory power(s), but the right to petition was primarily conceived as means to enforce equal treatment and opportunity of trade and commerce for the nationals of mandatory powers. It was later extended to the native populations upon the insistence of progressive pressure groups, yet they still had neither enforceable rights nor equal access to the Permanent Commission; the rules of procedure required native petitioners to submit their grievances to the mandatory, which transmitted them to the Permanent Commission with its response or comments.[67]

In addition, the chairman of the Permanent Commission had the power to decide which petitions deserved the Commission's attention and which "should be regarded as obviously trivial." The chairman based his decisions on the contents of the petitions as well as the authority or interests of their authors.[68] According to the Rules of Admissibility of Petitions, the grievances of the indigenous populations could not be accepted if they "contain[ed] complaints ... incompatible with the provisions of the Covenant and the Mandate Agreements; emanate[ed] from anonymous sources; [or] cover[ed] grounds ... covered by a petition recently communicated to the mandatory power and [did] not contain any new information of importance."[69]

Indeed, the San Sebastián agreement regarding the mandate was not "expressed in a form implying a legal obligation."[70] Paul Hymans acknowledged that it was difficult to see in what way the responsibility of the mandatories to native populations would be organized, or what measures could enforce it.[71] Accordingly, the responsibility of the League "before the public opinion of the civilized world" was in fact a moral one.[72] Specifically, the San Sebastián meeting ordered the mandatory powers to act responsibly on behalf of the League by fulfilling a threefold mission: to ensure the well-being of the native populations, to guarantee equal opportunity for trade and enterprise to the subjects of colonial powers, and to prevent the establishment of military and naval bases in the territories.[73]

The purpose of the mandate system was to cure colonial powers of their lingering monopolistic tendencies (designated as past irrationalism) with a new formula (trusteeship) based on the consent of other colonial powers (signified by the mandate agreement). Unlike the Independent State of the Congo (or Congo Free State), however, the mandate system vested sovereignty over the dependencies in the collectivity of colonial powers constituted by the League Council. The League in turn deputized its authority to a mandatory power that administered the territory and managed relations between colonial powers, settlers, and native populations. The mandate system went further by creating an instrument of supervision—the International Mandate Commission (also known as the Permanent Mandate Commission)—whose role was to oversee the compliance of mandatory powers with the goals and objectives of the mandate. Besides ensuring collective colonial exploitation, the commission also mediated conflict and, when required, promoted the "humane treatment" of indigenous peoples through limited health care, education, and a decent labor environment.[74]

THE MANDATE SYSTEM: PARTNERSHIP IN EXPLOITATION

The mandate system owed its form and structure to the dominant Orientalist and Africanist view that non-European societies were tribalistic and lacked the kind of political structures that the West would recognize.[75] This racist outlook also ranked the various dependencies according to their degree of social organization.[76] Woodrow Wilson's statements, the collective Western justification of the trusteeship, and Article 22 of the League Covenant all support this understanding of the mandate system, according to which the "most evolved" Ottoman Arabs were granted greater participation in their domestic affairs under the A mandate. Most African and some Pacific island territories were placed under category B or parallel legal arrangements. South West Africa and another group of German dependencies in the Pacific were ranked as C mandates, reserved for the "least evolved" of the colonized.

Some critics have ascribed the nature of the mandate system, in particular its gradation, to a political compromise between advocates of empire in the British dominions, notably General Jan Christian Smuts of South Africa and M. Massey of New Zealand on the one hand, and the Americans—Wilson and his advisers—on the other.[77] The proponents of this notion of compromise have subscribed to the ideological premise of the partitioned mandate system: that the differential degree of evolution—political, social, and otherwise—among the colonized justified the various types of mandate. In addition, they have argued that the formulation of the mandate occurred in an environment of conflict, confrontation, and compromise among colonial powers over practical economic and strategic concerns.

Indeed, political, economic, and strategic interests were central to the design of the mandate system and the ensuing allocation of territories. In this regard, one cannot help but notice that phosphate was the reason that Nauru, an eight-square-mile island in the South Pacific inhabited by two thousand people, was assigned to three mandatory powers. This view, however, omits key political developments in each region or territory that affected the determination of the degree of political control to be exercised by the victors. The three categories of mandate, it appears, were designed to reflect different political realities in the territories rather than different stages of development among the colonized. These circumstances were: the strength of the nationalists; the degree of political and economic involvement of European capital; and the existence of a political and religious elite predisposed to embrace values that intersected with Europeans' desires for the territories.[78]

The Open Door Policy

The vacancy left after World War I by Germany's defeat and Turkey's surrender of its former possessions offered a unique opportunity to eradicate the anarchy that prevailed under the Berlin colonial regime. Then Belgium violated the neutrality of the Independent State of the Congo, and other colonial powers responded by promoting their national interests at the expense of the "rule of law." Now contending colonial powers feared that, without a new regime, some of them might declare exclusive control over the resources of the new territories in Africa, Asia (particularly Persia, Mesopotamia, and Palestine), and the Pacific (Samoa, Nauru, and other islands).

The 1920 colonial regime was therefore founded on the principle of partnership and collective exploitation of the non-self-governing territories. Despite this general agreement to reduce the risk of intra-alliance rivalry, the Allies and associated powers were in disagreement regarding the principle of equality of treatment of each others' citizens and national companies. They also disagreed on the relations to be established between the mandatory powers and their new territories, especially the inhabitants. These opposing views, which dominated the postwar territorial debate, divided the founders of the new colonial regime into two camps. The first group, identified here as autonomists, advocated some degree of self-rule for the indigenous populations as well as stricter international oversight of the mandates. The proponents of this approach considered the proposed supervision of the mandate a means to preventing any form of annexation, which would be contrary to the "Open Door," the new ethos of colonial exploitation and international cooperation. This camp was opposed by annexationists, who defended the right of the victors to take outright control of the territories. The annexationists favored greater integration of colonial territories into the metropole.[79]

The United States was the chief advocate of territorial autonomy and liberal trade policy. President Wilson's objective in this regard reflected three conflicting American strategic and practical concerns. The first consisted of looser colonial control by the new mandatory administrations over the populations of the former German and Turkish dependencies. To this end, Wilson and his advisers supported the idea of trusteeship.[80] The trusteeship intended by Wilson provided a greater degree of participation by native populations. He thought of such participation as a means to ensuring the cultural survival of the colonized and, significantly, preventing the hegemony and protectionism of individual colonial powers.[81]

The second American design combined colonial administration with the spirit of unrestrained competition. This policy, known as the "Open Door," was inseparable from the general adjustment of all colonial claims. The United States was particularly concerned that agreements between Britain and France regarding the economic resources of the territories would, "as a practical matter, result in a grave infringement of the mandate principle which was formulated for the purpose of removing in the future some of the principal causes of international differences."[82] Wilson's proposal was contained in the fifth point of his peace proposal:

> a free, open-minded, and absolutely impartial adjustment of all colonial claims, based upon a strict observance of the principle that in determining all such questions of sovereignty the interests of the population concerned must have equal weight with the equitable claims of the Government whose title is to be determined.[83]

Wilson's advisers, notably General Edward House and George Louis Beer, special counsel on colonial matters, took this proposal through several stages of transformation to one essential point: that "any alien territory which should be acquired pursuant to the Treaties of Peace with the Central Powers, must be held and governed in such a way as to assure equal treatment in law, and in fact to the commerce of all nations."[84] In short, the Open Door policy gave economic effect to the juridical principle of trusteeship or mandate. This economic principle of the trusteeship remained its sole signifier, according to Duncan Hall, a former member of the League Secretariat. The colonial powers never defined the other principle of the trust, the just treatment of the native.[85]

Wilson and his advisers insisted upon the Open Door because they believed that unrestrained competition guaranteed equal economic opportunity to American businesses. It provided American businesses access to Africa, where the United States had no dependencies, and elsewhere. In this regard, American policy makers reflected the views of the business community, which had grown impatient with European protectionism. Both policy makers and businesses were convinced that the United States had the capacity to surpass its competitors in an open competitive market, and they especially feared any hindrance to the opportunities offered to U.S. capital by the ruined economies of Europe.[86]

Annexation and Pseudoautonomy

The American Open Door policy was rejected by France and by Great Britain and its dominions (Australia, New Zealand, and South Africa). These imperial powers preferred outright annexation of and greater political control over the former German and Turkish dependencies in Africa and Asia, where they were the primary colonial contenders. The British dominions in particular favored the annexation of German and other vacated dependencies contiguous to them. This annexationist sentiment culminated in the frenzied wartime British Round Table on the dependencies. This uniquely Anglo-Saxon forum, attended by American experts such as George Louis Beer and reputed defenders of the British Empire such as New Zealand's M. Massey, defined the position of the British dominions regarding colonial adjustments.

General Jan Christian Smuts of South Africa formulated the Round Table's annexationist position, according to which South Africa would incorporate South West Africa, Australia would control New Guinea, and New Zealand would extend its sovereignty to Samoa. Smuts's overall interpretation of the trusteeship began with his view of South Africa's future role in South West Africa: a territorial integration that did not require the international supervision suggested by Woodrow Wilson.[87] Smuts contended that the fulfillment of the sacred trust, in particular the obligation of the civilized to safeguard the welfare of the noncivilized, was a practical administrative matter. It required the outright annexation of the "German colonies in the Pacific and Africa [that] are inhabited by barbarians, who not only cannot possibly govern themselves, but to whom it would be impractical to apply any idea of political self-determination in the European sense."[88]

Smuts proposed that the British dominions be allowed to administer German territories such as South West Africa as if they were part of the empire for two additional reasons. One was the spatial connection between the vacated territories and their new masters. Annexation would be South Africa's reward for its liberation of South West Africa from German control. In his scenario, the natives "might be consulted as to whether they want their German masters back, but the result would be so much a foregone conclusion that the consultation would be quite superfluous."[89] Beyond this consultation, international supervision of the mandatory's authority was superfluous.[90] Finally, Smuts and other leaders of the dominions favored expropriation of the property of German settlers and seizure of official property in the former German territories as reparation for war damages.[91]

Political Realism: The A Mandate

While he advocated the annexation of contiguous dependencies by the British dominions, Smuts shared Wilson's overall approach to vacated and disputed territories. They agreed on the desirability of the trusteeship and, particularly, on the authority of the League to allocate trusteeship and to supervise its implementation. Unlike other annexationists in the British Empire, the South African also favored greater local control, a political tact that showed sensitivity to a rising tide of nationalism throughout the world.

The postwar sensitivity to nationalism was particularly useful in the Ottoman dependencies, where there was greater potential for a violent political explosion. The establishment of the A mandate under terms relatively favorable to the local populations can be traced to wartime maneuvers between Arabs, their rulers, and claimant colonial powers. These included British and French pledges to specific Arab leaders, as well as various other pacts that already existed between Arab leaders and their European counterparts; and Arab participation in the war effort and Arab attitudes thereafter.[92]

The involvement of Britain and France in the Middle East intensified at the turn of the century, with concerns over German expansion in that region. They first sought to counter German designs through diplomacy aimed at preserving their own strategic and economic interests.[93] To this end, Britain and France gained mutual agreements with Arab leaders, whose legitimacy they were compelled to recognize. These actions undermined Turkish authority, leading to the 1912 Anglo-French plan to eventually divide the Ottoman dependencies into zones of influence.[94]

In May 1916, as part of the effort to defeat Germany — and Turkey — Britain and France promised political autonomy to the ruling elites of the Ottoman dependencies, in effect encouraging a destabilizing armed revolt against the Turkish metropole.[95] The two Western powers cooperated with the leaders of the June 1916 revolt in the hope of asserting greater influence over Arab nationalists, in particular Hussain Ibn Ali, king of the Hedjaz and father of Emir Faisal. They viewed their influence over the moderate king of the Hedjaz as a means to control over Mecca, other holy places, and, subsequently, the Islamic world in general. Britain consistently promised political autonomy and recognition to Transjordanian and Saudi ruling elites in exchange for their support of the Allied war efforts. Later, London made a similar offer to the mufti as a reward for his support of British postwar plans in Palestine, particularly the establishment of a Jewish state there. France made similar commitments to the Syrians and the Lebanese.[96]

The prospect of Arab autonomy was attractive to many nationalist elites, and in this regard the European promise of self-rule coincided with the nationalists' desires. Yet, Arab nationalism ultimately stood in the way of British intentions in Palestine and elsewhere and blocked French plans for Syria. The 1916 Arab revolt and the request by King Hussain Ibn Ali for an empire of the caliphate increased his popularity throughout the Middle East. By 1919, the nationalist movement in the region was on its way toward unification under the leadership of the king of the Hedjaz.[97] The prospect of a unified Arab movement, even one led by the pliant King Faisal, posed a threat to the designs of the Allied powers, and this threat prompted the colonial powers to advocate the establishment of several autonomous zones led by rival rulers. To this end, France and Britain proposed in lieu of Faisal's Arabian empire a number of protectorates or autonomous territories to be placed under the trusteeship of the League of Nations.[98]

The Western plan to create protectorates also required the co-optation of ambitious rival Arab elites. In this regard, the Allied powers were confronted with both their wartime promises to Arab elites who supported Western interests in their peninsula and a more radical nationalism emerging from the 1916 revolt.[99] Under the circumstances, the colonial powers heeded the arguments of Wilsonian autonomists. They found in the staged autonomy of Arab communities a useful political instrument for retaining commercial and strategic interests. The solution to the European Middle East quagmire was reflected in section 4 of Article 22 of the Covenant of the League of Nations, which stated: "The communities formerly belonging to the Turkish Empire have reached a stage of development where their existence as independent nations can be provisionally recognized subject to the rendering of administrative advice and assistance by a Mandatory."[100]

Muted Annexation: The C Mandate

The League Council did not oppose extended colonial control in Africa and the Pacific, where local resistance was easily overcome through greater firepower by would-be mandatory powers and imperial rivalry was minimal. The mandatory powers were at liberty to integrate their new dependencies, categorized as B mandates, into specifically designed political and economic structures solely on the basis of their own needs and in accordance with the Open Door. The autonomy granted to the populations of these mandate B territories also depended upon the political designs of the mandatory powers.

Finally, the League Council established the C mandate as a concession to the annexationist forces of the British Empire, especially in Australia, New Zealand, and South Africa. The South African mandate over South West Africa was the result of practical political considerations,[101] the most significant of which was that South Africa had invaded and occupied the German protectorate in January 1915 as part of the British war effort.[102] The invasion gave Pretoria the advantage of effective control over potential competitors and bolstered Smuts's argument that annexation would maintain continuity and thus political stability.[103]

In his plea for annexation, Smuts conveniently drew from both old and new justifications of colonial expansion. He combined the older axioms of European sovereignty and obligation toward uncivilized natives with the more trendy notion of the trust—the obligation of the trustee toward the international community—but he convinced Wilson and other so-called autonomists on strategic grounds. The security-based plan advanced by Smuts in support of annexation addressed a particular U.S. concern: to deny Japan any military advantage in the Pacific Ocean. Wilson feared that Japanese incorporation of any South Pacific islands would be the first step toward military bases that would be used as launching grounds for attacks against the American continent and U.S.-controlled territories.[104] Wilson and his advisers House and Beer also argued that Japan could build up a strategic position from which it would attempt to control future trade in Asia.[105] The Americans were willing to counter Japan by allowing Australia and New Zealand to exercise greater political control over—to annex—their Pacific territories. The United States too would install military bases on the islands it controlled. In regard to the Pacific islands, in short, the Japanese military threat outweighed the benefits of the mandate, including the Open Door and demilitarization.

On the basis of their own strategic needs, American policy makers understood the military utility of contiguous territories. As a result, they accepted the South African desire to incorporate South West Africa. The Americans were also convinced that the commercial and trade advantages usually attributed to annexation did not apply in this case; British and American interests dominated local capital in South Africa, and this situation was expected to remain unchanged in a German-free South West Africa. Nonetheless, Wilson was not ready to sacrifice his most important postwar objective—an Open Door in mandate territories.[106] As a compromise, Beer and the British Lord Robert Cecil drafted a proposal for a category C mandate that owed its form more to the desire of annexationists than to the sentiments of free-traders. It had nothing to with the much touted Wilsonian idealism of political autonomy.[107]

THE SOUTH AFRICAN MANDATE

There are many indications that the South Africans got their annexation in all but name and that Wilson's mandate principle was "emasculated" in the case of the C territories.[108] The first indication is the lack of reference to the political rights of native populations and their general welfare in the last paragraph of Article 22 of the Covenant. Former League officials have confessed that the practical aspects of the League were irrelevant to the needs of the native populations of the territories. For instance, Duncan Hall, a former member of the League of Nations Secretariat, insisted that even if colonial powers had intended to fulfill unspecified obligations to the indigenous populations of the mandate territories, the underlying ideas and assumptions of the mandate pointed to the contrary.[109]

Safeguards for the Native Peoples

General Jan C. Smuts and other South African officials justified their wartime intervention in South West Africa by their commitment to the struggle against evil, in this case, their concerns for the indigenous populations who had undeniably suffered under German administration. South African officials argued that their country intervened in the protectorate in 1915 as a liberator and protector of the interests of local populations. This argument was easily accepted by other colonial officials and experts because South Africa's intervention occurred in the aftermath of German extermination of the Herero. Accordingly, the British dominion pointed to the treatment of Africans by Germany as a reason for its intervention.

Likewise, Smuts and others justified their postwar decision to annex the territory by "the sacred trust of civilization." They could point to a trail of multilateral negotiations and agreements in which embattled African leaders sought the cooperation of South African settlers in their wars against the Germans.[110] The South African government managed to convey the same impression to local populations. It presented itself as an agent of Britain whose sole purpose was to free the territory from German rule. Its campaign succeeded because Great Britain was a more credible alternative to Germany than the Afrikaners.[111]

South African officials carefully tailored their documentation of the requests by local populations as evidence that they were acting as liberators, not conquerors. In fact, the documentation of African sentiments presented to other colonial officials purposely blurred the distinction between African requests for "military assistance," on the one hand, and the surrender of political administration or external sovereignty, on the other hand, in order to support its own cause. The South African government did not underline the anticolonialist and anti-interventionist sentiments embedded in both African requests for protection and their calls for military assistance during German aggression. A careful reading of South Africa's documentary evidence indicates that whenever Africans appealed for protection or cooperation, the petitioners expected the British and South Africans to simply return the land and cattle stolen by Germans.[112]

South African behavior during the mandate brought criticisms from liberals, philanthropists, and other anticolonialists. Many critics protested South African conduct on the basis of Articles 22 and 23 of the Covenant. Article 22 committed League members to respecting freedom of conscience and prohibiting the slave trade, liquor, and arms traffic in the trust territories. Article 23 mandated the "just treatment of the native inhabitants ... fair and humane condition of labor ... the general supervision of the execution of agreements with regard to the traffic of women ... [and] the prevention and control of disease."

Other than vague references to the welfare of the native populations, neither Articles 22 and 23 nor related documents indicated the rules or procedures by which the trustee power was to fulfill its obligations. This lack of specificity encouraged South African excesses in the administration of the territory. South Africa's health policy, for instance, was limited to maintaining a vigorous labor force to meet its needs in industry and the mines; health care was aimed almost exclusively at the segments of the population directly involved in the colonial economy.[113]

In addition, few of the dispositions of the Covenant directly related to African welfare. The interdiction of fortification in mandate territories, for instance, was related to the fear that trustee powers might use mandate territories for aggression against rival colonial powers. The prohibition of military training for Africans was intended to preempt internal intrigues, in which enemy powers would enlist local allies in destabilizing each other.[114]

In fact, colonial officials were the first to admit the discrepancy between the ideals and the reality of the mandate. Paul Hymans, the first president of both the Assembly and the Council of the League, stated:

While it was important that the Mandatories possess a legal title, it was ... difficult to see in what way [the legal responsibility of the League] would be organized, or what measure would enforce it.... The responsibility of the League before the public opinion of the civilized world will in point of fact be a moral one.[115]

The Conqueror Trustee

Considered objectively, South Africa was not a trustee of the League but an occupying power whose goal was political and economic control. Its control of the territory began when its parliament enacted the Treaty of Peace and South West Africa Mandate Act, in 1919, months before the League officially awarded the mandate. The South West Africa Mandate Act granted broad authority over the territory and its peoples to the governor general of the British dominion.[116] These powers, according to the act, remained in effect until the League of Nations determined the terms of the mandate. Significantly, however, the Union of South Africa unilaterally legalized its 1915 de facto occupation of the former German protectorate.[117]

The League's decision to grant the C mandate only confirmed South Africa's prediction that nothing in the postwar arrangements proscribed the integration of the territory into its own. As a result, South African authorities enacted all relevant laws pertaining to the effective control of the territory. The 1927 Native Administration Act granted the governor general of South Africa the title of supreme chief of the natives of South West Africa. In this capacity, the colonial governor stood above the indigenous chiefs and leaders. He was endowed with the power to appoint and replace the chief native commissioner as well as the latter's subordinates within the territory—the native commissioners and their assistants. The governor was also entrusted with the power to determine the areas in which Africans lived, as well as the territorial boundaries of the areas occupied by the various ethnic groups.[118] The territory was under direct South African control until 1928, when the role of the governor general was delegated to a South African–appointed administrator within the territory. The new administrator inherited the powers of his predecessor.[119]

The end of South African control and the mandate was Western economic control. Beginning in 1922, South Africa strengthened the native reserves system instituted by Germany with the intent of further removing Africans from their lands.[120] The Germans had used the reserve system to facilitate the expropriation of African land for the benefit of imperial mining companies. Likewise, sections 13 and 14 of the South African Native Proclamation Act specified the conditions under which Africans could live on European farms outside of the reserves and the number of Africans each farmer was allowed to employ.[121] The terms of the Native Proclamation Act forced Africans to live in restricted areas, often without sufficient land to raise their cattle or practice agriculture. This proclamation and other acts that mandated the payment of taxes drew landless peasants, especially the adult male population, into the colonial economy as a pool of cheap wage laborers.[122] The transition from subsistence agriculture to wage labor did not occur without coercion. The dispossessed African populations were prohibited by law from moving from one area to another without authorization. Africans could be forced into wage labor if they were declared by the colonial administration to be squatting.[123]

South Africa consistently intervened to promote Western and settlers' economic interests. The role of the administration became prevalent as South Africa sought to promote a kind of commerce and industry unprecedented in its time for the indigenous populations. In the 1930s, for instance, South Africa introduced the Deeds Registries Proclamation as a means of further expropriating African lands.[124] The African Deeds Registries Act of 1937 was a modified version of one previously enacted by South Africa, which itself was inspired by a German law. In effect, the discovery in the 1860s and 1880s of diamond and gold prompted a rush of mining interests to the territory and a German imperial act that removed Africans from the lands desired by German interests. Similarly, the South African act removed all local entitlements and land rights and replaced them with a land tenure system with new land titles in order to enable the mining industry to acquire massive areas.[125]

The mandatory administration determined where Africans lived and worked. It defined the conditions under which Africans could own property, especially land and cattle, as well as the political and economic activities they could undertake. In this vein, it enacted a number of so-called native laws specifically designed to instill and maintain exploitative relations between the colonialists and each ethnic group within the territory.[126]

Political Control

The rate of expropriation of African land by European settlers and capital and the degree of political control of the mandatory invited African reaction and resistance. African reaction was more violent among the so-called squatters and wage laborers. The mandatory power responded to this situation in accordance with its authority under Article 22, paragraph 5, of the Covenant and the Mandate Agreement. These juridical clauses added the functions of defense, police, and security to the role of the mandatory.[127]

South Africa complied with the terms of the mandate by targeting the kind of political disturbances it feared endangered its control. In fact, the colonial administration insisted on the connection between political agitation and the reproduction of capital. It reported in 1936:

> It is common cause in South-West Africa that uncertainty as to the political future of the country is the basic reason for the dissatisfaction now prevalent. It retards the development of the country, makes investors of capital shy and has an unsettling effect on the inhabitants.... The smooth functioning of the Mandate System becomes practically impossible if such interference in the affairs of a Mandated Territory continues.[128]

In 1920, for instance, the Vagrancy Proclamation was adopted with the theoretical aim of preventing and suppressing "trespass, idleness and vagrance" among the "natives." The law was used to remove landless peasants (so-called squatters) from the property of settlers. This act was issued in a period of political unrest during which Africans attempted to retake control of the grazing lands from which they were initially ejected by German settlers.[129]

Like other colonial laws and regulatory acts, the 1930 Riotous Assemblies and Criminal Law Amendment Ordinance owed its existence to economic depression and the ensuing political tension between labor and capital in the territory. This act covered all potentially explosive political activities, including "labor organizing" and strikes. It considered both work stoppage and the refusal to return to work criminal acts. The act also punished any conduct or speech whose "natural and probable consequences" might be "the commission of violence by the public or the persons who witness the act or hear the speech." Finally, it gave magistrates broad authority to "prohibit any gathering by written notice or, if necessary, by oral public announcement" should they "fear that a public gathering will endanger the public peace."[130]

South African security legislation also targeted German settlers, who were angered by the terms of the peace treaty. The Undesirable Removal Proclamation empowered the mandatory to expel from the territory all persons deemed to be a security or political liability. The proclamation was aimed at people other than the natives who were considered "dangerous to the peace and order or good government of the territory" and those who "inflicted on anyone, or threatened anyone with, harm, hurt or loss to his person, property, feelings or reputation."[131]

Colonial Exploitation

Although South Africa was allowed under the authority of the peace treaty to confiscate the property of German nationals, it never fully exercised that right. Instead, the mandatory sought juridical and political ways to bring German nationals in line with the South African goal of colonial exploitation. It accomplished this objective through persecution and repression of German settlers on the one hand, and selective expropriation and legal protection of German interests on the other.

Specifically, South Africa exempted some German interests from the terms of the peace treaty because they had ties to British and South African capital. Long before the beginning of the war, many German interests, especially in the defunct German South West Africa Company, had been reconstituted under British law. Likewise, most German interests in the mining sector were held in conjunction with British capital at the time of South Africa's invasion in 1915.[132]

Other German interests survived the South African mandate as well. In the exercise of its authority, the mandatory power's desire to expropriate German nationals' property was tamed by its equally important need to supply South African markets with agricultural products and cattle and related items like hides.[133] Since the production and marketing of such products were dominated by German settlers, it was economically expedient for the mandatory to retain them within the territory.[134] In the same spirit, small shopkeepers and traders of German origin remained in the territory. Finally, once it satisfied the land needs of its own nationals (Afrikaner settlers), the new colonial power allowed nonantagonistic German settlers to keep their lands.[135]

South Africa applied the peace treaty in a manner consistent with its own self-defined national interests. Like other colonial powers, it did not allow German capital to compete with its own capitalist classes. Thus, South African capitalists and farmers received favorable treatment. After the mandate, Afrikaner farmers, for instance, were invited to settle "prime stock-farming land" no longer in the hands of the Germans. Most such lands were taken from German concession companies whose rights were repealed by the mandatory, but many Africans also lost their lands.[136] As a result of this policy, 10.4 million hectares—some 25 percent of the viable agricultural land in the so-called police zone, where African residency was prohibited—were allocated to about 1,500 new settlers by the middle of the 1920s.[137]

One sector of the South African economy that took full advantage of the mandate was the nascent mining industry. In 1915, the industry was in its formative years and operated in junior partnership with Western financiers. The arrangement was transformed during the mandate as this constituency gained increasing leverage in the colony and at home. This was the origin of the ascendance of Anglo-American and other mining corporations constituted under South African law. Once backed by loans from leading Western banks, these corporations mustered enough influence during the mandate to affect South African decisions, especially those pertaining to the exploitation of the mandate. The new South African mining industry presided over the demise of German interests only to acquire ownership of the vanquished companies.[138]

Other foreign interests also took hold of important interests, completing a trend that began with the passing of the South West Africa Company into British hands.[139] As an intrument of free trade, the mandate was designed to produce just this effect. In fact, one of the first actions of the mandatory was to transfer ownership of major mines to U.S.- and British-dominated capital. De Beers, for instance, acquired control over most of the diamond resources, while the copper mine at Tsumeb was bought by a consortium of U.S transnationals.[140] In the early years of the mandate, the transport sector was also dominated by a British firm, the Shell Trading and Transport Company, a large conglomerate that provided most of the oil distributed in the territory.[141] Finally, British financial institutions such as Barclays have been operating in Namibia since 1925.[142]

5

Constitutional Protection as Pretext

The outbreak of World War II revealed flaws in the international order and brought about a near-consensus worldwide about the necessity of restructuring it. Specifically, the defeat of Nazism and fascism reinforced the political currents hostile to totalitarianism and favorable to national self-determination. The Allies sought to preserve the status quo in Europe against the devastation of Hitlerism and fascism by instituting collective security in Europe and promoting Western hegemony through its cultural, legal, and intellectual values. They also attempted to secure Western hegemony through the mechanisms of the proposed international system: the United Nations.

In other respects, the juridico-political context of postwar restructuring remained an environment of open and concealed battles between opposing sides. The determination of the postcolonial regime opposed two unequal parties, the colonized and the colonizers, who distrusted one another and as a result positioned themselves politically and ideologically in order to influence or control the emerging postcolonial regime. Indeed, Africans' participation in the defense of freedom in Europe and their determination to obtain racial and national equality placed continued Western colonialism in a stark conflict with the declared ideals of the new order.

For their part, the Allies feared any association between colonialism and Nazism. They responded to the colonial question by consciously avoiding any perception of abuse in their own colonies, in the mandates, or in other dependencies they had wrested from Germany and other Axis Powers. Western powers were also sensitive to the nationalist charges about the lack of development or progress in the territories under their control. They reluctantly conceded the necessity of decolonization and national independence for the formerly colonized, yet they maintained a close supervisory role for themselves over these processes. The founders of the United Nations also replaced the mandate with an equally intrusive trusteeship system.[1]

DISCURSIVE STRUCTURES I

Early in the war, when the Allies showed obvious weakness and the Axis powers seemed invincible, the colonial powers appealed to the colonies for assistance. The proposed common front against Nazism and other forms of totalitarianism was not only greeted with enthusiasm in Africa, it gave credence to the Western promise of a postcolonial order in which racial and national oppression would be eliminated and an organization open to all nations established.

The War against All Forms of Oppression

World War I had intensified national consciousness and enlivened the drive to eliminate racial discrimination and national oppression. The League of Nations' response to national questions in Europe, its protection of European minorities, and, more importantly, its promise of eventual autonomy to the populations of mandated territories provided axioms, symbols, and juridical principles from which African intellectuals and activists could draw in their attempt to combat colonial rule. The League's response to African demands was disappointing, however, as colonial powers reneged on the promise that all peoples who contributed to the war would be considered at its conclusion for national autonomy.[2]

The interwar years witnessed a growth in Pan-African activism for national self-determination fueled by the revival of African culture, black nationalism (modeled after Garveyism and comparable movements), and anti-imperialism, as well as the support of Western critics of the imperial order.[3] African intellectuals and activists separated by ideology—nativists or separatists, socialist humanists, and communists—were divided over the appropriate political approach to national and world events. Nonetheless, they and others from the diaspora assembled the Second Pan-African Congress in three

European capitals (London, Brussels, Paris) in 1921 in order to propose concrete steps toward African liberation. These gatherings were followed by the Third Pan-African Conference—held in 1923 in London and Lisbon—and the Fourth Pan-African Conference, which met in 1927 in New York.[4] In general, these Pan-African forums blamed the League of Nations for failing to eliminate the primary cause of imperialism. They condemned the League Council for its opposition to the implementation of the doctrines of national equality and self-determination for the colonial dependencies. They also criticized the mandate system as a new form of foreign control aimed at preserving Western hegemony.

The Pan-Africanist movement failed to produce racial equality and national autonomy. It suffered from structural weaknesses, in particular insurmountable ideological differences among the participants. The movement also faced political repression from colonial powers both in Europe and in the colonies. Yet, it successfully transformed the political landscape in Africa, the American continent, and the Caribbean by placing racial equality, national autonomy, and self-determination at the center of postcolonial relations.

It was therefore with relative ease that Africans were persuaded by the colonial powers to enter World War II. The colonial powers asked for colonial troops to help fight racial discrimination (symbolized by Nazism) and totalitarianism (fascism). The horrors of Nazi war crimes against European Jews and other ethnic minorities injected an unprecedented racial dimension into the political discourse. The Western case against fascism, on the other hand, was viewed by Africans as a declared intention by the major powers to oppose all forms of oppression, including colonialism.[5]

The dramatic unfolding of the war, in particular the defeat of Nazism and fascism, affected Africans' attitude toward the emerging international order. The comparison between the struggle of Africans for national independence and the European war against Nazism was eloquently expressed by Leopold Sedar Senghor, then an African deputy in the French parliament:

> I would like to end this speech by assuring you of our determination to gain our independence and to let you know that it would be absurd and reckless to try to reverse our resolve. We are ready to resort to any means necessary to conquer our freedom—even violent. I would like to believe that France, which has just fought Hitler's racism, would not blame us for our decision.[6]

Indeed, by the end of the war, Africans and other colonized peoples expected the postwar order to establish equality among nations. This expectation increased in the popular African consciousness when hundreds of thousands of African soldiers lost their lives in the cause of European freedom.[7]

An Organization for all Nations

The African expectation of national self-determination was grounded discursively in several wartime Western declarations, in particular the 1941 Atlantic Charter and the 1942 Declaration by United Nations.[8] The order envisioned for the postwar era by the Allied powers was an international system of independent nations, free of oppression and domination and free to exercise their religions in dignity and justice, yet collectively committed to maintaining international peace and development.[9] In the 1941 declaration of principles known as the Atlantic Charter, the president of the United States and the prime minister of Great Britain based their hope for a better world order on the propositions that nations would seek no territorial or other aggrandizement and would respect the freely expressed wishes of colonized peoples for self-determination.[10]

The leaders of the Allied powers held another meeting in Moscow in October 1943 and issued the more specific Declaration on General Security, in which the participants pledged to respect the principle of sovereign equality for all "peace-loving" states. The new principle was to be the basis of a future charter organization open to all nonbelligerent nations.[11] That international organization came about as a result of proposals issued by the United States, Great Britain, and the Soviet Union at Dumbarton Oaks, in Washington D.C., on September 28, 1944. The Washington meeting was followed by a separate encounter between the United States, Great Britain, and China. The proposals that originated in these meetings were subsequently submitted to the four nations and then to the signatories of the Declaration by United Nations. A period of consultation followed to prepare for the United Nations Conference on International Organization, held in San Francisco beginning on April 25, 1945, which drafted the charter for the new organization, the United Nations. The United Nations came into existence on October 25, 1945, upon ratification of the Charter by thirty-nine nations.[12]

The UN Charter was an improvement upon the League Covenant in some respects. It retained the references of the Atlantic Charter to the right of peoples to self-government and the prohibition of force as a means of settling international disputes. The new document also reaffirmed the determination of the signatories of the earlier Declaration by United Nations to confront the challenges posed by Nazism and other aggressive policies in international relations.[13] On other points, however, including colonial exploitation, the Charter was also similar to the Covenant. Key Charter dispositions resulted from compromises based on competing national interests and the rivalry between the two dominant political economies (capitalism and communism), at the expense of the right to self-determination of colonial peoples and other dominated minorities.[14]

DISCURSIVE STRUCTURES II

In general, the post-World World II order protected the status quo in Europe and elsewhere against the devastation of Hitlerism and fascism. It also guaranteed Western hegemony by preserving the colonial order in the Third World.[15] With respect to the mandate system, the victors secured their hegemony by maintaining its essence — corporate colonial unity and cooperation among colonial powers. The Allied powers proposed a colonial agenda that emphasized freedom of trade and navigation, prohibition of force as a means of settling territorial disputes, and disarmament of the dependencies. Freedom of trade in the colonies was dependent upon a redefinition of colonial relations and a definitive settlement of colonial issues such as those involved in the mandated territories.

With regard to postcolonial self-determination, the colonial powers and their ideologues, lawyers, and others who conceived the new international system anticipated their battle against the colonized and their sympathizers in the West. They responded to postwar anticolonialism with a twofold strategy. First, they designed the rules and procedures of the emerging international system, the United Nations, in a manner consistent with Western domination. Second, the new norms of international relations perpetuated the values and interests of the dominant Western classes as international standards. In the ideological realm, the sanctification of Western culture and values was grounded in the myth that, in the evolution of cultures and the values essential to them, the other races were bound to develop in the direction followed by Europeans. This logic was instrumental in determining the trusteeship system as well as the rules and procedures of decolonization. It also served the greater end of imposing legal and cultural norms upon the others for the sole purpose of political control and economic domination.

New Roles for Colonial Powers

The drafters of the UN Charter violated the spirit of national equality by vesting central authority and fundamental powers in the Security Council, in particular its permanent members: initially, Britain, France, the United States, and the USSR.[16] This situation was a consequence of the concentration of world power and the hegemonic impulses of the Allied powers. Beginning with their 1944 Dumbarton Oaks meeting, Great Britain, the United States, and the Soviet Union decided to join with China and France in assuming guardianship of global security as well as the protection of the emerging international system. At the San Francisco conference, where the UN system was formed, the new world powers rejected any proposal that did not recognize a special position for them. According to Francis O. Wilcox, a U.S. congressional consultant to the San Francisco meeting, the larger powers built the "principle of great-power firmly into their new structure, by consciously channeling the authority of the international organization into the hands of the permanent members."[17]

The new world powers realized their ambition for hegemony when they constituted themselves into an executive organ of the United Nations, the Security Council. The official rationale was that a smaller body was more apt to act quickly, without the hindrance of long debate, which was bound to occur in the General Assembly.[18] Consequently, the founders of the UN system concentrated decision-making powers in the hands of five nations (China, Britain, France, the Soviet Union, and the United States) by granting them virtually executive privileges in matters regarding international security and other issues of global concern.[19] The five permanent members of the Security Council alone had the power under Articles 42 and 43 to enforce decisions pertaining to "threats to the peace, breaches of the peace, and acts of aggression." As Security Council members, according to Charter Article 39, they possessed the authority to determine the relevance of any situation to the peace or breach of it.[20] Their decisions in this regard were declared binding on all UN members, who were required to carry them out.[21] In addition, under Article 12, the Security Council could declare itself competent in any matters it considered relevant to the peace, even if such matters were under consideration by the General Assembly. In such an event, the General Assembly, which represents the whole UN membership, must defer to the Security Council, at least until the Security Council asks the General Assembly to make a recommendation.[22]

The manner in which the permanent members were to exercise their vote was defined by Charter Article 27 and Rule 30 of the Provisional Rules of Procedures. According to Article 27 (3), the "decisions of the Security Council on all matters shall be made by an affirmative vote of seven members [of eleven] including the concurring votes of the permanent members." The general rules of Article 27 intended the negative vote of a permanent member to disqualify the Security Council from considering any matter before it. In such circumstances, UN rules and procedures allowed other organs to declare themselves competent. It may be assumed that the Charter intended this as a means of encouraging unanimity among the permanent members on substantive security and peace issues.

Security Council rules were specifically designed to avoid paralysis. Charter disposition and other general rules of law required the permanent members to honor their obligation as guardians of the peace by avoiding the appearance of conflicts of interest. In any decision under Chapter VI, particularly paragraph 3 of Article 52, a permanent member or any other state party to a dispute was expected to abstain from voting. In other words, the Charter and the general principles of law prohibited a permanent member that was party to a situation from adjudicating in its own cause.[23]

The Charter recommended two solutions to potential conflicts of interest, usually when a permanent member was either a party to or directly interested in the outcome of a conflict. The first solution was for the member to observe its obligation to be neutral by not attending the related Security Council meetings. In the event that a member chose to attend Security Council proceedings related to a conflict to which it was a party, Charter rules required the permanent member to abstain voluntarily from discussion of the substance and from related procedures and votes.

Honor, Veto, and Conflicts of Interest

Within the UN's first five years, the permanent members of the Security Council developed a body of precedents regarding their role based on practices, procedures, and customs not anticipated by other members. Specifically, the permanent members interpreted the meaning and application of the negative vote more broadly than prescribed by the Charter.[24] This new view of the negative vote, or veto, reached through an agreement by four permanent members, excluding China,[25] perverted the spirit of the Charter with respect to conflict resolution by extending the application of the veto beyond substantive matters: "If any member raises an objection regarding the procedural character of a certain resolution, a vote is taken to determine its nature."[26]

Charter dispositions and other UN rules limited the use of the veto to substantive matters in order to allow for free and unrestricted debates. Yet, under the Four-Power Declaration, a permanent Security Council member could declare the preliminary question of whether the question under consideration was substantive or procedural to be a substantive matter and, accordingly, veto any further debate.[27] Great Britain exercised this privilege during the Corfu Channel dispute, which opposed it to Albania. The British Security Council delegate violated the spirit of the Charter by arguing that neutrality constituted an infringement upon his country's rights ("I am deprived of my vote under Article 27, paragraph 3") and declared that "the vote which we are going to take is a purely procedural one and ... I can exercise my vote."[28] The Belgian president of the Security Council concurred with the British delegate that Article 27 did not prevent parties to a dispute from voting except in regard to the peaceful settlement of disputes.[29]

The ability of the permanent members both to determine whether a matter was procedural or substantive and to veto consideration of it in either case was dubbed by its critics the "double veto."[30] Its practice has prompted many critics to note that the international community lacked protection against the abuses of the permanent members: "Any permanent member would be able to veto the determination that it had committed an act of aggression."[31] Indeed, the Syrian president of an earlier Security Council session predicted that it would give rise to utter abuse: "A permanent member could say that any procedural question is a substantive one and it would cast its vote against the majority, and the Security Council would not be able to accomplish anything."[32]

With regard to colonial matters, the double veto provided the colonizers with the means to control UN policy making and its outcomes. Predictably, the colonizers used this privilege frequently, violating the neutrality required of a party to a conflict or dispute.[33] The colonial powers were aided in their abuses of power by two contradictory provisions of the Charter. One stipulated that a permanent member was required to abstain only when a dispute involved itself and other states. A dispute in this context was defined as a contest or conflict between two or more states.

In contrast, a permanent member that was party to an international situation had no obligation to abstain in related Security Council proceedings. The Charter defined an international situation as a tension that did not meet all the criteria of a dispute.[34] The distinction between a conflict and a situation was that a situation did not involve more than one state. According to this distinction, most crises that opposed colonial peoples to their colonizers fell under the category of a situation and, therefore, were not subject to the rules governing conflicts of interest. In short, the Charter did not provide any protection to colonial peoples against the abuses of their oppressors.

Exploitation without Obligations

The Allied powers overhauled the mandate system and replaced it with the trusteeship system in an atmosphere of colonial suspicion and Western profession of sensitivity. Accordingly, the trusteeship system was intended as a substitute for formal annexation in (a) all formerly mandated territories, (b) the territories detached from the defeated belligerents, and (c) colonies voluntarily placed under the system by the ruling colonial powers. Like the mandate system it replaced, the trusteeship was in practice another form of colonial control, primarily organized around the military, political, and economic interests of colonial powers. The trusteeship system promoted past corporate colonial unity and cooperation. It implemented the freedom of trade and navigation, the prohibition of force as a means of settling territorial disputes, and the disarmament of the dependencies.

The primacy of colonial interests was underscored during the formulation of the trusteeship system by the division of the trust territories into ordinary and strategic trusts.[35] This distinction between the two types of trusts was founded upon the degree of accountability of the trustee power, signified by the modes of supervision and the related procedures of examination of the required annual reports. The colonial powers controlled the strategic trusts with little accountability to the international community other than through the Security Council, which they dominated.

The Allied powers attributed the supervision of the ordinary trust territories to the Trusteeship Council under the authority of the general UN membership. This council comprised permanent and nonpermanent members. The permanent members included the permanent Security Council members and all other administering powers of previously mandated territories. The nonpermanent Trusteeship Council members were to be chosen for three-year terms. They have been drawn primarily from the general UN membership.

Theoretically, the purpose of the Trusteeship Council was to promote the political, economic, social, and educational advancement of the natives of ordinary trust territories. In this regard, the trusteeship system retained two fundamental aspects of the mandate system. First, the postwar powers granted colonial peoples the right to petition the council on matters related to their well-being and the administration of the territory.[36] Second, the trust powers were required to submit to the Trusteeship Council an annual report, on the basis of which the council evaluated their performance.[37]

The drafters of the UN Charter professed to best preserve the interests of colonial peoples in the trust territories by moving away from the legalistic approach of the mandate. They introduced new procedures regarding the annual reports and improved the mechanisms of conflict resolution. Specifically, the Trusteeship Council was allowed to exercise discretion in dealing with conflicts arising from the administration of the trust. It was permitted by UN rules to deal with such matters selectively and on an ad hoc basis, depending upon the specific circumstances in the territory.[38] Contrary to the conventional wisdom, however, the move away from legal formalism, characteristic of the League of Nations' approach to conflict resolutions, did not necessarily protect the colonized from abuses. According to one critic, the problem of accountability remained the same as before: the international community, outside of the trust powers, lacked the means to verify that the administering powers complied with the rules set forth by the council. Moreover, the international community did not possess the authority either to enforce those rules or to implement programs that conformed to a minimal understanding of the "well-being of the peoples."[39]

Hindsight now shows that colonial relations worsened under the trusteeship system. The move away from the formalism of the mandate enabled colonial powers to divest themselves of most of the requirements of the mandate, including the legally defined duties of the trustee. According to natives who petitioned the Trusteeship Council during its early existence, the trustee powers intensified their exploitation of the territories after they were no longer restrained by intrusive prescriptions.[40] Specifically, native petitioners from the African trust territories of South West Africa, Togo, and the Cameroons claimed that the colonial powers increased their land expropriations through excessive grants, concessions, and various forms of monopoly given to interested colonial parties.[41]

A MANDATE IN DISPUTE

As a growing number of formerly colonized peoples achieved formal independence, the General Assembly was increasingly dominated by countries that had in common only their colonial past and their opposition to overt foreign domination. Although the capacity of the new nations to affect change within the international order was limited, their presence within the General Assembly frustrated the attempts of the colonialists to maintain neocolonial rule in Africa and elsewhere. The increasing number of formerly colonized nations within the international body caused a slow reversal of the ideological pendulum in favor of racial and national equality.[42]

The white minority government of South Africa was particularly concerned by this trend and distrusted the general UN membership and especially the supervisory body of the trusteeship system. Indeed, South Africa anticipated the General Assembly's rejection of its racist policy of apartheid, which it implemented at home and in South West Africa. It feared that the "hostility of the non-white world toward South Africa" would alienate the Western nations.[43] South Africa feared that in their opposition to its policies in South West Africa, the new nations would make full use of their numerical (thus voting) strength in the United Nations, as well as of their actual and potential economic and strategic importance.[44] The hostility of the nonwhite world can be explained without reference to the merits of apartheid. Indeed, "for Afro-Asians, the possibility that [apartheid] has any merits can scarcely arise. It is the policy of white men governing black; and the only good thing that white men still wielding authority in Africa can do is to abdicate in favour of the non-white majority."[45]

South African suspicion of the group it called the Bandung or Afro-Asian confraternity progressively led to its resistance to the UN proposals that it submit the administration of the former mandate of South West Africa to the supervision of the Trusteeship Council. This rejection of the council's authority led to an open confrontation between South Africa and the great majority of the international community.

South Africa under Pressure

The General Assembly first tackled the question of South West Africa (now Namibia) in December 1946.[46] In accordance with its authority under the Charter, the assembly proposed that South Africa assume its international responsibility and its obligations to the peoples of the territory by placing Namibia under the international supervision of the Trusteeship Council.[47] South Africa rejected the proposition at once because it distrusted the motives of the UN general membership. Its position was stated in terms of legal technicalities, in particular its interpretation of the authority of the Trusteeship Council and of the class C mandate, which was Namibia's status under the League Covenant.

Essentially, South Africa claimed that the mandate it received from the League had lapsed as a result of the collapse of the 1919 world order and that, having been entitled by the Covenant to "administer the territory as if part of its own body," it had the right to annex Namibia to or integrate it into South Africa. In effect, it contended that Namibia was not affected by the dispositions of the Charter pertaining to non-self-governing and mandate territories. In sum,

South Africa recognized no obligation to submit the territory to the authority of the Trusteeship Council.[48]

The General Assembly responded to South Africa's challenge by adopting resolution 338 (IV), which appealed to the International Court of Justice for an opinion. The court issued an advisory opinion on July 11, 1950, that vindicated the General Assembly's position. The court advised that:

> The Union of South Africa continues to have international obligations stated in Article 22 of the Covenant of the League of Nations and in the Mandate for South West Africa as well as the obligation to transmit petitions from the inhabitants of that Territory, the supervisory functions to be exercised by the United Nations, to which the annual reports and the petitions are to be submitted.[49]

The court was guarded—indeed, conservative—in its 1950 opinion. Although it recognized the supervisory role of the General Assembly, the International Court of Justice limited that role to the extent permitted under the League Covenant, decreeing that the degree of supervision the assembly exercised over Namibia "should not ... exceed that which applied under the Mandates System, and should conform as far as possible to the procedure followed in this respect by the Council of the League of Nations."[50] Nonetheless, South Africa remained wary of the General Assembly and refused to abide by the opinion of the court and submit to the Trusteeship Council.[51]

The lawyer representing South Africa argued that the General Assembly "cannot arrange for the immediate substitution of the United Nations as mandator, or for the immediate transfer of any mandate functions to the United Nations." Pursuing the logic that the UN was not successor to the League, he added:

> If it is right to say, as I submit it is, that a mandatory relationship, without a mandator, is something juridically impossible, it must follow that the mandates lapsed when the League disappeared. Both Organizations were content to rely, instead, upon the expressed intentions of the mandatories, and their good faith in carrying out those intentions.[52]

The government of South Africa was also convinced, as were other mandatory powers, that the mandate was intended for the primary benefit of the mandatory.[53] Significantly, South Africa rejected the revisionist notion that the class C mandate, like the other two categories of mandate, was intended to promote the welfare of the native. It argued with some justification that "the Mandate ... was not accepted by the peoples of South West Africa, but was imposed upon them from without; and the rights which they acquired under the Mandate they acquired as individuals but not as a legally competent community."[54] South Africa insisted that Article 22 of the Covenant placed the emphasis on the word *Territory,* not on "community and people." The mandate merely covered a territory formerly belonging to an enemy nation, Germany. Accordingly, a political status for the native population could not be inferred from either Article 22 or the mandate agreement.[55]

It was also South Africa's position that the General Assembly as a whole, and colonial powers in particular, could not dispute its right to alter the status of the territory, especially if changes corresponded to the "wishes of the population."[56] Here, too, South Africa could point to established Western practice. In effect, Britain and France had implemented similar transformations in Lebanon, TransJordan, and Syria that changed the status of these territories to nationhood. Those powers did not consult with or seek the cooperation of the League although that organization had not yet dissolved. In fact, the League welcomed the changes *post facto.* The UN recognition of the changes undertaken by France and Britain in the Middle East, especially the alteration of the status of Palestine, emboldened South Africa to pursue its plans for annexation of Namibia. In the words of its lawyers, the sole point of the debate was to determine the conditions under which South Africa would obtain international recognition for whatever status it chose for Namibia.[57]

This was the context in which the governments of Ethiopia and Liberia undertook action before the world court. In effect, they were frustrated by South Africa's delays and bad faith as well as by the inaccessibility of the court to the people of Namibia. The statist bias of the international system in particular justified their action, which was introduced on behalf of the native populations of Namibia. The action of Ethiopia and Liberia at the time seemed to be the last resort for a permanent settlement because Namibians did not have the option of applying to the International Court of Justice. Because Namibia was not a state, it could not apply directly to the court.

Furthermore, as inferred earlier from the Charter, the question of Namibia was in legal parlance a situation and not an international conflict; an international conflict was defined as a dispute or a contention among states.[58]

Since the statist bias prevented stateless communities from applying to the court, Liberia and Ethiopia stepped in. They told the court that "in so far as they were Members of the League of Nations at the time of the League dissolution, and are Members of the United Nations," they had a dispute with South Africa concerning the interpretation and application of the international mandate.[59] Finding grounds for action was only the beginning; next Ethiopia and Liberia had to disprove previous South African claims.

The crucial point of contention was whether South Africa could be trusted to serve the interests of the African populations of Namibia. Citing South Africa's domestic policy of apartheid, Ethiopia and Liberia sought to prove that the government in Pretoria was not qualified to be entrusted with the future of African peoples.[60] They interpreted the meaning and intent of the international trust according to its most liberal implications, carefully drawing from previous world court rulings and opinions that maintained that the mandate had survived the dissolution of the League because "its purposes have not yet been achieved."

In its 1966 reply to Liberia and Ethiopia, the world court did not consider the substance of their arguments. Instead, the court insisted that neither Ethiopia nor Liberia was directly affected by South Africa's actions and therefore had no legal grounds for application to the court.[61] The opinion was consistent with the court's past opinions in particular and Western jurisprudence in general. Indeed, whether the mandate had survived the dissolution of the League or not, the reality was that the mandate was conceived as a colonial instrument, and its oversight therefore lay in the hands of mandatory powers and the League Council. In this sense, the trust itself was colonial, not universal.

The 1966 ruling set off a wave of furor among supporters of Namibian rights within the General Assembly. On October 27, 1966, an anticolonialist coalition adopted a resolution that terminated the trust that the international community, through the League, had bestowed upon South Africa. Resolution 2145 (XXI) stated that "South Africa has failed to fulfil its obligations in respect of the administration of the Mandated Territory and to ensure the moral and material well-being and security of the indigenous peoples, inhabitants of the South-West Africa, and has, in fact, disavowed the Mandate."[62] The General Assembly proposed reinstatement of the international status of Namibia and thereby brought the territory under direct UN responsibility. The resolution also referred to a previous resolution that condemned apartheid and racial discrimination as a crime against humanity.[63] In this, the resolution was in line with the position initially taken by Ethiopia and Liberia.[64]

South Africa's Defiance

In spite of the rebuff of the international community, South Africa maintained its control of the territory and pursued its policy of apartheid at home and in Namibia. In fact, South Africa likened apartheid to self-determination—or, more appropriately, self-rule—which met its obligations under the rules of the trust of civilization. The official doctrine stated:

> The policy of separate development envisages the creation of a number of Bantu territorial units with an increasing measure of self-government. The basic principle to be applied in this connection is that Europeans living in the native areas will be citizens of the European State; Natives living in the European area will be integrated into the political machinery of the various native areas.[65]

The Dutch Reformed Church has been most frequently cited as the cornerstone of the ideology of the kind of racial superiority espoused by South Africa. Indeed, any analysis of apartheid must first look inward to the white government's view on the matter and the effects of the implementation of apartheid on the various communities of South Africa and Namibia. While apartheid is uniquely South African, the teachings of the Dutch Reformed Church alone have not explained the official discourse of separate development. The policy of apartheid pointed to a more complex phenomenon that extended beyond South Africa to the world of colonial powers as a whole. Racial segregation has been, in the words of one South African lawyer, an invaluable element of the cultural heritage white South Africans shared with other white colonialists around the globe.[66]

The policy of apartheid, also known as separate development or apartness, was grounded in the belief that Africans were inherently inferior and inspired by the kind of paternalism that required European administration of Africans and their affairs. The colonial powers maintained that Africans could not survive the harsh adversarial conditions of the modern world, especially if they were to compete with whites. South African lawyers and other ideologues relied extensively upon the scientific "findings" with which other Western colonialists justified racism in order to shore up their own credibility in the international community. South Africa continued to bring to the World Court expert witnesses to justify the appropriateness and legitimacy of its policy of apartheid. Thus, during the 1966 pleadings, one expert quoted a U.S. study that claimed to have found strong evidence that "the average Negro is significantly less intelligent than the average white."[67]

Although this study was not conclusive as to the actual "mental capacity" of Africans, it was intended to cast doubts on the wisdom of integrating different racial groups under the same political and economic structures; if the races had to coexist, Africans must be under the guidance of Europeans. Such an order was mandated by nature itself: "between the populations which are mixed but separated by origins, traditions, and social conditions, there is no other alternative than gradual assimilation, disappearance through servitude or massacre."[68]

Modern sociology, which once defended slavery and segregation in the United States, was also incorporated into South African arguments before the world court. One finding reported to the court was that "men react selectively to their fellow men, in the sense of seeking the association of some and avoiding the association of others. Selective association is necessarily based on some observable differences between those whose association we seek and those whose association we avoid."[69] According to this source, race identification was the most important sociological factor of socialization:

> Physical differences persist to foster social distance which characterize out-group avoidance. Even a superficial consideration of race relations, i.e., contact between black and white, in the United States and Britain, indicate that the Negro, one in class, language, religion and general culture with the host people, remain in essentially caste

status, facing overt or covert prejudice in their day to day contacts with their co-nationals.[70]

That South Africa always looked outward to Australia, New Zealand, and the United States for ideas concerning apartness was confirmed during the court proceedings. South Africa insisted in its oral arguments that the political and economic success of Australia and similar states lay in their capacity to maintain "civilized standards, and ... the Western way of life" without being "swamped by primitives."[71] One South African official, who interpreted the Australian colonial experiment as a success story, argued that harmonious relations among the races were possible only under the conditions of a "politically qualified franchise" for Africans, colored, and Asians.[72]

Another South African official maintained that racial separation in South Africa and Namibia was intended to "avoid insoluble problems which arise from [the] inability of Europeans and non-Europeans in any one country to merge successfully into a single harmonious community."[73] The two races, he argued, should live separately in a partnership in which the white race would "contribute the knowhow" and the black race, the labor force.[74] This official explained that it was for this purpose that South Africa needed a federal system of government in which the white minority would act as "guardian" of their African "wards." In this arrangement, whites would assume responsibility for federal policies and therefore provide the majority of legislators in the state. Africans would be represented on the basis of their ethnic origins and would be responsible only for matters directly related to them.[75]

Thus, the apartheid government developed a number of areas for so-called racially homogeneous national communities. The areas reserved for Africans were subdivided into several reserves or native areas, according to so-called ethnic affiliations. The proponents of apartheid claimed that the reserves were necessary "in view of the extremely heterogenous composition of the non-White population"; they prevented "friction amongst the various [African] groups" and the domination of other groups by whichever groups rose to prominence.[76]

The policy of national reserves was not invented by the apartheid regime. It was begun in South Africa by the British and in South West Africa by the Germans at the turn of the century when it provided white settlers with the means to ensure white political and economic domination over Africans. Apartheid was uniquely adapted to the specific conditions of South Africa, but its purpose remained the same as that of its antecedents.[77] In the words of one official, "colour [race] is only an element, albeit a very important one, in an evolving social and economic process rather than [the] problem itself. We are faced with a process of development that has to be lived with, rather than with an intellectual problem which can be solved and disposed of."[78]

THE ODENDAAL ALTERNATIVE

In the years 1962–63, following the accusations by Ethiopia, Liberia, and other countries that it had neglected its responsibility to promote the welfare of native Namibians, South Africa ordered a commission to inquire into ways of accomplishing that objective without compromising the mandatory's control. The Odendaal commission, named for its chair, Frans Hendrik Odendaal, was asked to make recommendations "on a comprehensive five year plan for the accelerated development of the various non-White groups of South West Africa, inside as well as outside their own territories."[79] The task of the Odendaal commission was twofold. It was instructed first to evaluate South African efforts and accomplishments in the territory in the domains of population growth, welfare, health services, agriculture, education, communications, and economic development.[80] Then the commission was to propose a means of improving the "material and social welfare" of the natives, as well as the "further development and building up" of African homelands or native reserves.[81]

The report produced by the Odendaal commission satisfied the apartheid regime but disappointed its critics: it emphasized the necessity both to modernize apartheid and to maintain the territory dependent upon South Africa. The report suggested that the welfare of Namibians was best assured by the continued presence of South Africa as a modernizing force and by the supremacy of the white minority in Namibia.[82] The external modernizing role of the apartheid regime was complemented by the obligation of the white minority in Namibia to "guide the development of Africans towards self-determination ... within their respective groups."[83]

In the years that followed the Odendaal report, the apartheid regime created several additional homelands. It also reconfirmed the

South African need to determine the appropriate form of government for the native populations according to its own evaluation of the traditions of each group. Such traditions in turn determined the relations of the natives to the central white administration and its economy.[84]

The Odendaal plan reserved a total of 40 percent of the territory for the Africans, who made up 90 percent of the population. The African area was divided into eleven Bantustans, or homelands, scattered within the police zone and the northern area. The police zone, the area occupied by the white minority, contained most of Namibia's prime land resources. The white settlers owned 43 percent of the territory even though they represented only about 10 percent of the population. As the mandatory power, Pretoria took direct control of the remaining land area.[85] This land allocation affected the political economy of the colony. All of the mineral riches were located in the area reserved for the white minority, and five thousand white ranchers appropriated 37 million hectares of the best agricultural and ranching land. In contrast, 150,000 Africans households had access to only 5 percent of the viable farmland in the far north.[86]

As in the past, the dependence of Namibia was key to South Africa's plan.[87] The Herero, Nama, and other Bantustans dispersed within the police zone provided the labor force for the white economy. Africans who lived in the northern area, in the Kaokoland, Okavango, Ovamboland, and the Caprivi, also migrated to the police zone to seek employment. This situation was integral to the South African plan. In effect, by neglecting the northern economy, the colonial authority created a relatively underdeveloped area that depended upon the white economy in the south.[88] Finally, South Africa created the conditions for the total dependence of the colony for its domestic capital.[89]

The economic policy endorsed by the Odendaal report allowed South Africa and its allies to further entrench their control of the territory's natural and human resources. In effect, the Namibian economy was heavily controlled after World War II by South Africa and its allies; the South African administration protected the foreign investors who directed the economy from without. According to the Odendaal report, the share of foreign businesses of Namibia's total import amounted to 80 percent by 1963. The modern mining sector was dominated by American, British, and German capital; foreign interests had full monopoly over the exploitation of diamond, copper, uranium, and other natural resources.[90] By the 1960s, transnational corporations and other foreign economic interests completely dominated the economy of Namibia.[91]

A New Wave of Resistance

The post–World War II anticolonialist resistance began within the traditional leadership and the churches. It initially consisted of a series of social protests against specific colonial policies. These protests were joined later by educated Africans, mainly urban and mine workers. By the end of the 1950s, the nationalist movement included intellectuals in liberal careers such as law and teaching.[92]

A key component of the 1950s nationalist movement was the South West African Student Body (SWASB), whose members were inspired by the struggle of the African majority against apartheid in South Africa, where they themselves had studied. The Namibians were impressed by the 1952 Defiance Campaign organized by the African National Congress and the South African Indian Congress in response to the "unjust laws" of apartheid. Upon their return home, the young nationalists of SWASB founded the South West African Progressive Association (SWAPA) in association with other militant intellectuals. The Windhoek-based organization was founded in the aftermath of the 1952 and 1953 contract workers' strikes. SWAPA worked to instill a unifying ideology of national liberation in the minds of the working class, which was ethnically more representative of the diversity of the general population than any local organization. It also sought to join the traditional leadership in a struggle against colonial oppression that cut across old ethnic and sectional lines.[93]

SWAPA brought labor organizations over to the nationalist cause when it made South Africa's brutal repression of legitimate trade unionism an element of its protest. The nationalists and labor also objected to the contract labor system that deprived northern indentured laborers of their rights—including the right to choose their jobs and employers, and to resign from or change jobs. For the nationalist associations, cheap labor and deepening poverty exemplified the African condition under colonial domination. They encouraged workers to identify the semiofficial labor recruiting arm of the mining corporations, the South West Africa Native Labor Association (SWANLA), with colonial interests.[94]

By the mid-1950s, Namibian students and labor activists had created a noticeable popular base, from which the Ovamboland People's Congress (OPC) was founded in 1957. Renamed in 1958 the Ovamboland People's Organization (OPO), it received the support of the South African Communist Party, the Federal Party, and the African National Congress. OPO's internal program consisted of confronting South African colonialism in all its manifestations. The organization also campaigned outside of South Africa and Namibia to seek support for the struggle against exploitation and repression.[95]

Resistance to colonial exploitation widened in 1959, when an alliance of intellectuals, urban youth, and the Herero-based Chiefs' Council was joined by several activists from OPO and other organizations to form the South West Africa National Union (SWANU). One of SWANU's objectives was to bring into the nationalist movement the regional organizations in the south, center, and north of the territory.[96] Soon after it was formed, the new united front was confronted with South Africa's decision to remove the black population from the township of Katutura, an area near Windhoek. SWANU decided to resist the forced removal, and in conjunction with the mass protest against removal a procession of African women marched to the residence of the administrator in defiance of the police on December 10, 1959. The following day many more people joined in the protest. The police intervened, shot into the unarmed crowd, and killed at least eleven Africans.[97]

Popular anger followed the Katutura massacre, but the popular front could not agree on strategies. According to one source, the Chiefs' Council did not share the radicalism of the young militants of SWANU. The front also suffered from continued South African repression. It finally fell apart in 1960. OPO subsequently reconstituted itself as the South West Africa People's Organization (SWAPO) with the much broader objective of national unity and national independence from colonial exploitation.[98]

From its creation in April 1960, SWAPO pressured South Africa to end its occupation of the territory. To this end, it mobilized world opinion as well as organized an internal armed resistance through the People's Liberation Army of Namibia (PLAN). SWAPO won major successes, particularly on the diplomatic front. In 1973, for example, the UN General Assembly recognized SWAPO as the "authentic representative of the Namibian people."[99] The most significant victory of SWAPO and its supporters against the apartheid state was the 1966 General Assembly vote to terminate the mandate.

Against the Winds of Change

Although the General Assembly's decision to terminate the mandate came as a blow to the international image of South Africa, it did not deter the country from attempting to retain the initiative over any settlement in the colony. Subsequent events in southern Africa diminished the ability of the apartheid state to maintain control over Namibia. One event that changed the strategic and political landscape was the capitulation of Portugal to the nationalist forces of Angola and Mozambique after years of armed resistance.[100] The end of colonial rule in Angola and Mozambique reduced the number of white-minority regimes in southern Africa to three—Rhodesia, South Africa, and Namibia—as well as exposed the effects of apartheid on the region.

South Africa first responded to these events by trying to shore up its own reputation as a colonial power and soften international reactions to its continued occupation of Namibia. South Africa pretended to comply with General Assembly demands to implement self-rule in Namibia and even abandoned its advocacy of annexation and instead tried to install a Namibian government that would be subservient to Pretoria. It sought an internal agreement with a select group of Africans who consented to a dominant role by white-dominated political parties in postapartheid Namibia. The result was the Turnhalle Constitutional Conference.[101]

The Turnhalle Conference was held between 1974 and 1976, after a tripartite consultation between the government of South Africa, the South African Department of Bantu Affairs, and the executive committee of the South West Africa National Party (SWANP). A right-wing political party, SWANP was composed of white Namibian settlers who had a close association with South Africa's ruling National Party.[102] The tripartite consultation was enlarged later to include so-called traditional chiefs. The African chiefs were chosen by SWANP and persuaded to join in the forthcoming conference.[103]

According to the initiators, the Turnhalle talks had many objectives, all related to the exercise of self-determination by the people of Namibia. The first aim was to discuss a constitutional future for a self-governed Namibia. One item on the agenda was the determination of communal rights for the various ethnic and racial groups. In the view of SWANP leaders, the constitution was to reject any formula that might "enforce a new dispensation" for any group.[104]

The constitutional concept of group rights proposed by SWANP did not imply equality among the various ethnic and racial groups; it was introduced by the white minority in order to protect its own rights against any fundamental change in the power structure. The concept presumed that Africans and Europeans had different needs, as did different ethnic African groups. The presumed differences required specific group rights, such as representation in a future government. The government would be federal, based on racial and ethnic representation. Each ethnic authority would have "the greatest possible say in its own and national affairs which would fully protect the rights of minorities." This particular articulation and understanding of group rights was the only sure way to "do right and justice to all," according to South Africa and the white Namibian minority.[105]

The Turnhalle Conference also proposed a central government that would be a by-product of the ethnic and regional authorities; that is, the parliament would represent both the white constituencies and the Bantustans. Significantly, the members of this parliament would not be elected directly. Rather, they would be chosen according to rules of procedure established by their respective ethnic and racial governments. The executive authority of the central government would rest in a council of eleven members, each one representing an ethnic group.

During the conference, there emerged two tendencies among the white delegates regarding the decision-making processes and the role and authority of the central government. One tendency favored a decision-making process in which all questions would be decided unanimously, with each group having the power of veto. This group foresaw little role for the central government in allocating resources in the political process. The Action Front for the Preservation of the Turnhalle Principle—Aktur—favored this principle of decision by absolute consensus. The decision-making procedure advocated by the Democratic Turnhalle Alliance (DTA) would institute a two-tier power relation between a so-called Bantustan Confederation and the white constituency. In this scheme, decisions would be made by a simple majority, granting the central government a significant role in policy decisions. Despite their different approaches, however, the objective of both parties remained the same: the preservation of the rights and privileges of whites in a postcolonial Namibia.[106]

The Turnhalle Constitution was never implemented because of other setbacks suffered by South Africa. The first was military defeat in Angola. In early 1976, South Africa invaded Angola in order both to destroy SWAPO forces in that country and to boost the fortunes of the rebel forces of the National Union for Total Independence of Angola (UNITA). This aggression was decisively repelled by Angolan troops, aided by Cuban internationalists.

South Africa also lost international support when it used its bases in Namibia as a springboard from which to launch attacks against the nearby "frontline states," in particular Zambia. This behavior cost Pretoria much-needed Western support, especially among the Western Security Council powers, which had quietly supported the Turnhalle constitutional reform. Pretoria's aggression was particularly bewildering to its supporters because it coincided with growing anticolonialist climate within the United Nations. Prior to the South African aggression, several Western nations, including Britain, France, West Germany, and the United States, had granted semidiplomatic recognition to the Democratic Turnhalle Alliance by allowing it to open offices in their respective countries. Now even these powers could not immediately endorse the internal settlement schemes of Turnhalle nor publicly defend their client's actions.[107] Much to the dismay of Pretoria, the Security Council in 1976 unanimously adopted a resolution that went beyond the usual condemnation of apartheid to establish the principle of South African withdrawal and independence for Namibia.[108]

Following the Security Council resolution, South Africa, eager to break out of its international isolation, implemented a new version of the "internal settlement" in the hope of keeping international pressure at bay. The aim of South Africa's cosmetic reforms was to reduce the likelihood of UN intervention.[109] In this context, the Pretoria government appointed Justice Marthinus T. Steyn as the new administrator general of Namibia in 1977. The new administrator had full powers to reform the laws of the territory. The reform consisted mostly of removing from the statute books the laws most objectionable to the international community and replacing them with new emergency laws: Steyn introduced martial law zones within the territory after abolishing some discriminatory laws.[110]

The powers of the administrator general varied as a function of internal and international pressure. Beginning in mid-1979, as a reaction to a 1978 Security Council resolution, the South African official lost some of his powers to a so-called interim government. When the interim government collapsed in 1982, South Africa selected a transition government that was unique in the history of the territory in that it included some black Namibians. One of the roles of the transition government was to draft a new constitution for Namibia, contingent upon South African approval. In January 1986, South Africa convened a National Constitutional Council to draft the constitution. The heavy-handed attempts of the apartheid state to control Namibia's future continued through the 1989 elections, which led to the independence of the former colony.

AMBIVALENCE TOWARD DECOLONIZATION

Postwar decolonization occurred within an order typified by a realignment of power within the UN system between the Western and Eastern (communist) blocs. This distribution of power created unease among the colonized and the formerly colonized. Africans, Asians, and other Third World peoples feared that the permanent Security Council members would be in a position to abuse their newly acquired power if it were not checked by that of the General Assembly.[111] They suspected that the unchecked powers of the Security Council would be detrimental to their own interests. Indeed, the Western colonial powers intended to control the process of decolonization in order to ensure the hegemony of liberalism and the affirmation of free trade among integrated national and geoeconomic spaces. Still, as the basis of the emerging international political economy, these spaces remained hierarchically differentiated into core and peripheral national and regional economies.

Reactions to Declining Hegemony

Despite increasing international opposition to South African occupation of Namibia, there never was a consensus concerning the role of the former mandatory in the process of decolonization, nor even regarding the meaning and extent of self-determination for the former mandate territory.[112] The intensity of the pressure on and criticism of the apartheid state, however, was an indication of the declining support for old-fashioned foreign rule. The retreat from outright colonial rule also marked the beginning of the end of the authority of colonial powers as an entity.

The diminishing authority of colonial powers in world affairs was due in part to the fact that, prior to the collapse of the Soviet Union, they did not have full control of international organs that under previous international regimes had been their exclusive domain: the Security Council and the Trusteeship Council, for example. The lack of full control over UN policy-making organs posed procedural and structural obstacles that colonial powers had to overcome in order to determine policy. With respect to decolonization, for instance, the former colonial powers had to contend with both Third World nations and, more significantly, the communist states, which were at least rhetorically opposed to political privilege bestowed by colonial domination.[113] To the extent that Soviet and Chinese leaders disputed the legitimacy of the capitalist states of Europe, especially their expansionist policies, their presence within the Security Council had measurable effects for colonial peoples seeking independence.[114]

Until 1971, when the People's Republic of China was admitted as a permanent member, the Soviet Union alone among Security Council members had officially dissociated itself from the Western objective of maintaining capitalist hegemony through colonial exploitation. For instance, the General Assembly resolution known as the Declaration on the Granting of Independence to Colonial Countries and Peoples was the result of a speech delivered by Soviet premier Nikita Khrushchev at the assembly's fifteenth session. The speech was followed by a debate that led to the submission of a draft declaration by the Soviet premier and culminated in the passage of resolution 1514 (XV), "whose contents were drafted and submitted by forty-three nations, mainly African, Asian and Latin American."[115]

Even though the Soviet Union and China had not fully abandoned expansionist policies, they opposed colonial expansion and economic exploitation as practiced by the West in Africa. The ruling elites of China and the Soviet Union disputed the legitimacy of Western capitalism and especially its expansionist policies, in ways that coincided with the aims of anticolonial and nationalist movements in Africa. The presence of the socialist states within the Security Council therefore not only eroded the necessary colonial consensus, it provided an opening, and at times support, for anticolonial forces such as SWAPO. The alliance between African nationalists and the socialist bloc endangered Western interests and compelled the West and its client state of South Africa to design a multifold policy that consisted of cooperation with the United Nations whenever it was convenient but also political confrontation and compromise in order to retain previously enjoyed privileges.

Selective Recourse to the Security Council

One approach to controlling the outcome of decolonization was selectively to rely on the Security Council as a policy instrument. This selective reliance on the Council was key to protecting so-called vital Western interests while allowing for formal decolonization in Namibia. Western powers pushed and obtained support for Security Council resolutions that did not essentially affect their interests.

One policy area in which international consensus was easily obtained was the rejection of apartheid. Even South Africa's allies did not want to be associated with a government that openly advocated racial discrimination. After the June 21, 1971, world court ruling that South African occupation of Namibia was illegal, a near universal consensus emerged on the necessity to eliminate apartheid. The court ruling, it has been said, was one important factor in the unanimous approval of Security Council resolution 385 (1976), which uncompromisingly called for Namibian independence.

On the other hand, Western powers used their remaining strength, including the veto, to block Security Council resolutions they perceived to be incompatible with their own interests (and South Africa's). Western powers used the veto repeatedly against resolutions related to decolonization in Southern Africa. Between June 1971 and June 1987, for instance, the United States vetoed fifty-one resolutions, nine of them directly related to apartheid policies or South African aggression against its neighbors.[116] One resolution pertained to the arms embargo against South Africa; six dealt exclusively with the situation in Namibia.[117] Other Western powers have similar records. During the years 1975 to 1987, every draft resolution concerning Namibia that was vetoed by the United States was likewise vetoed by France and Great Britain.[118] Only once did France differ with Great Britain and the United States on the Namibia question.[119]

Western powers pursued their dual policy of cooperation and confrontation with the United Nations at the expense of Namibians. For instance, when South Africa objected to the procedures laid down in Security Council resolution 385, Britain, France, and the United States reversed themselves by proposing instead a modified version, resolution 435 (1978). Similarly, when South Africa unilaterally organized elections in Namibia in 1978, in violation of resolutions 385 and 435, the same Western powers would not join in denouncing Pretoria's actions. Since they had sponsored resolution 435, Western powers chose to abstain from—instead of vetoing—the condemnation. The move was motivated solely by practical concerns for their own credibility.[120]

South Africa's allies also employed other strategies to weaken opposition to their control of the process of decolonization. They initiated alternative international forums that they dominated and that competed with UN organs. The most visible was the Western Contact Group. The ostensible aim of the group was to mediate the process of Namibia's independence, and it was technically authorized under Article 35 of the UN Charter.[121] Its timing and role in the decolonization process, however, indicate that the Western decision was politically motivated: it was primarily an effort to remove the Namibian negotiations from the auspices of the Security Council and the General Assembly.

In effect, it was in 1977 that the permanent Western members of the Security Council obtained a golden opportunity to take command of the Namibia issue. The occasion was the entry of Canada and West Germany to the Council for two-year terms as nonpermanent members. Canada and West Germany (the Federal Republic), like other Western members, had vested interests in Namibia. Therefore, they joined the three permanent Western members in forming a consultative group known as the Contact Group or Western Five.[122] Although the Contact Group held its legitimacy and authority from the Charter, its existence subverted UN procedures of conflict resolution, especially the conflict-of-interest clause. The formation of the Contact Group violated the general principle of law according to which states that had interests in specific policy areas had the international obligation to abstain from promulgating or promoting policy prescriptions that "may involve deliberate truncation of" other states' rights.[123]

Indeed, the Contact Group countries used their political and military assets within the international community to obstruct policy prescriptions they did not support. The first act of the group was to propose a Western plan for Namibian independence that had been drawn up outside the UN framework. The first draft of the proposal was issued in January 1978, in anticipation of the "proximity talks" initiated and mediated by the foreign ministers of the five between representatives of South Africa and SWAPO.[124] This draft retreated from the main elements of Security Council resolution 385.[125] It also moved away from the comprehensive settlement of previous UN plans by replacing the international organization as the key negotiator of decolonization. The Contact Group plan made two substitutions to the UN plan: the role of the United Nations changed from "administering authority" charged with "implementation of Resolution 385 under the guidance of the Security Council" to a mere party to the decolonization process, and the Contact Group usurped the guidance role of the council, which was left with an oversight function.[126]

The Western plan made several concessions to South Africa. One was the extrication of the enclave of Walvis Bay from the settlement process. This action implicitly endorsed Pretoria's contentious position that the seaside enclave was not an integral part of Namibia.[127] The Contact Group also included the South African-appointed administrator general in the decolonization process as an independent party separate from South Africa.[128] This action was tantamount to accepting as a fait accompli Pretoria's annexation of the territory.[129]

Partial Impartiality

The Western Five also endorsed South Africa's insistence that UN participation in the settlement process be based on its strict adherence to impartiality. Pretoria had accused the UN Transition Assistance Group (UNTAG) of partiality to SWAPO. UNTAG had been set up to assist the special representative of the secretary general in carrying out the UN mandate in compliance with resolution 435.[130] Pretoria presumed that UNTAG was incapable of assuming its responsibility to be impartial because of the influence of the General Assembly within it. Besides concerns over its composition, South

Africa suspected the status of UNTAG security and police forces, which were to be sent to Namibia prior to elections.

The Western Five used the occasion of the Geneva preimplementation meeting to try to soothe their ally. The multiparty meeting, proposed by the secretary general, was held in January 1981 in order to bring the parties to the Namibian settlement to an understanding. The parties were expected to draft a "declaration of intent" that would determine the obligations of the parties as well as "ensure the impartial discharge [by the United Nations] of its responsibilities," especially with regard to the supervision of the election.[131] The meeting was dominated by a controversy about the determination of the parties to the process and the implications of UN impartiality to SWAPO. The controversy was the result of a South African demand that the determination of the parties to the settlement be extended beyond the initial three participants—itself, its appointee the administrator general of Namibia, and SWAPO.[132]

The Contact Group agreed with South Africa's position even though it made the initial determination of the parties that were invited to the Geneva meeting. In effect, the Western Five and Pretoria insisted that the so-called internal parties be admitted to the settlement process "on an equal basis with [SWAPO]" because they viewed in such participation a means to further isolate the liberation movement.[133] The reason officially invoked to justify the participation of the internal parties was that they not only represented the true wishes of the majority of Namibians but also would be significant players in the proposed elections.

According to a Contact Group memorandum, the impartiality of the United Nations, especially UNTAG, involved an equal consideration of the views of SWAPO and the internal parties as well as an inclusion of these parties in any preindependence discussions.[134] The internal parties were represented by a group of Namibians, white and black, who accompanied the delegation of the administrator general. In the opinion of many, the internal parties had been created with the assistance of South Africa in an effort to subvert resolution 435 and the international campaign for decolonization in Namibia. So, in their majority, the internal parties were constituted to oppose SWAPO.[135]

The same memorandum sought to end UN support for SWAPO. The termination of existing UN programs was viewed by the Western Five and South Africa as essential to impartiality. Specifically, the memorandum advocated the withdrawal of financial support for the Namibian program of the UN Department of Public Information. The funds allocated to this program served to mobilize political support for South Africa's withdrawal from Namibia.[136] Such an action would have put SWAPO, which was then based outside the territory, at a disadvantage vis-à-vis the so-called internal groups and perhaps would have delegitimized the organization as the "authentic representative" of the Namibian people.

The question of impartiality and representation was not resolved satisfactorily. Pretoria and its allies demonstrated their displeasure by effectively preventing the drafting of the much anticipated "declaration of intent" concerning the schedule of Security Council resolution 435. On the other hand, SWAPO and its supporters were disappointed by the partiality of the Contact Group definition of impartiality, which totally ignored South Africa's position in the conflict—as an occupier, an administrator, and a party to the negotiation, all at once.[137]

The Contact Group continued to negotiate with and support South Africa long after the failed Geneva preimplementation meeting. In April 1981, South Africa's defense and foreign ministry officials met with their counterparts from the U.S. State Department to discuss future strategies. During this meeting, Rolof Pik Botha, Pretoria's foreign minister, raised new conditions related to white Namibians' concerns about the right to property, an independent judiciary, freedom of religion, the preservation of their language, and the quality of education under a future majority-ruled Namibia.[138] He suggested constitutional guarantees that would have protected whites, especially in the event of a SWAPO-led government. The two parties discussed the possibility of drafting a constitution for Namibia that, according to the South African option, would precede any other step in the settlement process—especially the preindependence election.[139]

After consideration of the South African proposals, the United States changed the position it held prior to the pre-implementation meeting. Drawing its own conclusions from the April meeting, the United States began to insist that while Security Council resolution 435 was the basis for transition to independence, its dispositions alone could not be the basis for the full settlement.[140] This reversal in U.S. position prepared the ground for the various understandings that were later attached to resolution 435 and other UN settlement plans.

Partial Constitutional Protections

In October 1981, the Contact Group moved to supplement the terms of resolution 435 with the constitutional guarantees demanded by South Africa. They insisted that all parties subscribe to the institution of a multiple-party system and the protection of the property rights of the white minority as a condition to their participation in the process. The proposals included in the "Principles Concerning the Constituent Assembly and the Constitution of an Independent Namibia" were submitted to the Security Council and the secretary general to be appended to resolution 435. According to the first phase of the plan, groups and political parties wishing to participate in the elections should adhere to a Declaration of Fundamental Rights that included inter alia equality before the law, protection from arbitrary deprivation of private property, the right to associate for political or trade purposes, and the freedoms of speech, movement, association, and press.[141]

Following the adherence of the parties to the constitutional principles, the preindependence elections would be held to determine a constituent assembly, on the basis of either proportional representation or an "appropriate determination of constituencies," or even a combination of the two. The second option was a euphemism for South African choice of ethnic or racial representation. The assembly thus elected could modify the preindependence conditions or adopt a new bill of rights only if it obtained a two-thirds majority.[142]

The new Western proposal satisfied some whites who rightly believed that under the political circumstances in the territory SWAPO could not obtain a majority in the assembly without a system of direct representation. They based their arguments on the fact that the territory was divided along ethnic and racial lines and, moreover, many of the Bantustan chiefs had been appointed by the Pretoria-backed administration. These chiefs also had some affiliations with the so-called internal parties.

Despite the political reality in the territory, the majority of whites remained doubtful of the outcome of the elections. They were concerned about the possibility of a two-thirds majority victory by SWAPO, which might provide the antiapartheid nationalist organization with the opportunity to draft or revise any preindependence constitution. In this context, the unmitigated application of the electoral principle of one vote per person in a system of direct representation remained anathema to the majority of white Namibians and to South Africa. Even the guarantees proposed in the Western plan could not appease them.

The Contact Group submitted a revised version of its previous proposal on December 17, 1981. In the new version, the principle of universal and equal suffrage was replaced by a "one person–two votes" formula, inspired by the West German electoral system. According to the new proposal, one set of votes would determine half of the seats in the assembly, assigned according to the proportion of the votes received. The second set of ballots would determine the seats to be held on the basis of single-member constituencies "containing as nearly equal a number of inhabitants as is practicable."[143]

As the Western-mediated negotiations evolved, it became clear to SWAPO and other antiapartheid organizations that motives other than concerns for a free election and constitutional guarantees caused the Contact Group to constantly alter the independence plan. Indeed, the group was pursuing a two-track policy aimed at accomplishing the same goal, retention of South Africa's and other Western nations' interests in Namibia. The first track in the strategy of South Africa and its allies was an attempt to deny SWAPO an electoral victory in nationwide balloting. Initially, they attempted to achieve this by setting up a complex electoral procedure that would be incomprehensible to a largely illiterate Namibian population.[144] These powers had predicted that the margin of the electoral victory of the nationalists determined the potential for an independent SWAPO-led Namibia to reduce its dependence upon South African and other Western interests. The Western Five had estimated that if SWAPO failed to reach the two-thirds majority, property and other socioeconomic relations would remain intact, leaving whoever governed the country to a peripheral role in an economy largely dominated by the white minority and foreign interests. Under these conditions, foreign interests in Namibia did not have to fear popular pressure on SWAPO to effect change in the structure of capital and the economy in order to meet the needs of the dispossessed majority of Namibians.[145]

The second track of the Western plan was an insurance policy against the dreaded two-thirds SWAPO victory. To this end, South

Africa and its allies brought into the decolonization debate issues not directly related to independence or self-determination. The most significant extraneous factor that the Contact Group nations injected into the independence plan was their insistence upon preindependence constitutional protection of minorities' rights. The Western Five set the endorsement of such constitutional guarantees by political parties as a precondition of their participation in the election.[146]

In the ensuing debate over the need for constitutional guarantees for minorities' rights, the United States and its allies made the link between the proposed Declaration of Fundamental Rights, other specific guarantees for minorities, and the protection of property rights and related privileges very clear. In the context of Namibia, the rights and privileges to be protected were those the whites had come to enjoy under colonial rule. Significantly for the Western Five, the white minority was in the main integrated into the international economy, which the Western powers privileged over the rights of the majority of Namibians. In fact, the Western mediators specifically rejected, or refused to consider, SWAPO's interpretations of the so-called fundamental freedoms and human rights in conjunction with Namibian decolonization. In the organization's view, the concepts of human rights and fundamental freedom included socioeconomic justice and the fundamental narrowing of the gap between European settlers and their African associates, who in the past enjoyed privileges, and the large majority of the African masses, who have been dispossessed through colonial mechanisms.[147]

Conclusion
The Challenges of Postcolonialism

With the independence of Africa's last colony, Namibia, two contradictory precepts have come to dominate the authoritative Western discourse on postcolonialism. The first is that the post-World War II international regime has restored sovereignty and self-determination to the formerly colonized.[1] This postulate is based on the jurisprudential notion that the current norms of international relations and law are founded upon the principles of political autonomy and juridical equality among national entities.[2] At the same time, the vast majority of authoritative scholars and practitioners recognize that most former colonies do not possess the requisite attributes of statehood.[3] These postcolonial states are "not authorized and empowered domestically,"[4] that is, they are composed of diverse ethnic and cultural subgroups that continue to maintain tenuous relationships with central authorities. In addition, beyond the basic juridical protection against outside intervention, these entities lack tangible capabilities to deter other states or to act freely in the international arena. In sum, they have a shortage of the institutional features that characterize fully sovereign Western states.[5]

The postulated accomplishment of the postcolonial regime and the deficiencies of the process of decolonization are empirically interconnected. Yet, they remain rhetorically disjointed in the hegemonic Western metaphysics, reflected by the dominant political and international legal theories. The related authoritative discourse considers postcolonial institutional deficiencies to be intrinsic to the constitution of the new states. This means that the organic shortcomings of the former colonies are independent of deliberate preindependence strategies and tactics adopted by the protagonists of decolonization. This discourse also rejects the contention that the structures of the present international system limit the capacity of African nations to achieve self-determination and full sovereignty. It effectively minimizes the stifling effects of the subjection of Third World entities to a global political, cultural, scientific, and technological apparatus that guarantees Western hegemony within a hierarchical international order.

The rhetorical separation of these two postcolonial realities (decolonization and organic defects) has been essential to the perpetuation of four authoritative claims and propositions. The first is an emotive Western claim to postcolonial redemption and moral rectitude. This claim, grounded in a philosophical commitment to the status quo, is widely supported by a multitude of Western theorists and professionals from a range of theoretical perspectives. These publicists reject views or utterances that conflict with Western hegemony. The second authoritative claim is that African and other Third World crises are solely the result of inadequate domestic leadership. In the ideological instance, this discursive position suggests that African and other non-Western elites lack the intellectual training and cultural foundation to develop programmatic solutions to internal economic destitution and political chaos on the one hand, and to international problems on the other.

The empirically dubious claim regarding the capacity of Africans and other Third World peoples to govern has provided the basis for two equally tenuous and complementary propositions. One is the intimation that Western models ultimately offer the only reasonable alternative to the current state of international affairs. In this regard, Western policy makers and policy advocates have suggested that the survival of developing nations depends upon their submission to the mandates of the present hegemons. The other proposition is that Western philosophy, science, and culture remain the sole guarantors of international stability and prosperity.

Although lacking empirical necessity, the metaphysical dissociation of postcolonial crises from the deficiencies of decolonization has been sustained by a philosophical commitment to the status quo. It is my contention that this theoretical and ideological position conflicts with the proclaimed objectives of the present international regime: peace, stability, interdependence, multilateralism, international co-existence. In particular, Western perceptions of the self and others, signified by the claims and propositions outlined here, have undermined the quest for sound solutions to two categories of post-colonial international crises. The first category consists of conflicts resulting from the breakdown of legitimacy, themselves attributable to the lack of resources essential to nation building. These domestic contestations often lead to political chaos affecting other states. The second category emcompasses conflicts that originate in outside interference. They are the result of either outright subversion by hegemonic powers or destabilizing pressures by Western-dominated international institutions. In particular, the proposed authoritative solutions to these crises demand the further erosion of African (and Third World) self-determination and sovereignty as a prerequisite to attaining the objectives of the international regime. This postcolonial project would afford an insurmountable advantage to the West within hierarchical international structures. Once unquestioned, this ethically deficient postcolonial regime has increasingly come under scrutiny in the Third World, and as a result has called the very survival of the Western-inspired international order into question.

LIBERAL RESPONSES TO POSTCOLONIALISM

The plurality of liberal supporters of the present international regime embraced the precepts of the authoritative discourse. As a result, they generally refute the notion that the processes that led to national autonomy in the former colonial empires have bearing both on the continuing Western hegemony within the international order and on ongoing postcolonial crises in the former Western empires.[6] These scholars and publicists assume that current Western supremacy and the ascendancy of capitalism outside Europe resulted from natural evolutionary processes. Thus, supposedly less efficient non-Western institutions, especially local instruments and standards for use, possession, and exchange, simply collapsed during contact with Europe. Similarly, non-Western norms are presumed to have simply disappeared as a result of the natural progression of the laws of production and exchange.[7] Thus, they dismiss as irrelevant the view that the international system adversely affects the capacity of the new nations to muster sufficient resources for their survival.

This position is founded on two mistaken assumptions. The first considers the rules of the "game" of international relations to be apolitical, atemporal, and ahistorical. In this context, the authoritative liberal representation of decolonization is based upon the assumption that the postwar international system consists of clearly defined neutral rules. Decolonization is assumed to have taken place within mutually agreeable conditions between the formerly colonized and the colonizers. It is said to typify a free exercise of the popular will of the colonized, that is, self-determination. Accordingly, national independence was the result of a sovereign act that the formerly colonized opposed to the claims of former colonial powers. Finally, the majority of legal and political theorists have assumed that the advent of national independence in the former dependencies completed the civilizing qua Enlightenment project of a universal order based on rights and liberties. Many liberals continue to advance this view, although the applicable procedures and rules of international law allowed the colonial powers to manipulate the entire process of decolonization. In fact, the imperialist powers selectively imposed jurisprudential rules of entitlement with the deliberate intent of maintaining their own hegemony within the new regime.[8]

The second assumption, more insidious, posits that the Western founders of the rules of international relations and law are rational and that others are not. This assumption, in turn, has led to the suggestion that Western leadership within the international order is necessary to peace, international stability, and security. The imperative of this leadership is said to be grounded in superior Western ethos, culture, economy, and technology. The supposed desirability of Western leadership is the basis of most liberal solutions to current international crises. This position, however, ignores both Western control of the relevant decision-making organs of the international system and the conduct of the hegemonic powers in fulfilling their role as guardians of the peace.

Echoing these assumptions, Robert Jackson rejects any association between the international system and the misfortunes of the new states. In *Quasi-States: Sovereignty, International Relations, and the Third World,* he argues that the misfortunes—lack of resources, poverty, and vulnerability—of the new nations are rooted in cultural, technological, environmental, and other factors.[9] In particular, he attributes the inability of African and other Third World nations to fully exercise sovereignty and self-determination within the postcolonial international system to a case of precipitous decolonization: the primary cause of current African crises is that the postcolonial states on that continent lacked the required political maturity at the time of national independence. In this evolutionary paradigm, political maturity is signified by the preeminence within society of socioeconomic classes favorable to the reproduction of civil society and constitutional institutions.[10] These assimilated elites are expected to ascend to existing political, intellectual, and moral norms. Such prospective Third World rulers would support democratic institutions, liberal values, and interdependence within an international order dominated by the West. Because of the absence of the evolutionary requisites for national autonomy, Jackson claims, African nations and others have been led by authoritarian and corrupt rulers throughout their independence.

In Jackson's view, Western powers have been unduly charitable to quasi states and their leaders by granting full sovereign immunity to Third World leaders, allowing them to persist in extralegal and antidemocratic actions. Although they have acted within the normative boundaries of the international system in this regard, the consequences of their action have been disastrous. The most significant effect of granting sovereign privileges to postcolonial rulers is that the beneficiary elites have remained unaccountable for their violations of human rights and international conventions. As a result, these ruling classes have submitted neither to the will of their own populations nor to the mandates of the international community, substituted for Western powers. It is therefore anachronic that by granting full immunity to the formerly colonized, the former colonial powers have in effect undermined the very liberties and rights that form the foundations of the present international system. Indeed, according to Jackson, Western powers have recently been deprived of the legal and political standing to intervene in the Third World in order to prevent the descent of its ethnic and national entities into economic destitution. They have been unable to prevent incompetent and irresponsible governing elites from bringing about domestic chaos and, subsequently, crises of international proportions.

Jackson's analysis of postcolonial Third World crises and the dynamics of the international system omits the deliberate hegemonic strategies pursued by Western powers during colonial rule and decolonization, which continue to dominate postcolonial international relations. This omission is consistent with the position that postcolonial independence restores juridical equality through the application of Western-inspired principles. Jackson argues that this restoration of equality also institutes rational processes (e.g., free negotiations and open policy options) to the relations between former colonial powers and the formerly colonized.[11] This liberal position assumes that the former colonies were not, and continued not to be, affected by the policies pursued by Western powers during decolonization. The Namibian case sufficiently demonstrates, however, that decolonization was not an unconstrained exercise by the formerly colonized of a universally applicable right to self-determination. The UN debate concerning Namibia was driven primarily by the desire of Western nations to maintain the existing hierarchies of the international order and the attempt by Third World nations to subvert those structures.

Nevertheless, liberals must dismiss the conduct of colonial powers during decolonization as irrelevant in order to propose that Western leadership is both desirable and essential to prosperity, peace, and the stability of the international order. The reality is that the role played by the former colonial powers fell short of their legal obligation under the UN Charter. Their juridical transgressions were complemented by a moral ambivalence vis-à-vis postcolonial self-determination. As elsewhere in Africa, the Western Contact Group strategically exercised its oversight functions in favor of particular socioeconomic classes, as well as racial and ethnic groups. Concurrently, it placed political and legal restrictions on local populations that limited their capacity to exercise their rights in the postcolonial order. It complemented these actions with economic, political, and military pressure intended to coerce noncomplying communities into conformity.

The uses and abuses of Western leadership during the transfer of power in the Third World have had grave implications for both theory and the current state of affairs in international relations. In this regard, there exist historical connections between Western visions of postcolonialism and the related political strategies on the one hand,

and the emergence of the so-called quasi states within the international order on the other. In ideological disputes and political confrontations within the United Nations, Western powers opposed all models of decolonization and international relations that conflicted with their expectations. Indeed, these states envisioned a postcolonial regime in which the needs of the other coincided with the requirements of their own national interests.

In the specific case of Namibia, the Contact Group used its controlling position within the Security Council to effectively usurp the process of decolonization from the more representative General Assembly. The declared intent of this group was to restore temperance and impartiality to the debate. In fact, its aim was to establish and admit to the international system organically deficient postcolonial entities, unable to play a significant role either domestically or in the international order. The means to accomplishing this postcolonial regime included preconditions to organizing elections and, ultimately, granting self-rule to the indigenous populations. When the Contact Group was opposed by the general UN membership, these Western states deployed procedural rules, dilatory tactics, and political intimidation in order to implement their particular vision of postcolonialism.

The Restructuring of Empire

Western conduct during decolonization conflicts with the liberal claim of Western ethical rectitude. Beginning with European postwar reconstruction efforts, the former colonial powers and their allies intended to reform but not eliminate empire. Decolonization was to allow for a transition from territorial claims to new forms of control built upon past philosophical foundations including political, legal, and cultural assimilation of the colonized into the structures of the global system. By determining the political and constitutional settings of national independence, Western powers virtually dictated the terms of postcolonial relations. These terms were intended to preserve structural links between Western economies and those of their former dependencies. In general, they promoted the hegemony of the West and the dependence of the former colonies. They seldom ensured interdependence.[12]

The preferred strategy of the hegemonic Western powers in the case of Namibia was to assist South Africa in creating an "authentic" ruling elite, agreeable to its postcolonial project. Concurrently,

Western Contact Group nations deliberately applied their influence within the United Nations in order to undermine the political and juridical positions of the leading nationalist movement, both internally and internationally. The South Africa–supported Democratic Turnhalle Alliance (DTA) and a group of African elites offered an advantage over the South West African People's Organization (SWAPO) in this regard. The white-dominated DTA maintained the strongest ties to the colonial economy and, by extension, to the international political economy. Likewise, the so-called black internal groups, a coalition of local chiefs and colonial appointees, were expected to position themselves between the colonizer and the colonized and act according to their own class interests by defending the status quo. According to this scenario, this future ruling elite would maintain the regulations and political structures that sustained existing property relations. The leaders would also promote political alliance with the West.[13] In exchange for their cooperation, South Africa and its Western allies would remove the controversial aspects of colonial rule.[14]

The objective of the Western Contact Group was to implement new mechanisms of control built upon past legal, cultural, and intellectual foundations. In particular, the imposition of the jurisprudence of state succession presumably enabled the hegemonic powers to protect civil society from the encroachments of future governments. Since they assumed that SWAPO was inimical to their own economic interests, Contact Group states compelled the nationalist organization to adhere to preindependence constitutional principles that clearly delineated the public sphere, where state intervention was permitted, from the private spheres.[15]

Significantly, the Western-inspired constitutional principles committed the future government and state to promoting a model of economic development that precluded a complete restoration of Namibian self-determination. The designers of this dependent capitalist model limited the role of the state to the protection of domestic capital and the enforcement of existing privileges as a collective good.[16] They also considered colonialism, whatever its effects, to be a political fact beyond the reach of postcolonial governments, courts, and lawyers. As a result, they denied African demands for postcolonial compensation and restitution on the grounds that they were unconstitutional. In sum, Western powers deemed SWAPO's preindependence political agenda, in particular its desire to reverse the effects of colonial exploitation, to be inappropriate.

The Western strategy for hegemony extended beyond the attempt to contain domestic politics in the postcolonial states within constitutional boundaries. For instance, the imposition of the jurisprudence of state succession burdened Namibia with the duty to fully honor the public debts incurred by South Africa during its administrations. Like other postcolonies, Namibia was obligated to uphold the rights of public servants to pensions and other benefits. The new Namibian state and government were also juridically bound to protect selective individual rights and liberties including the economic rights of the minority white population. These entitlements were acquired during years of deliberate exploitation that violated both individual Namibian rights and UN injunctions. They were also the foundation upon which this minority group built its own domestic influence.

In contrast, the Western Contact Group opposed plans by the General Assembly and the Non-Aligned Movement to restore the rights of the black population, including the return of land, compensation, and other restitutions. Western powers suppressed Namibian idioms of ownership and local juridical contexts of property and dismissed the historical contexts of the acquisition of property and wealth by empire builders like Adolf Luderitz and the white settlers who followed in their footsteps. As a result, the decolonization process presumably granted political autonomy to Namibians, but it deprived the Herero, Nama, and others of political and juridical protection. Ironically, SWAPO's acceptance of the preindependence conditions makes that organization an accessory to the violation of the rights of the majority of its own political base.[17]

Evidently, the juridical foundation of the postcolonial state was not congenial to universal justice. By suppressing colonial subjectivities and histories of property, the new juridical system prevented the nationalist party from envisioning alternative models involving the restructuring of the postcolonial domestic regime.[18] Postcolonial Namibia, like other African countries, was left without the legal, political, and economic resources with which to play a meaningful role in the global order. Without resources or juridico-political standing in the international order, African governments also lost (at least for a time) the opportunity to restructure the basis of civil society in a manner that restores rights and dignity to the majority of their populations.

This postcolonial marginality has affected the ability of Namibia and other African nations to function as sovereign members of the international community. This condition is bound to last for the foreseeable future, regardless of the competence or integrity of African leaders. The post–national independence mismanagement and corruption cited by Jackson and others has only compounded the African postcolonial condition. Indeed, postcolonial marginality has given rise to organically unstable and dependent states. The politically and economically dependent African states have remained in an intermediate stage between the vestiges of the past (traditional institutions) and the postcolonial realities of debt, social strife, civil war, starvation, and disease.[19]

INDETERMINACY AND CONTINGENCY

For their part, critical legal scholars (be they empiricists or theorists, realists, Marxists, or even poststructuralists) reject both the precepts of the authoritative discourse and the view that international law reflects objective processes. In general, they recognize the ethical and normative deficiencies of current international law. They have also been cognizant that the norms of international law have varied according to geography, the requirements of the global economy, and the balance of power in international politics. Nearly all but a small minority, however, share the premise that Western jurisprudence may provide the basis for meaningful reform under the current international order. They believe, arguably, that the norms and principles of the international system are mostly indeterminate and contingent.

Critical Realism and Its Uncertainties

Most critical realists begin with the view recently expressed by Olive P. Dickason in regard to European use of jurisprudence during the conquest and settlement of the New World. In "Concepts of Sovereignty at the Time of First Contacts," Dickason argues that, for every law or recognized practice claimed by colonizing nations to legitimize their positions, one can make challenges or counterclaims equally based in valid legal precedents.[20] This thesis is the basis of Henry Reynolds's argument that Australian colonial jurisprudence, by facilitating the dispossession of Aborigines and allowing other kinds of injustices against them, typifies a sinister use of international legal norms.[21]

Reynolds and Dickason differ in one significant way. Reynolds insists that international law embodies consistent ethical axioms and pronouncements on civil rights and liberties. He is convinced that international jurisprudence may provide the basis for postcolonial justice in Australia and, perhaps, elsewhere. He believes that the rights of the Aborigines of Australia (in particular their title to land) can be harmonized with those of the government of Australia.[22]

While it is not within the scope of this book to discuss Reynolds's views regarding Australia, the contention that contemporary international jurisprudence may provide solutions to postcolonial tensions and conflicts elsewhere contains a basic flaw. In Dickason's view, international law is replete with contradictory principles and doctrines, many of which appeared under specific circumstances to facilitate Western imperialism.[23] In this context, any expectation of a satisfactory reconciliation would have to rest on faith in both international and domestic institutions. The first foundation of this leap of faith is that the United Nations and its decision-making organs objectively evaluate the common purpose, or threats to it, and allocate resources and punishment accordingly. This has not been the case.

The second basis of the faith in postcolonial reconciliation of rights within the present international system is that national courts and other institutions of adjudication would render dispassionate and objective rulings. Supporting this assumption, Richard Falk maintains that technological development and increasing interdependence has positively affected the U.S. Supreme Court in this regard. This court, he claims, frequently has had to rely on international consensus in cases involving American claims against foreign countries.[24] He also claims that other national courts, in the West and elsewhere, have begun to apply legal doctrines and authoritative opinions creatively in postcolonial cases in which conventional law offers no solutions. He illustrates his assertion with evidence that courts have relied "upon norms and standards contained in instruments that are not legally binding according to traditional notions."[25]

Although Falk makes a convincing case, his arguments run counter to the more dominant and alarming trend. In effect, the doctrines and opinions considered authoritative by these national (and municipal) courts have been based exclusively on Western jurisprudence. Likewise, courts have generally referred to juridical instruments supported by their own national governments. In most instances, Western institutions have shunned the opinion of the majority of nations, including the declarations of the General Assembly and other broad-based international organizations.[26] They have not followed the emerging theoretical consensus that the formal acts of such institutions as the General Assembly "are either *evidence* of the existence, or are themselves *constitutive*, of either conventions, customs, or general principles within the scope of Article 38."[27]

This fact has not deterred radical critics who draw on Marxism, literary analysis, and poststructuralism. They argue that the postcolonial settings of intercommunal relations are complex. They contend that international relations no longer lend themselves to simple binary oppositions. Consequently, it is not appropriate to attempt to change the course of international relations and the international legal system on the basis of the confrontation between the former antagonists. The means to transforming international law, it would seem, rest in complex interactions among multilateral coalitions organized around the objects of their concerns. This contention is based on fact and ideology.

Indeed, both the imperial powers and those they colonized can be identified empirically (historically) and discursively to be composite and heterogeneous. Each camp holds a somewhat ambiguous and problematic position vis-à-vis the totalizing systems of imperialism. Likewise, the learned classes of the oppressor do not represent the authentic voice of their societies any more than those of the oppressed express their societies'. Both groups make only contentious claims in the name of the nation.[28] African leaders who struggled to wrest political power from the colonial powers, it seems, have only a slightly better claim on that power than their colonial counterparts. This argument bears consideration, especially in light of the abuses of human rights that have befallen independent Africa.

In the ideological instance, Western poststructuralists have reached beyond the dichotomies of totalizing systems in order to offer what they perceive to be practical solutions to everyday life. Michel de Certeau, for instance, argues that too much has been made of the structures of demonology upon which the learned cultures of Europe built their totalizing systems. He contends that praxis depends on mechanisms of usage that exceed the structures of such systems. In general, the users of systems such as international law have successfully subverted the meanings of their norms through manipulation and inversion.[29]

Contentious Juridical Innovations

Those who claim that the norms of totalizing systems are ultimately indeterminate may take comfort in the resourcefulness of Third World nations and dependent peoples. During decolonization, the new nations and dependent peoples overcame two apparent obstacles: Western control of the decision-making organs of the international order and the subjective nature of international law. Third World nations found solace in their numerical advantage. Indeed, the former colonies possessed diverse cultural backgrounds, ideological perspectives, and moral orientations that set them apart from their former oppressors, and also distinguished them from one another. They shared a hostility to foreign rule and in varying degrees were receptive to anticolonialist discourse.[30] In this regard, they surmounted the liabilities inherent in the existing balance of power by exploiting the atmosphere of ideological contestation between the two rival hegemonic blocs. Thus, the protagonists of full decolonization accepted the support of China and the Soviet Union and other sympathetic nonpermanent members of the Security Council.

With an absolute majority within the General Assembly, postcolonial states contributed to shaping the decolonization debate. The new states formed various advocacy groups whose common goal was to reverse the effects of colonial exploitation.[31] In general, the agenda of such groups as the Non-Aligned Movement and the Group of Seventy-Seven conflicted with the interests of hegemonic powers. This agenda was discursively grounded in the unfulfilled postwar ideals of national equality, democracy, multilateralism, and postcolonial interdependence. These Third World groups increased the role of the new states in formulating the rules and ethos of international relations and successfully designed international instruments to assist dependent nations in their quest for independence.

First, noting the absence of jurisprudence regarding decolonization, Third World groups joined the former communist bloc in developing new doctrines, principles, and rules of procedure.[32] To this end, these General Assembly members took advantage of the silences, vagueness, and ambiguities of the law of nations. Specifically, the nationalists referred to statements in the preamble of the UN Charter asserting the equality of nations and prohibiting foreign control.[33] For instance, they sponsored the 1960 resolution 1514 (XV), which stated that "alien subjugation, domination and exploitation" denied fundamental human rights and was contrary to the UN Charter.[34] This Declaration on the Granting of Independence to Colonial Countries and Peoples, also known as the Khrushchev resolution, affirmed the right of colonial peoples to "freely determine their political status and freely pursue their economic, social and cultural development."[35] As in other instances, the sponsors of this declaration carefully discounted contradictory Charter dispositions, including Articles 73 and 76, that support colonialist positions.[36]

The vagueness of the preamble to the Charter and other international instruments enabled colonial peoples and their supporters to isolate given legal principles from the general strictures of the international system in order to broaden their meanings into new doctrines.[37] In short, colonial and postcolonial peoples were not deterred by the Western origin of the requirements, regulations, and rules guiding decolonization. In fact, Africans and other Third World peoples inverted legal norms previously used against them in order to undermine Western positions. This discursive act was also an *attempt* to liberate postcolonial legal thinking from the genealogical strictures and epistemological apparatus of Western systems.

The anticolonialist bloc was most successful in creating new institutions to implement decolonization. It used General Assembly sessions and working committees as platforms from which to redefine the conditions of self-government. The Non-Aligned Movement and like groups compelled the General Assembly to broaden the purpose of the petitions addressed to the United Nations by the native populations. The assembly also revised UN procedures with regard to the analysis of developments in the dependencies[38] and dissolved the Committee on Information from Non-Self-Governing Territories, transferring its functions, under the terms of the 1963 resolution 1970 (XVIII), to the Special Committee on the Granting of Independence to Colonial Countries and Peoples. In addition, the General Assembly established a committee to monitor compliance with its Declaration on the Granting of Independence to Colonial Countries and Peoples.

Following the 1966 revocation of the mandate, the General Assembly ordered the Special Committee to oversee South Africa's and other nations' compliance with resolution 2326 (XXII) requesting immediate decolonization of Southern Africa and insisted that all member states and international organizations "use their influence with the Government of South Africa in order to obtain its compliance."[39] The UN general membership established the Council for Namibia in May 1967 under the terms of its resolution 2248 (S-V). The council was charged with the administration of the territory under the executive responsibility of a commissioner appointed by the General Assembly.[40] The council was endowed with the power to promulgate laws, decrees, and other regulations consistent with its role. It was to be replaced with a legislative assembly following elections conducted on the basis of universal adult suffrage.[41] The council also oversaw the UN Institute for Namibia, which provided an alternative to the mediocre education that Namibia's black population received under South African administration and research to assist Namibians in formulating postcolonial policies and programs.[42] Finally, the Non-Alignment Movement and other sponsors of General Assembly acts empowered representative Namibians to manage their own affairs. Thus, in 1973, outmaneuvering opponents, they voted to recognize SWAPO as the "authentic representative of the Namibian people."[43]

The Limits of Juridical Innovation

Third World nations benefited from the vagueness and ambiguities of the law, which allowed them to create a body of norms that complemented or contradicted existing ones. Yet, these postcolonial states suffered setbacks in their struggle because their opponents had the means to exploit the flaws and ambiguities of international law much more effectively. The postcolonial nations were engaged in a relentless struggle for control of the discourse of international relations. Both sides resorted to the same mechanisms of innovation and confrontation, yet Western powers possessed an insurmountable advantage. The reaction of the Third World countries to decolonization denoted a new tendency in the international order; they acted in an authoritative and creative manner that shed new light on the talent and capacity of the UN general membership. Western powers, who did not share the enthusiasm of their former dependencies, took steps to counter the moves of their antagonists. Unlike the former colonies, they were, as permanent Security Council members, empowered by the Charter to make executive decisions. In contrast, General Assembly resolutions are said to have only recommendatory force, that is, they do not entail binding obligations.[44]

Western powers were therefore in a position to overturn General Assembly achievements.[45] They could also ignore the recommendations and opinions of assembly-appointed committees. Such was the case when the Council for Namibia attempted to protect the territory's resources from abusive exploitation prior to independence. In 1974 the council was sufficiently alarmed by the intensity of foreign exploitation of Namibian resources to take action. In its Decree No. 1, this administering body declared:

> No person or entity, whether a body corporate or unincorporated, may search for, prospect for, explore for, take, extract, mine, process, refine, use, sell, export, or distribute any natural resource, whether animal or mineral, situated or found to be situated within the said Territory without the consent and written authority of the United Nations Council for Namibia or of any person authorized to act on behalf of the said Council.[46]

Typically, Western powers questioned the constitutionality of this administrative act.[47] In particular, they argued that the Council for Namibia was not competent to issue such an order. Nor could the council or the General Assembly legally enforce this and similar decisions. Predictably, Western-based multinationals never complied with the decree.

Claiming lack of precedent or law, Western powers moved to prevent any legal action against their own abuses, including the mismanagement of the Namibian "trust" and the devastations of decades of colonial rule. They rejected any discussion of prosecution of violators. Yet, the economic clauses contained in Part X of the Treaty of Versailles provided a jurisprudence for prosecution. Under its rules, the victors of World War I compelled the aggressor states, such as Germany, to compensate their victims — for loss of property, debts, other rights and interests, and other contractual obligations.[48] According to this clause, Namibians would have received compensation for proven expropriation or denial of basic rights that had economic implications. This clause, and others from various treaties, could have been broadened to include the appropriation by settlers of collective property: land and natural resources.[49] Other international instruments, including the convention against genocide, could have formed the basis for prosecution of other human-rights abuses.[50]

The Namibian debate demonstrates that self-determination was not an indeterminate juridico-political concept during decolonization. It shows that not all theoretical perspectives or practical possibilities were translated into praxis. Whereas in the Western context the *teleos* of autonomy had been the affirmation of the self,[51] decolonization was subject to external requirements, in particular the preservation of the national interests of the former colonizers.[52] Indeed, the process of decolonization was fraught with open and concealed battles. In their quest for continued hegemony, Western powers deployed all means—textual interpretations as well as military, economic, and political leverage—to reduce the expression of self-determination to a neocolonial state.[53] In contrast, the formerly colonized lacked—or, more appropriately, were deprived of—the juridical and material capacity to restructure international relations.

SELF-DETERMINATION AND POSTCOLONIALISM

The postwar context of postcolonialism was a complex environment of mulitidimensional political conflicts, diverse political forces, and conflicting ideologies. African opposition to colonialism and critique of its discourse varied in form and content according to the nature of foreign control, the local power configuration, the dominant ideologies, and the strategies of the nationalist forces. African nationalists were divided by their attitudes and dispositions to world and national events, including the general anticolonial atmosphere that followed World War II. The nationalists offered differing views of colonialism and the dominant Western culture, including international law. Likewise, their views of Western philosophy and science differed greatly; they did not all reject the authoritative discourse of international relations and its assumptions. They also held conflicting views of the distortions and silences of Western discourses regarding Africa.

Only a fraction of African elites advocated a restructuring of the present regime or sought a fundamental transformation of international praxis. As Robert Young writes, the majority of the anticolonialists "derived their notion of nation and self-determination from the Western culture that is being resisted."[54] These African elites appropriated Western political and juridical idioms, which they attempted to adapt to their own struggle.[55] The current postcolonial crises suggest that the results of the dominant African strategy have been mixed at best. Its failure to fully restore African sovereignty and self-determination has had significant political and theoretical implications.

Interdependence, or New Marginalization

The primary objective of the African anticolonial discourse was to affirm African subjectivity (*personalité africaine*) at home and abroad.[56] Its secondary aim was to contribute to the creation of a postcolonial environment favorable to the ideal of interdependence among national communities. These goals inspired various strategies of resistance to colonial rule and postcolonial national policies. Beginning in the 1940s, one segment of the African elite espoused the Enlightenment concepts of difference, universalism, interdependence, and free will as bases of both their critique of colonialism and their postcolonial project. African socialists (Julius Nyerere, Kenneth Kaunda, Kwame Nkrumah) and literary figures in the Negritude movement (Aimé Césaire, Leopold Sedar Senghor) had infused their notions of African consciousness and black culture with notions of difference and universalism. Meanwhile, conservatives like Jomo Kenyatta and Felix Houphouet-Boigny emphasized liberal policies, goodwill, and interdependence between Africa and the West as means to emancipation and self-affirmation.[57]

These self-styled progressive and conservative intellectuals sided with Western humanists in arguing that the Western models of interdependence were the solutions, to the backwardness of formerly dependent territories. The majority of African leaders shared the evolutionist views of development and progress that subordinated self-rule to the existence of institutions characteristic of the liberal state.[58] Many African elites led their associations and organizations into renouncing (or denouncing) the so-called radical ideas that advocated the total restructuring of the international system. These leaders championed a model of anticolonialism that sought political liberation — that is, the end of foreign control — as an end. They hoped that the emerging nations would inevitably transform intercommunal relations by virtue of their presence within the international system. Some African elites and their organizations severed their ties to progressive and radical elements of Western societies in response to official demands. They hoped to obtain in return Western goodwill, assistance, and postcolonial interdependence. Under the leadership of Houphouet-Boigny, the Rassemblement democratique africain (RDA) opted for this model of postcolonialism.[59] The largest and leading anticolonial movement in French Africa, the RDA terminated its parliamentary affiliation with the French Communist Party and other progressive organizations. This parliamentary affiliation had offered the African nationalists a working relationship with radical French critics of colonialism within the French National Assembly, the Assembly of the Union, and the Council of State. The movement also expelled its radical elements, gave up its claims for redress of colonial wrongs, and abandoned its prior objections to the French Union.[60] In return, Houphouet-Boigny and his backers received encouragement from French sympathizers in thinking that political and economic ties—France's goodwill and support for postcolonial development efforts—would continue.[61]

The French political establishment encouraged the RDA's actions by promising in return a postcolonial collaboration between itself and African elites. In particular, the French government promised to embrace RDA leaders and their political agenda. In the initial phase of this collaboration, France offered postcolonial association between the metropole and Africans within a French Union. Later, this offer was replaced with one of national independence within colonial territorial boundaries. Both choices had intended consequences (and, perhaps, unintended ones that are beyond the scope of this study). The most significant was Africans' adoption of Western jurisprudence and cultural idioms as the basis of their relations with the metropole. They also espoused the Western evolutionist view of postcolonial state formation typified by a Western-style government based on the constitutional protection of select liberties and rights. In sum, the African elites surrendered political and economic initiative and subscribed to a discourse that legitimized the liberal state, proscribed any form of ownership other than capitalist, and recognized colonial structures and boundaries.[62] France and its Western allies also obtained from their African partners the affirmation of free trade among integrated but differentiated national spaces of core and peripheral national economies. This final African conversion all but guaranteed continued Western supremacy on the continent.

The official postcolonial project competed with more radical Pan-Africanist ideas. The radical Pan-Africanists suspected that political independence under the circumstances described here would amount to little change. They claimed that national independence would change only what Gayatri C. Spivak has described in a different context as "the geographical conjuncture of Western imperialism."[63] African leaders such as Ruben Um Nyobe, Gabriel d'Arboussier, and Boubou Hama feared that postcolonial French projects would marginalize Africa within the postcolonial regime. The leader of the Union des populations du Cameroun and the two RDA legislators were critical of the structures of the decision-making institutions of the French Union and demanded greater democracy within the colonial-era National Assembly and the Assembly of the French Union as a necessity for equal partnership. They also insisted on similar requirements for African participation in future international organizations. They were hostile to Western attempts to perpetuate the hegemony of a few nations within the emerging juridico-political systems.

Um Nyobe, for instance, criticized the UN system, particularly the trusteeship system, for its discrimination against the dependent peoples it presumably protected.[64] Like many African activists, he objected to the fact that the postwar international organization provided few decision-making roles for the formerly colonized. The Securtiy Council and other power centers of the international order stripped collective participation and partnership of their essence, he said; the new order was predicated on juridical constructions that depended on the inequitable power structures of past centuries.[65] He and other activists felt that the UN Charter offered few mechanisms with which to enforce national equality (and decolonization) or mandate multilateral participation on issues of global concern.[66]

For their part, d'Arboussier and Hama (prior to the 1950 RDA disaffiliation) rejected the French Union as a model of equitable interdependence. They noted that under the tricameral legislative system, the National Assembly, where Africans had no significant presence, performed the essential decision-making function. This division of legislative authority enabled the French political establishment to ignore dissenting Africans in key policy areas, including Vietnam, the security of the Union, and the postwar plan for reconstruction. They also indicated dissatisfaction that French heritage had been imposed as the cultural context of discourse and rejected the notion that French law superseded African norms.[67]

Despite these objections, the French establishment's and RDA's views of postcolonialism prevailed from the 1950s to the early 1970s. African colonies achieved political independence, having surrendered the will and organizational capacity to fundamentally affect the international environment. With RDA cooperation, France and its allies instituted a postcolonial regime that maintained past hierarchies under new forms. Aided by their Western allies, RDA and other African elites substantially improved the general condition of their respective countries. During the early era of independence, Ivory Coast leaders, like those of Kenya, Zaire (under Mobutu Sese Seko), and other countries, generally maintained the economic structures inherited from colonialism. Their strategy consisted in building a modern import-substitution sector from the existing economic base. Initially, the income from the export of primary goods and raw materials gave them access to capital and technology, which in turn facilitated growth. The performance of African elites was relatively successful during the years of economic expansion in the West, when the demand for raw materials and primary agricultural products was high.[68]

During this era, Western powers criticized individual African leaders, but they generally condoned political corruption, economic mismanagement, and human rights violations by their self-proclaimed African allies. They frequently supported — and in many cases installed — abusive local rulers. The impact of this policy was mitigated, however, by relative economic growth in many African countries prior to the late 1970s. Then, as a result of a prolonged economic recession, the industrialized nations altered their commitments to Africa and preindependence hope gave way to a general malaise fueled by an insurmountable economic depression and a decline in living standards. This condition, compounded by disease, drought, famine, and debt, subsequently generated economic and political chaos.

Western reactions to the African crisis have rested upon a certain liberal pragmatism that subordinates ethics to economic and political self-interest. Western-dominated international institutions such as the International Monetary Funds (IMF) and the World Bank have proposed programs of privatization, austerity, and economic restructuring that have focused solely on rectifying perceived weaknesses in African cultural, economic, and political institutions. Significantly, the African debt, both inherited and misspent, has provided a new rationale for direct intervention in Africa. Where once chartered companies claimed empires for Europe, the IMF and the World Bank now extract from Africa what the West needs: political submission. These institutions have demanded the partial or total surrender of African sovereignty to external (and to a lesser extent internal) capital or its agents as a condition to debt restructuring. Finally, these measures have weakened the foundations of African states in significant ways. The austerity measures in particular have targeted expenditures instead of needs and brought Africa to the brink of collective suicide by famine, disease, social and political unrest, and so on.[69]

Neoevolutionism and Its Discontents

Like their decision-making counterparts, Western theorists who subscribe to the authoritative discourse have deliberately responded to decolonization and postcolonial crises. Liberals generally begin their analysis of the present crisis with an outright indictment of the performance of Third World leaders. Although it is empirically indefensible, this condemnation has been central to the philosophical rejection of any principled criticisms of either Western policies or the international system. The first objective of this philosophical hostility to non-Western criticisms has been essential to ensuring the centrality of Western hegemony and national interests in the discourses of international law and international relations. The second has been to eliminate the possibility of change through multilateral dialogue or intersubjectivity involving the critical segments of Third World elites.

The critical Third World perspectives have been delegitimized as irrelevant—or are suspected of seeking the destruction of the West. As a result, authoritative Western scholars quietly stood by as the former colonial powers applied undemocratic means to weed from nationalist movements so called radical elements. In the former French empire, for instance, successive metropolitan governments persecuted radical anticolonialists, that is, the associations and organizations that advocated total transformation of praxis through repression and political bribery.[70] These secular and religious forces—progressive nativists, communists, Islamists, and others—have been revived by the deepening African crisis. By eliminating these African perspectives, the French establishment virtually eliminated any viable alternative to the now discredited domestic political elites.

The secular proponents of African radicalism generally maintained that postcolonial self-determination required a process that guaranteed a high degree of African sovereignty and, in fact, decolonization of the international system itself. They desired a total transformation of postcolonial relations (and its discourse) into mutually beneficial interdependence.[71] The postcolonial world they envisioned also figured in part in the 1942 Declaration by United Nations—a world of independent nations, free of oppression and domination, free to exercise their religions, in dignity and justice, yet collectively committed to maintaining international peace, development, and the freely expressed wishes of independent peoples and nations.[72]

The liberal position vis-à-vis African critics has not changed in the postcolonial era. In general, liberals have been suspicious of Third World proposals to either restructure the international order or change existing norms. Their arguments against non-Western initiatives have varied from contempt to outright misrepresentations of Third World views regarding international relations. This general reaction is reflected in Western discussion of the initiatives undertaken by postcolonial nations during the 1970s. These initiatives were generally intended to redress the inequities of the international system. Some Third World recommendations purported to correct the trade imbalance between poor and developed nations and to foster the development of the poor nations. The 1974 New International Economic Order, for instance, would have established balance in the decision-making processes regarding international economic transactions, guaranteed fair exchanges between the industrial North and the South, and protected the former colonies against abuses from a few hegemonic powers.[73] In another instance, during the 1982 Law of the Sea Convention, the majority of Third World nations insisted on a rational management of "common property resources" for the general welfare of the international community. Besides creating a Seabed Authority to manage maritime resources, the initial international version of the Law of the Sea protected the territories of the former dependencies (particularly their maritime economic zones and the embedded natural resources) from the dominion of the advanced nations.

Other proposed reforms would have preserved for the human race the resources that lay outside of national boundaries, whether at sea or in space.

These reform efforts were defeated by the nations that stood to lose their influence. Western nations opposed the proposed reform measures on narrow political and strategic grounds often unrelated to the issues at hand. Yet, liberal critics of these Third World initiatives seldom examine the merits of Third World arguments in their entirety. Instead, the majority attributes the failure of Third World initiatives for reform principally to their scope and methods. Robert Jackson suggests that the New International Economic Order was unduly ambitious in that it attempted to replace "free trade and cumulative justice [with] economic democracy and distributive justice."[74] He also claims that by proposing such drastic changes in the international regime, proponents failed to appreciate the rational Western approach to international affairs.[75] As a result, the industrialized nations found the proposal unacceptable.

In general, liberal arguments against Third World initiatives have echoed two principal tenets of the colonial discourse. The first is that Western (and Westernized) decision makers are rational. The second is that the non-Western(ized) other is irrational by nature. Accordingly, Western theory once cast Africans as the equivalent of European witches and other outcasts. Jackson now likens the afflicted Africans to a hybrid between the proverbial menacing multitudes and the undisciplined Western underclasses.[76] Like nineteenth-century philanthropists, he recommends positive Western assistance to the deserving multitudes on humanitarian grounds.

Having cast Africans and other Third World nations as beggars, Jackson advocates solutions to Third World–based international crises that parallel Western affirmative action programs. As in domestic assistance programs, the recipient states of Western aid (their leaders in particular) should be obligated to act as directed—that is, "responsibly." In this context, *responsibility* and *accountability* are synonymous with submission to foreign mandates like structural adjustment programs, liberalization, and privatization. Indeed, Jackson's solutions depend on the political wisdom that Western models and idioms (juridical precedents concerning debt repayment and rights) remain the best answers to postcolonial problems. He yearns for "a greater variety of international statuses including more intrusive forms of international trusteeship" that "might have rendered the post-colonial situation less unsatisfactory."[77] In their absence, he endorses the "right of humanitarian intervention," a form of postimperial interference that is said to be necessary to the prevention of gross violations of human rights, in particular genocide.[78]

Legitimacy and Cultural Contestations

The new liberal humanism would have been unimpeachable had it been based upon equal dignity among the various communities and individuals. Equality assumes that the same standards are applied to all members of the international community; that individual nations accept responsibility for their own actions; and that states submit to reciprocal treatments. Implementation requires analytical detachment from national interests and self-interest. This is contrary to the liberal commitment to a particular political order, which depends on two presumptions, both unfounded. The first is the moral superiority of Western institutions. The second, based on the first, is Western innocence, that is, the absence of responsibility for events elsewhere.

The reticence of authoritative Western scholars to accept responsibility (individual or national) has been denounced by a growing number of critics on various grounds. Olivier Russbach finds the refusal of Western theorists to account for the actions of their own governments to be culpable on two counts.[79] One is that Western nationals have unduly surrendered their democratic responsibilities by refusing to take responsibility for the actions of their chosen governments. In addition, these "free citizens" have unnecessarily refrained from holding their elected officials accountable for the abuses of self-assigned international mandates, including the much vaunted moral leadership within the international order.[80] Second, Russbach and other members of the Association européenne droit contre raison d'état fault Western nationals for failing to take advantage of international legal dispositions in order to enforce their nations' obligations to other communities and their members. They claim that existing legal norms, however flawed they may be, may still provide solutions to the majority of international conflicts and situations. (These may include unsettled postcolonial claims.) Thus, Russbach and others are critical of Western legal scholars' role in the reproduction of the privileged interests of Western societies.[81]

The argument that authoritative Western theorists have been unwilling to envision perspectives in international relations other than those consistent with Western hegemony and official mandates has been made in Africa. The so-called African radicals assumed fifty years ago that Western elites failed to identify the real threats to global security and interdependence because they involved the actions of their own governments. The primary danger to postcolonial peace, these African elites said, was the Western tendency to claim rights and privileges on the basis of a discourse of rights and liberties, and concurrently to demand that others surrender their rights and privileges for the sake of moderation and goodwill. Frantz Fanon and others predicted that while Europe was generally ready to relinquish official colonialism, its dominant classes would not be willing to forgo their privileges in the postcolonial era: it was not realistic to expect Western elites to suspend their tendency to exploit others, nor were they likely to conceive of a world order that did not support their desire to maintain their own privileges.[82]

A half-century later, Claude Marchant joins these Africans in arguing that Western policies toward the Third World, in particular the reactions to local crises, threaten to irreparably undermine the legitimacy of both international law and the present international order. He notes with displeasure the withering away of the notion of human solidarity in the West. Unfortunately, he writes, the Western drift away from the ideals of humanism has been matched by cultural dislocation in the rest of the world, and the resulting cultural contestations between the West and the rest of the world are the ultimate danger to the survival of the human species.[83]

Indeed, these conflicting dispositions between the West and others have already had chilling effects on international stability, multilateral interdependence, and cross-national intersubjectivity. Official Western responses to postcolonial crises in Africa have revealed programmatic flaws in preindependence liberal propositions of global partnership and economic interdependence. The corresponding theoretical perspectives have left doubts about the veracity of the liberal discourses on rights, liberties, justice, and peace and have weakened the credibility of Western-proposed models of interdependence as solutions for Africa's "ills." Finally, they have undermined the liberal propositions for interpersonal politics as a means to overcoming national and racial barriers within the international order.

The absence of comprehensive global solutions has placed the postcolonial ruling elites on the defensive. They surrendered political, intellectual, cultural, and economic independence for the sake of cooperation, but instead of cooperating, their Western partners pursued their own quest for power and abandoned political imagination, theoretical innovations, and interpersonal goodwill. In the meantime, African nations remained trapped in an intermediate state between "tradition and the projected modernity of colonialism."[84] They became territorial spaces where, according to Samir Amin, the "vestiges of the past, especially the survival of structures that are still living realities (tribal ties, for example), often continue to hide the new structures (ties based on class, or on groups defined by their position in the capitalist system)."[85] The internal difficulties of African rulers have been compounded by mismanagement and corruption. Now lacking political and financial support from their former Western allies, they are no longer in a position to justify foreign mandates, including International Monetary Fund conditions, to their people.

Postcolonialism in a New World Order

A growing number of the credible nonruling African elites have lost faith in the possibility of African self-determination within both the present international system and the global order. Pioneering this trend, Samir Amin notes that the West has historically taken advantage of Africa when it was most vulnerable. It was therefore not surprising that Western powers should manipulate the present African crises in order to maintain their own hegemony. Amin argues that the unilateralism of decision making in regard to the African debt and the near-dictatorial manner in which IMF and other foreign mandates are implemented in Africa are consistent with past Western tendencies to exploit and subjugate Africa. As supporting evidence, he points to the universalization of capital accumulation by the West, the burden imposed on Africa and other Third World peoples in debt payment schemes, the resistance to power sharing and collective decision making in international affairs, the attempts to retain monopoly of new technologies, and the appropriation of outer space and the seas by juridical means. As a result of these Western actions, the only available avenue for survival, Amin suggests, is for Africa to "disconnect" itself from the international order in strategic policy areas—including global regulations regarding trade, finance, capital, intellectual property, transfer of technology, and so on—that perpetuate Western dominance within the international system.[86]

Amin's agenda may appear to be unrealistic, but the view that Africa needs to create for itself the space for autonomous and self-sustaining development has support among a growing number of Africans. Eden Kodjo has revisited the basic tenets of Pan-Africanism; in *Africa Tomorrow,* the former secretary general of the Organization of African Unity proposes that Africans pursue an independent course of action whenever possible. Although he does not advocate total disconnection, Kodjo's policy suggestions exceed Amin's. So doubtful is he of the intentions of the superpowers that Kodjo proposes that Africa develop its own nuclear umbrella in order to defend its future gains, if not to survive.[87] These and other Pan-African projects have a growing appeal because the arguments upon which they are based are grounded in the African experience. Over the past five centuries, as it has been incorporated into the global order, Africa has prospered best, it may be argued, when it was least connected to the international system.

Amin predicted in 1986 that, barring cultural rejuvenation among progressive secular forces, Islamic and other fundamentalist forces would rise to fill the void left by the discredited ruling elites.[88] Indeed, the rise of the Islamic Salvation Front and the upheaval in Algeria in the early 1990s can both be attributed, generally, to popular mistrust of the international regime and Western support of corruption and authoritarianism—and, more specifically, to dislocations caused by the mandates of Western-dominated international institutions. To many in this movement, the postcolonial Algerian crisis itself and the Western response to it are elements of an anti-Muslim "conspiracy" that is said to be a component of a more global anti-Third World policy that disregards the basic human rights and needs of the vast majority of the world's people. This argument is echoed among Islamic fundamentalists in Tunisia, Morocco, and Libya, as well as by non-Islamic groups, including disaffected unemployed youths in urban centers throughout Africa. These groups often contrast Western attitudes toward the plight of the African masses with their past support for specific racial groups (in Southern Africa), socioeconomic classes (primarily in East and Central Africa), and unrepresentative client rulers (generally in Francophone Africa).

The rise of these two nonestablishment tendencies, the fundamentalist religious groups and radical secularists, has been received with discomfort in the West. Policy makers are alarmed that these forces have propelled the current democratic revival in Africa and have referred to the outcome of democratic processes in such places as Algeria and Angola as "negative trends."[89] Indeed, one can deduce from the tone of the national democratic forums that the majority of Africans perceive a link between greater participation in domestic political processes, popular accountability, and decentralization of statist institutions on the one hand, and structural changes in the global homeland on the other. Most Africans expect to include respect for communal differences, multilateralism, or at least coexistence.[90]

The imperatives of democratic reform in Africa have appeared on the surface to run counter to the existing Western economic and security interests on the continent. Although this perception is generally unfounded, it will continue to prevail for as long as policy makers and others are unwilling to experiment with new approaches to the questions of identity, democracy, pluralism, cooperation, and global responsibility. Empirical consistency and concern for the future of the globe — and the human species — dictate that we link issues of national concern, including sovereignty and self-determination, with those of global concern, in particular the restructuring of the international system. Humanity may be facing a global environmental challenge on a par with unparalleled political mistrust and cultural dislocations. These challenges require new intellectual tools. They demand that we rethink our approaches to global security, peace, and stability. In the long term, scholars will have to design new fields of study, new analytical methods. At present, however, we must revisit our intellectual assumptions, and perhaps our political agendas, in order to promote a new vision of human solidarity and global interdependence. We might still save ourselves from global catastrophe if we apply self-determination and multilateralism to the future course of international relations.

Notes

INTRODUCTION

1. This approach is illustrated in the majority of the essays compiled by Prosser Gifford and Wm. Roger Louis under the titles *The Transfer of Power in Africa: Decolonization, 1940–1960* and *Decolonization and African Independence: The Transfers of Power, 1960–1980.*

2. Francis H. Hinsley, *Sovereignty.*

3. David Strang, "From Dependency to Sovereignty: An Event History Analysis of Decolonization, 1870–1987."

4. L. C. Green and Olive P. Dickason, *The Law of Nations and the New World,* pp. 4–141 passim.

5. See Gifford and Louis, *Transfer of Power* and *Decolonization and African Independence.*

6. According to Christopher Miller, a "'discourse' is not a category equal or opposable to 'language,' 'speech,' 'writing,' 'thought' or 'idea.' It participates in all of these but is not reducible to any of them. There is no 'discourse' in the sense that there is a classical system of tropes known as 'rhetoric'; there are only *discourses,* forming themselves according to the shape of their objects. To speak of a discourse is thus to express a critical attitude, a bias toward reducing utterances to their 'paper reality,' understanding them as contingent and overdetermined rather than necessary and immutable." Christopher Miller, *Blank Darkness: Africanist Discourse in French,* p. 61.

7. Robert H. Jackson, *Quasi-States: Sovereignty, International Relations, and the Third World.*

8. See, for instance, A. W. Singham and Shirley Hune, *Namibian Independence.*

9. Solomon Slomin, *South-West Africa and the UN: An International Mandate in Dispute.*

10. Ronald Segal and Ruth First, eds., *South West Africa: Travesty of Trust.*

11. For elaboration on this point, see Umozurike O. Umozurike, *International Law and Colonialism in Africa.*

12. Anthony Pagden, ed., *The Languages of Political Theory in Early-Modern Europe,* p. 17.

13. James Boyd White, *Heracles' Bow: Essays on the Rhetoric and Poetics of the Law,* p. xv.

14. Talal Asad, "Anthropology and the Analysis of Ideology."

15. Ibid.

16. Ibid.

17. Peter Mason, *Deconstructing America: Representation of the Other,* p. 182.

18. Georg Jellnek, *L'Etat moderne et son droit.*

19. Peter Hulme, *Colonial Encounters: Europe and the Native Caribbean, 1492–1797,* pp. 2–4.

20. Mason, *Deconstructing America.*

21. Janet L. Abu-Lughod, *Before European Hegemony: The World System A.D. 1250–1350,* pp. 2–6.

22. Mason, *Deconstructing America,* p. 41.

23. Robert Young, *White Mythologies: Writing History and the West,* p. 4.

24. Eric Cheyfitz, *The Poetics of Imperialism: Translation and Colonization from the Tempest to Tarzan,* p. xiii.

25. Tragically, Kirkpatrick Sale observes, these scientists and humanists did not pause "to observe, to learn, to borrow the wisdom and the ways" of peoples they perceived to be "heathen ..., half naked and befeathered, ignorant of cities and kings and metal and laws, and unschooled in all that the Ancients held virtuous." Kirkpatrick Sale, *The Conquest of Paradise,* p. 367.

26. The norms and principles of the international order have historically applied to identifiable objects of intercommunal interactions. These objects may be a specific issue (for instance, sovereignty) or geographic area (in this case, Africa). The totality of the norms and principles that apply to such an issue or area constitute a regime. For further reference, see Stephen Krasner, "Structural Causes and Regime Consequences: Regime as Intervening Variable," and Richard Falk, "Regime Dynamics: The Rise and Fall of International Regimes."

27. Young, *White Mythologies,* pp. 2–5.

28. Sale, *Conquest of Paradise*, p. 368.
29. Ibid.
30. Mason, *Deconstructing America*, p. 4.

1. GENESIS, ORDER, AND HIERARCHY

1. Johannes Fabian, *Time and the Other: How Anthropology Makes Its Objects*, p. 144.
2. S. C. Saxena, *Namibia: Challenges to the United Nations*, pp. 215–49.
3. Richard A. Falk, *The Status of International Law in International Society*, pp. 126–84.
4. Fabian, *Time and the Other*, p. 144.
5. Charles Henry Alexandrowicz, *An Introduction to the History of the Law of Nations in the East Indies*, pp. 49–59.
6. Charles Henry Alexandrowicz, *The European-African Confrontation*, pp. 4–7.
7. Ibid. p. 5.
8. Henry Reynolds, *The Law of the Land*, p. 46 and passim.
9. For a summary of this realist view, see David M. Trubek and John Esser, "'Critical Empiricism' in American Legal Studies: Paradox, Program, or Pandora's Box?" and David Trubek, "Where the Action Is: Critical Legal Studies and Empiricism," p. 578 and passim.
10. Ibid., p. 2.
11. Falk, *Status of International Law*.
12. Ibid., pp. 130–45 and passim.
13. See, for instance, Green, "Claims to Territory in Colonial America," in L. C. Green and Olive P. Dickason, *The Law of Nations and the New World*.
14. Ibid., pp. 14–20.
15. Ibid., p. 79.
16. Ibid., p. 66.
17. See, for instance, James Boyd White, *Heracles' Bow: Essays on the Rhetoric and Poetics of the Law*, and Anthony Pagden, ed., *The Languages of Political Theory in Early Modern Europe*.
18. Umozurike O. Umozurike, *International Law and Colonialism in Africa*, p. 11.
19. Ibid., pp. 1–12.
20. Ibid., passim.
21. Michel Foucault, *The Order of Things: An Archaeology of the Human Sciences*, pp. ix–xxiv and passim.
22. Ibid., pp. 72–73.
23. Ibid., pp. xiii, 72–73.

24. Anthony Pagden, "Dispossessing the Barbarians: The Language of Spanish Thomism and the Debate over the Property Rights of the American Indians," in *Languages of Political Theory*, p. 81 and passim.

25. Green and Dickason, *Law of Nations*, pp. 168–81.

26. Louis Comisetti, *Mandats et souveraineté*, pp. 18–38.

27. Christopher Miller, *Blank Darkness: Africauist Discourse in French*, pp. 16–48.

28. Olive P. Dickason, "Concepts of Sovereignty at the Time of First Contacts," in Green and Dickason, *Law of Nations*, pp. 145–56.

29. Janet L. Abu-Lughod, *Before European Hegemony: The World System* A.D. *1250–1350*, p. 11.

30. Ibid.

31. Peter Mason, *Deconstructing America: Representation of the Other*, p. 18.

32. Eduardo Galeano, *Memory of Fire: Genesis*, p. 46 and passim.

33. Green and Dickason, *Law of Nations*, p. 4.

34. Galeano, *Memory of Fire*, p. 46.

35. Ibid., p. 6.

36. Green and Dickason, *Law of Nations*, p. 181.

37. Foucault, *Order of Things*.

38. Ibid.

39. Bartolome de las Casas, *The Devastation of the Indies: A Brief Account*.

40. "By what right and by what justice do you hold the Indians in such a horrible bondage? Aren't they dying, or better said, aren't you killing them, to get gold every day? Are you not obliged to love them as yourselves? Don't you understand this, don't you feel it?" Antonio de Montesinos quoted in Galeano, *Memory of Fire*, p. 57.

41. Casas, *Devastation of the Indies*.

42. See Leonardo Boff, *Jesus Christ Liberator* and *Liberating Grace*; Gustavo Gutierez, *The Power of the Poor*.

43. In contrast, Pope Paul III pledged the faithful to exemplary actions. In his 1537 bull *Sublimis Deus* Pope Paul III declared that despite European rights to dominion over Indians and other non-Europeans, these people were human beings endowed with both soul and reason.

44. The papal bulls did not delineate the extent of the rights that the Portuguese and Spaniards were to have over the "natives" of the territories they had acquired. They indicated only that the "natives" would be taught "good customs." Galeano, *Memory of Fire*, p. 46.

45. Pagden, "Dispossessing the Barbarians ...," p. 79.

46. "Everyone ought to continue as he was when he was called. Were you a slave when your call came? Give it no thought. Even supposing you

could go free, you will be better off making the most of your slavery."
Corinthians 7:21–22.

47. Mulford Q. Sibley, *Political Ideas and Ideologies: A History of Political Thought*, chapter 8, "The New Testament and Early Christianity."

48. Casas, *Devastation of the Indies*.

49. For instance, Queen Elizabeth I, a Protestant, contested the primacy of the pope in international relations, in particular "his authority to bind Princes who owe him no obedience." Green and Dickason, *Law of Nations*, p. 11.

50. Benedict Anderson, *Imagined Communities: Reflections on the Origin and Spread of Nationalism*.

51. Peter Hulme, *Colonial Encounters: Europe and the Native Caribbean, 1492–1797*, p. 4 and passim.

52. Herein lies the beginning of modern history, which, according to Todorov, has been pathetically characterized by, among other things, the African slave trade, the genocide of the indigenous peoples of the new continent, the horrors of the two world wars in the twentieth century, and the Holocaust. Tzvetan Todorov, *La Conquête de l'Amérique*, chapter 1, "Découvrir," pp. 11–58.

53. Miller, *Blank Darkness*, p. 59.

54. This distinction among various forms of love is Jean-Jacques Rousseau's, as quoted in Paul de Man, *Allegories of Reading*, pp. 168–90.

55. Paul de Man has described three positions of self-centeredness: a subject might simply love itself and remain indifferent to others; it could compel others to love it as it loves itself; or it might love others in a reciprocal exchange of love. The first and the last forms of self-love are based on the ethos of difference. The second form is potentially pathological. It suffers from oblivion to the other and therefore carries the danger of confrontation between the self and the nonself. Ibid., pp. 168–90.

56. Pagden, "Dispossessing the Barbarians," p. 80 and passim.

57. Fabian, *Time and the Other*, p. 3.

58. Miller, *Blank Darkness*.

59. Dennis W. T. Shropshire, *The Church and Primitive Peoples*, p. xviii.

60. Mason, *Deconstructing America*, p. 20 and passim.

61. Douglas Lorimer, *Colour, Class and the Victorians*, pp. 16, 145.

62. Hulme, *Colonial Encounters*.

63. H. L. Malchow, "Frankenstein's Monster and Images of Race in Nineteenth-Century Britain."

64. Mason, *Deconstructing America*, p. 43.

65. Hulme, *Colonial Encounters*.

66. Mason, *Deconstructing America*, pp. 41–58 and passim.

214 · NOTES TO CHAPTER 1

67. Ibid., pp. 41–58 and passim.

68. Hulme, *Colonial Encounters*.

69. Ibid.

70. Daniel R. Headrick, *The Tools of Empire: Technology and European Imperialism in the Nineteenth Century*.

71. Norman Dwight Harris, *Europe and Africa*, p. 17 and passim.

72. "Inevitably the European self is amenable to further analysis in terms of categories like 'learned culture' and 'popular culture.' ... The terms 'learned' and 'popular' refer to the forces at work in the battle over knowledge/power, and not to the cultural products themselves." Mason, *Deconstructing America*, p. 42.

73. Talal Asad, "Anthropology and the Analysis of Ideology."

74. Ibid.

75. Sibley, *Political Ideas and Ideologies*, pp. 372–73.

76. Locke discusses the empirical relation between experience and the external senses in "Of Ideas in General and Their Original," in John Locke, *Human Understanding*, p. 379.

77. John Locke, *Two Treatises of Government*.

78. David Hume, *Treatises on Human Nature*, pp. 399–455 and passim.

79. David Hume, *An Inquiry Concerning Human Understanding*, p. 55.

80. Stephen Jay Gould, *The Mismeasure of Man*, pp. 40–41.

81. J. H. Brumfitt, *The French Enlightenment*, pp. 27–43.

82. Ibid.

83. Montesquieu, Charles-Louis de Secondat, baron de la Brède, *Oeuvres complètes*, p. 232 and passim.

84. Ibid., passim.

85. Montesquieu, *Lettres persanes*.

86. Ronald Grimsley, *From Montesquieu to Laclos: Studies on the French Enlightenment*, p. 12.

87. Ibid., p. 491.

88. Harris C. Payne, *The Philosophes and the People*.

89. Ibid., pp. 7–17.

90. Ibid., pp. 7–17 and passim, for the many definitions given to the term *people* during the Enlightenment.

91. Ibid., p. 20.

92. For instance, Rousseau warned the Polish authorities not to free the serfs by decree "until you have freed their souls." Jean-Jacques Rousseau, *Oeuvres complètes*, p. 974; see also Marie-Jean-Antoine-Nicolas, marquis de Condorcet, *Oeuvres complètes*.

93. Henri Brunschwig, *Enlightenment and Romanticism in Eighteenth Century Prussia*.

94. Ibid., p. 6.

95. Ibid., p. 15.

96. Immanuel Kant argued that the people needed as much enlightenment as philosophers. By popular enlightenment, he meant public instruction of the people about their duties and their rights—natural right as well as those that derive from ordinary common sense—with respect to the state to which they belong. *Kant's Political Writings*, ed. Hans Reiss, p. 186.

97. In Kant's philosophy, the realms of the senses and those of understanding are situated at different levels. Thus a lived experience does not necessarily lead to an understanding of the social phenomena that make up such an experience. The two extreme ends, sense and understanding, "must be brought into contact with each other by means of the transcendental function of imagination, because, without it, the senses might give us phenomena, but no objects of empirical knowledge, therefore no experience." Immanuel Kant, *Critique of Pure Reason*, p. 114; also see pp. 109–27.

98. Reiss, ed., *Kant's Political Writings*, p. 17.

99. Brunschwig, *Enlightenment and Romanticism*, p. 42.

100. Ibid.

101. Casas, *Devastation of the Indies*.

102. Quoted in Gould, *Mismeasure of Man*, p. 41.

103. Anderson, *Imagined Communities*, pp. 76–90.

104. Ibid.

105. Cheyfitz, *Poetics of Imperialism*, pp. 52–60.

106. Ibid., pp. 57–60 and passim.

107. Malchow, "Frankenstein's Monster," p. 93.

108. Ibid., passim.

109. It was fashionable then for social scientists, ethnologists, historians, and anthropologists to inject Darwinian evolutionism and Newtonian mechanics into their studies and knowledge of humans. In this episteme of natural history, "the exercise of knowledge was projected as the filling of spaces or slots in a table or the marking of points in a system of coordinates in which all possible knowledge could be placed." Fabian, *Time and the Other*, p. 8.

110. Ronald Robinson, *Africa and the Victorians: The Official Mind of Imperialism*, pp. 2–3.

111. Ibid, p. 3.

112. Kwame Anthony Appiah, "Race," in Frank Lentricchia and Thomas McLaughlin, *Critical Terms for Literary Study*, pp. 276–78.

113. There were occasional objections to the simplistic views of Africa. Despite his own cruelty and harsh treatment of Africans, Henry Morton Stanley wrote of his admiration for the diversity of customs and habits in Africa. He equally admired the diversity of the African climate and geography, and he disputed claims that Africa was "one single place stocked with

leopards, hyenas, crocodiles, etc." Henry M. Stanley, *In Darkest Africa,* vol. 2, pp. 73–111.

114. Ibid., pp. 71–111.

115. Miller, *Blank Darkness,* pp. 20–25, 59.

116. A. R. JanMohamed, "The Economy of Manichean Allegory: The Function of Racial Difference in Colonialist Literature," p. 70.

117. Mason, *Deconstructing America,* p. 41.

118. In the seventeenth century, reports of humans with tails in Africa were common in Europe: "They all had tails, about forty centimeters long and perhaps two or three in diameter; this organ is smooth; among the cadavers there were those of many women who were formed in the same fashion; aside from this, they, the women were the same as other Negroes." Miller, *Blank Darkness,* p. 4.

119. Shropshire, *The Church and Primitive Peoples.*

120. Upon the insistence of philanthropists, the Berlin Conference undertook to abolish the slave trade inside Africa, to prohibit the sale of alcoholic beverages and firearms, and to protect the natives. Emile Banning, *La Conférence Africaine de Berlin et l'Association Internationale du Congo,* pp. 6–12 and passim.

121. Johannes Fabian, "Hindsight: Thoughts on Anthropology upon Reading Francis Galton's Narrative of an Explorer in Tropical Africa (1853)."

122. Great Britain, Parliamentary Papers, *Natives of South-West Africa and Their Treatment by Germany,* pp. 12–14.

123. Francis Galton, *Memories of My Life,* pp. 138–51; Fabian, "Hindsight." Also see Derek W. Forrest, *Francis Galton: The Life and Work of a Victorian Genius.*

124. The Anthropological Society later presented him with two medals for his services. Fabian, "Hindsight."

125. Galton, *Memories of My Life,* pp. 138–51.

126. Ibid.

127. Ibid., p. 228.

128. Ibid.

129. James Chapman, *Travels in the Interior of South Africa: 1849–1863,* p. 20.

130. Pagden, "Dispossessing the Barbarians," pp. 17, 79.

2. PARTIAL RECOGNITION TO THE BARBAROUS

1. See for instance, L. C. Green, "Claims to Territory in Colonial America," in L. C. Green and Olive P. Dickason, *The Law of Nations and the New World,* and Charles Henry Alexandrowicz, *An Introduction to the History of the Law of Nations in the East Indies* and *The European-African Confrontation.*

2. Green, "Claims to Territory," pp. 17–20 and passim.

3. See Alexandrowicz, *European-African Confrontation*, p. 5 and passim.

4. Umozurike O. Umozurike, *International Law and Colonialism in Africa*, p. 49.

5. Ibid.

6. Alexandrowicz, *Law of Nations*, p. 14.

7. Janet L. Abu-Lughod, *Before European Hegemony: The World System* A.D. *1250–1350*, pp. 306–8.

8. Ibid., p. 308.

9. Ibid., pp. 306–8.

10. Alexandrowicz, *Law of Nations*, p. 3 and passim.

11. Ibid., p. 3.

12. Green, "Claims to Territory," p. 106.

13. See also Peter Mason, *Deconstructing America: Representation of the Other*, pp. 18–25.

14. Eduardo Galeano, *Memory of Fire: Genesis*, p. 46 and passim.

15. Johannes Fabian, *Time and the Other: How Anthropology Makes Its Objects*, pp. 3, 26.

16. Ibid., p. 3.

17. For a general discussion of the seventeenth-century epistemological replacement of the classical mode by one that depended on sign systems, see Michel Foucault, *The Order of Things: An Archaeology of the Human Sciences*, pp. 128–62 and passim.

18. See Jacques Derrida, "White Mythology: Metaphor in the Text of Philosophy," in *Margins of Philosophy*, pp. 207–72.

19. Edward Said, quoted in Mason, *Deconstructing America*, p. 34.

20. Anthony Pagden, ed., *The Languages of Political Theory in Early-Modern Europe*, p. 15 and passim; James Boyd White, *Heracles' Bow: Essays on the Rhetoric and Poetics of the Law*, p. 33.

21. Olive P. Dickason, "Concepts of Sovereignty at the Time of First Contacts," in Green and Dickason, *Law of Nations*, p. 185.

22. On the relation between the subjects of a discourse and ideological categories, see Stuart Hall, "The Problems of Ideology: Marxism without Guarantees," p. 39.

23. The definition of subjectivity depends upon four elements: (1) the will to act or refrain from action; (2) the consciousness of the undertaking and knowledge of its possible consequences; (3) the power to undertake or refrain from undertaking a particular act; and (4) the consequences of the acts that could be attributed to the subject, even if the subject is not cognizant of some of them. Jean-Claude Coquet, *Le Discours et son sujet*.

24. Fabian, *Time and the Other*, p. 26.

25. Basil Davidson, *Black Mother, Africa: The Years of Trial*, p. 53.

26. Ibid., p. 53 and passim.

27. On the rules of possession during conquest, see Henry Reynolds, *The Law of the Land*, pp. 1–54, and Alexandrowicz, *Law of Nations*, pp. 150–57.

28. Quoted in Reynolds, *Law of the Land*, pp. 9–22.

29. J. Westlake, *International Law*, pp. 105–7; also see Reynolds, *Law of the Land*, p. 12.

30. Green and Dickason, *Law of Nations*, p. 17.

31. Kay B. Warren, *The Symbolism of Subordination*, p. 7 and passim.

32. Alexandrowicz, *Law of Nations*, p. 99.

33. Ibid., p. 154

34. J. H. W. Verzijl, *International Law in Historical Perspective*, vol. 7: *State Succession*, p. 249 and passim.

35. Umozurike, *International Law*, p. 39.

36. Verzijl, *Historical Perspective*, p. 249 and passim.

37. Ibid., passim.

38. By the time European hegemony was complete, the extent of Asians' political authority was circumscribed by their usefulness in the European quest for influence. Alexandrowicz, *Law of Nations*, p. 23.

39. Ibid., pp. 14–18.

40. Ibid.

41. Westlake, *International Law*, p. 40.

42. The Western view of treaties to which Africans were party depended upon the limited juridical capacity conferred on Africans. The semijuridical incapacity of Africans diminished the validity of engagements made by Europeans with them. See Westlake, *International Law*, part 1, p. 40, and Green and Dickason, *Law of Nations*, pp. 47–48.

43. Indeed, cooperation among colonial powers became increasingly important with rapid industrialization and the advent of capitalism. See Alexandrowicz, *Law of Nations*, p. 85.

44. Ibid., pp. 150–57.

45. I am indebted here to Fredric Jameson's discussion of the significance of conceptual canons for interpretation. See Jameson, *The Political Unconscious: Narrative as a Socially Symbolic Act*, pp. 17–102 and passim.

46. A. P. d'Entrèves, *Natural Law: An Introduction to Legal Philosophy*, p. 31.

47. For a summary of the Grotius-Freitas debate, see Alexandrowicz, *Law of Nations*, pp. 49–59.

48. Hugo Grotius, *The Freedom of the Seas; or, The Right which Belonged to the Dutch to Take Part in the East Asia Trade*, introductory note.

49. Grotius, *Freedom of the Seas*, p. 16.
50. Ibid., p. 15.
51. Ibid., p. 11.
52. Ibid., p. 10.
53. J. M. Kelly, *A Short History of Western Legal Theory*, pp. 219–43 and passim.
54. Alexandrowicz, *Law of Nations*, pp. 49–59.
55. Ibid., p. 44.
56. Ibid.
57. East Indians, in this context, occupied a special position between the native populations of the New World and Africa on the one hand and Europeans on the other. Being the least "barbarous" of the infidels, East Indians were granted special treatment typified by their greater political authority and right to dominion. Green and Dickason, *Law of Nations*, pp. 181–85.
58. Grotius, *Freedom of the Seas*, p. 9.
59. Moses Bensabat Amzalak, *Trois Précurseurs portugais*, pp. 39–95; also see Alexandrowicz, *Law of Nations*, p. 44.
60. Seraphin de Freitas, *Justification de la domination Portugaise en Asie*, pp. 3–15.
61. According to Freitas, Portuguese discoveries began in Africa in 1410, with the sighting of "Mount Laena" in present-day Sierra Leone. Ibid., pp. 15–16.
62. Ibid.
63. Ibid., p. 16.
64. Ibid, p. 18.
65. Ibid., pp. 20–22
66. Ibid.
67. Ibid.
68. Amzalak, *Trois Précurseurs*, pp. 39–95; also see Alexandrowicz, *Law of Nations*, p. 44.
69. Alexandrowicz, *Law of Nations*, p. 44.
70. Ibid., p. 54.
71. Jameson, *Political Unconscious*, pp. 17–102.
72. Todorov argues that the human status of non-Europeans was first denied, and then altered, through a threefold process. This process can be situated at three levels: values, praxis, and the episteme. Tzvetan Todorov, *La Conquête de l'Amérique: La Question de l'autre*, p. 191.
73. Pagden, ed., *Languages of Political Theory*, p. 15, and White, *Heracles' Bow*, p. 33.
74. For further analysis of the limits of interpretation and the production of meaning, see George Aichelle Jr., *The Limits of Story*.

75. Eric Cheyfitz, *The Poetics of Imperialism: Translation and Colonization from the Tempest to Tarzan*, pp. 50–57.

76. Ibid.

77. Pagden, ed., *Languages of Political Theory*, p. 15; White, *Heracles' Bow*, p. 33.

78. See also White, *Heracles' Bow*, p. 121 and passim.

79. See Jameson, *Political Unconscious*, pp. 17–102.

80. Ibid.

81. United States Declaration of Independence, quoted in Steffen W. Schmidt et al., *American Government and Politics Today*, Appendix A.

82. Frantz Fanon, "Racism and Culture," in *Toward the African Revolution*, pp. 25–44.

83. See, for instance, Stephen Krasner, "Structural Causes and Regime Consequences," and Richard Falk, "Regime Dynamics: The Rise and Fall of International Regimes."

84. "International law was used to facilitate, or acquiesce in, the imposition of both [slavery, fifteenth to nineteenth centuries, and colonialism, nineteenth and twentieth centuries] afflictions; it was also, paradoxically, used to eradicate the first and, presently, the second" only to allow other forms of domination. Umozurike, *International Law*, p. 1.

85. Ibid., p. 3.

86. Fabian, *Time and the Other*, p. 12 and passim; also see Valentin Y. Mudimbe, *The Invention of Africa: Gnosis, Philosophy, and the Order of Things*, p. 2.

87. Patrick Brantlinger, "Victorians and Africans: The Genealogy of the Dark Continent," p. 181 and passim.

88. Kader Asmal has argued that "from the end of the sixteenth till the nineteenth century, companies formed by individuals and engaged in economic pursuits were invested by the State to whom they were subject with public powers for the acquisition and administration of colonies." They were bestowed with governmental and legislative powers for the sole purpose of facilitating their activities and obligating European states on behalf of their citizens. Kader Asmal, "Juridical Aspects of the Berlin Conference (1884–1885): Contribution to a New Legal Order," pp. 12–15.

89. Daniel Headrick, *Tools of Empire: Technology and European Imperialism in the Nineteenth Century*.

90. Bruce Fetter, ed., *Colonial Rule in Africa: Readings from Primary Sources*, pp. 3–21 and passim; Alexandrowicz, *European African Confrontation*, p. 27.

91. Walter Rodney, *How Europe Underdeveloped Africa*.

92. Mudimbe, *Invention of Africa*, pp. 16–22.

93. Anderson, *Imagined Communities*, pp. 20–21, 86–103.

94. James Lorimer, *The Institutes of Law: A Treatise of the Jural Relations of Separate Political Communities*, preface to the second edition.
95. Lorimer, *Jural Relations*, pp. 93, 98.
96. Ibid., p. 98.
97. Ibid, pp. 101–2.
98. Ibid., p. 103.
99. Ibid., p. 102.
100. Ibid.
101. James Lorimer, *The Institutes of Law: A Treatise of the Jurisprudence as Determined by Nature*, pp. 246–59.
102. Ibid., p. 259.
103. Lorimer, *Jural Relations*, p. 102.
104. Ibid.
105. Ibid.
106. Lorimer, *Jurisprudence*, pp. 419, 425–36.
107. Ibid., p. 414.
108. Ibid., pp. 425–36.
109. Edith Sandhaus, *Les Mandats C de l'Empire Britannique*, p. 3.
110. Ibid. Art. 4: "Each [European] State reserve[d] the right to dispose freely of its property and to grant concessions for the development of the natural resources of the territory, but no regulations on these matters shall admit of any differential treatment between the nationals of the Signatory Powers."
111. R. Y. Jennings, *The Acquisition of Territory in International Law*, p. 4.
112. Ibid., p. 41 and passim.
113. J. H. Baker, *An Introduction to English Legal History*, pp. 263–64.
114. Likewise, postcolonial international agreements concerning others have focused on the ways in which European (and now Japanese and American) laws can be applied to the other in the interests of the subject's security. Charles Lipson, *Standing Guard: Protecting Foreign Capital in the Nineteenth and Twentieth Centuries*, p. 14.
115. For illustrations of such colonial processes, see Morton J. Horwitz, *The Transformation of American Law: 1780–1860*, pp. 160–210.
116. Baker, *English Legal History*, pp. 263–64.
117. In the Americas, as elsewhere, the acquisition of territories and lands was the core motif of colonial conquest. The acquisition of land implied the exercise upon its inhabitants of a cluster of privileges and rights related to power and power relations. The law of the land, whether related to contracts or not, was slanted toward the larger end of power and control. This view of land rights, it is believed, has its origin in England, where, in the Middle Ages, "rights to real property meant jurisdiction as well as

ownership." See, for instance, Lawrence M. Friedman, *A History of American Law*, pp. 202–5.

3. NATIVES' RIGHT TO DISPOSE OF THEMSELVES

1. Umozurike O. Umozurike, *International Law and Colonialism in Africa*.

2. Edouard P. Engelhardt, *Etude de la Déclaration de la Conférence de Berlin relative aux occupations africaines*, p. 20.

3. Geoffrey de Courcel, *L'Influence de la Conférence de Berlin sur le droit colonial international*; Duncan Hall, "The League Mandate System and the Problem of Dependencies," *Studies in the Administration of International Law and Organization*.

4. Congo Reform Association, *Indictment against the Congo Government: Report of the King's Commission of Inquiry and the Testimony Which Compelled It*, p. 9.

5. Dennis W. T. Shropshire, *The Church and Primitive Peoples*.

6. Arthur Conan Doyle, *The Crime of the Congo*, p. 8.

7. Emile Banning, *La Conférence Africaine de Berlin et l'Association Internationale du Congo*.

8. Douglas A. Lorimer, *Race, Class and the Victorians*, pp. 12–28.

9. Ibid., pp. 5–12.

10. Charles Henry Alexandrowicz, *The European-African Confrontation*, pp. 5–12.

11. Banning, *Conférence Africaine*, pp. 18–22.

12. Ibid., p. 20.

13. Francis H. Hinsley, *Sovereignty*, pp. 214–35.

14. Christopher Miller, *Blank Darkness: Africanist Discourse in French*, pp. 5, 61, and passim.

15. See Courcel, *L'Influence de la Conférence de Berlin*.

16. On the distinction between the right of peoples to dispose of themselves (*le droit des peuples de disposer d'eux-mêmes*) and the right to self-determination (*droit à l'autodétermination*), see Courcel, *L'Influence de la Conférence de Berlin*, p. 85.

17. General Act of Berlin, Article 11 (February 26, 1885).

18. Daniel R. Headrick, *The Tools of Empire: Technology and European Imperialism in the Nineteenth Century*, p. 110.

19. Ruth M. Slade, *King Leopold's Congo*, pp. 84–118.

20. U.S. Senate, *Message from the President of the United States Transmitting a Report of the Secretary of State Relative to Affairs of the Independent State of the Congo* (ca. 1885), p. 7.

21. Ibid., p. 7 and passim.

22. S. E. Crowe, *The Berlin West African Conference: 1884–1885*.

23. Courcel, *L'Influence de la Conférence de Berlin*, p. 41.
24. Ibid.
25. Great Britain, Parliamentary Papers, *Natives of South-West Africa and Their Treatment by Germany*, p. 13.
26. Doyle, *Crime of the Congo*, p. 7.
27. Arthur Berriedale Keith, *The Belgian Congo and the Berlin Act*.
28. Courcel, *L'Influence de la Conférence de Berlin*, p. 85.
29. Ibid., p. 271; my translation.
30. Headrick, *Tools of Empire*, p. 116.
31. Doyle, *Crime of the Congo*, p. 3; also see Headrick, *Tools of Empire*, pp. 196–98.
32. U.S. Senate, *Message from the President*, p. 7; see also J. du Fief, *La Question du Congo depuis son origine jusqu'aujourd'hui*, pp. 15–18.
33. M. F. Lindley, *The Acquisition and Government of Backward Territory in International Law*, p. 26.
34. The United States justified its participation by noting that "an American citizen (Henry Morton Stanley) first revealed the importance of the Congo country." Turkey, for its part, demanded to participate by reason of its interests in Northern Africa. See Kader Asmal, "Juridical Aspects of the Berlin Conference (1884–1885): Contribution to a New Legal Order," p. 20.
35. U.S. Senate, *Message from the President*, p. 26.
36. The flag of the association was adopted for the independent state. Riccardo Pierantoni, *Le Traité de Berlin de 1885 et l'Etat Independant du Congo*, p. 193.
37. Ibid., p. 196.
38. Courcel, *L'Influence de la Conférence de Berlin*.
39. Pierantoni, *Le Traité de Berlin de 1885*, p. 195.
40. Keith, *The Belgian Congo and the Berlin Act*, p. 63.
41. Ibid., p. 27.
42. Ibid., pp. 65–82; Courcel, *L'Influence de la Conférence de Berlin*, p. 38.
43. Benjamin Gerig, *The Open Door and the Mandates System*, pp. 34–41.
44. This form of extraterritoriality was practiced in Asia centuries before it was applied to Africa, in the nineteenth century. Lindley, *Acquisition and Government*, chapter 1; Malcolm Shaw, *Title to Territory in Africa*.
45. Asmal, "Juridical Aspects of the Berlin Conference," pp. 2, 28.
46. This legal concept has its roots in the decision of Lord Cromwell to establish his rule over the Commonwealth of Ireland (1653–59).
47. Courcel, *L'Influence de la Conférence de Berlin*; Banning, *La Conférence Africaine de Berlin*.

48. Hall, "The League Mandate System," p. 93.

49. Engelhardt, *Etude de la Déclaration*, p. 19.

50. Miller, *Blank Darkness*, pp. 5, 61, and passim.

51. Most Africans who entered into agreements with Europeans did not understand the intentions of their "protectors." Umozurike, *International Law*; Great Britain, Parliamentary Papers, *Natives of South-West Africa*, p. 13; Asmal, "Juridical Aspects of the Berlin Conference," p. 18.

52. Courcel, *L'Influence de la Conférence de Berlin*, p. 85.

53. Ibid.

54. Ibid., p. 38.

55. Engelhardt, *Etude de la Déclaration*, p. 19.

56. Asmal, "Juridical Aspects of the Berlin Conference."

57. Umozurike, *International Law*.

58. The Rhenish Missionary Society had hoisted the Prussian flag as early as 1864. Four years later it asked for the protection of the German *Reich*. More than ten years after the German *Reich*'s act, Britain and other colonial powers recognized Germany's influence over the territory. See Horst Drechsler, *Let Us Die Fighting*, p. 18; also see Asmal, "Juridical Aspects of the Berlin Conference," pp. 2, 28.

59. Asmal, "Juridical Aspects of the Berlin Conference," p. 7.

60. Great Britain, Parliamentary Papers, *Natives of South-West Africa*, pp. 14–17; Heinrich Vedder, *South West Africa in Early Times*, pp. 418–26.

61. Vedder, *South West Africa in Early Times*, pp. 418–26.

62. Ibid.

63. Willem Jordaan was apparently assassinated by an Ovambo ruler, Chief Nechele, in retaliation for expropriation of Ovambo land. Great Britain, Parliamentary Papers, *Natives of South-West Africa*, p. 16; also see Vedder, *South West Africa in Early Times*, p. 413.

64. Great Britain, Parliamentary Papers, *Natives of South-West Africa*, p. 18.

65. William O. Aydelotte, *Bismarck and British Colonial Policy*, p. xi.

66. Great Britain, Parliamentary Papers, *Natives of South-West Africa*, p. 13; Vedder, *South West Africa in Early Times*, pp. 418–26.

67. Georg M. Gugelberger, preface to *Diary and Letters of Nama Chief Hendrik Witbooi: 1884–1894*.

68. Great Britain, Parliamentary Papers, *The Wishes of the Natives of the German Colonies as to Their Future Government*.

69. Great Britain, Parliamentary Papers, *Natives of South-West Africa*, pp. 77–79.

70. Ibid., p. 17.

71. Dr. Heinrich Ernst Göring, the commercial controller of the company—later imperial commissioner—was also endowed with "certain

limited powers and jurisdiction over German settlers in the country." Aydelotte, *Bismarck and British Colonial Policy*, p. 22; also see p. 18.

72. Ibid., p. 32.

73. J. H. Esterhuyse, *South West Africa 1880–1894: The Establishment of German Authority in South West Africa*, pp. 73–74.

74. Ibid.

75. Vedder, *South West Africa in Early Times*, pp. 478–507.

76. Great Britain, Parliamentary Papers, *Natives of South-West Africa*, p. 5.

77. Ibid., p. 32.

78. Alexandrowicz, *European-African Confrontation*, p. 5.

79. Gugelberger, *Diary and Letters*.

80. Drechsler, *Let Us Die Fighting*.

81. Ibid., p. 23.

82. Ibid.

83. Ibid., pp. 23–24.

84. Great Britain, Parliamentary Papers, *Natives of South-West Africa*, p. 15.

85. Ibid.

86. Drechsler, *Let Us Die Fighting*, p. 25.

87. Esterhuyse, *South West Africa 1880–1894*, pp. 46–98.

88. Ibid., pp. 88–116.

89. Drechsler, *Let Us Die Fighting*, p. 31.

90. Ibid., p. 22.

91. Ibid., p. 37.

92. Asmal, "Juridical Aspects of the Berlin Conference," p. 13.

93. Great Britain, Parliamentary Papers, *Natives of South-West Africa*, pp. 15, 18.

94. Esterhuyse, *South West Africa 1880–1894*, pp. 46–98.

95. Aydelotte, *Bismarck and British Colonial Policy*, pp. xii–xiii.

96. Ibid., pp. 16–18.

97. Ibid., p. 17.

98. Ibid., p. 18.

99. Drechsler, *Let Us Die Fighting*, p. 47.

100. Ibid., p. 49.

101. Ibid., p. 89.

102. Ibid., pp. 69–71.

103. Ibid., p. 69.

104. Ibid., pp. 69–71; also see Great Britain, Parliamentary Papers, *Natives of South-West Africa*, pp. 23–28.

105. Helmut Bley, *South-West Africa under German Rule: 1894–1914*, p. 81.

106. Hinsley, *Sovereignty*.

107. Maharero was the name of the elder leader of the Herero people. Kamaherero was apparently his title. See Drechsler, *Let Us Die Fighting*, pp. 19, 24.

108. Ibid., p. 19.

109. Ibid., pp. 21–26.

110. Ibid., p. 26.

111. Great Britain, Parliamentary Papers, *Natives of South-West Africa*, pp. 42–43.

112. Peter H. Katjavivi, *A History of Resistance in Namibia*, pp. 7–8, and Great Britain, Parliamentary Papers, *Natives of South-West Africa*, p. 43.

113. Drechsler, Let Us Die Fighting, p. 50.

114. Great Britain, Parliamentary Papers, *Natives of South-West Africa*, pp. 42–43.

115. Ibid.

116. Drechsler, *Let Us Die Fighting*, p. 50; South West Africa People's Organization, *To Be Born a Nation*, p. 153.

117. Great Britain, Parliamentary Papers, *Natives of South-West Africa*, p. 43.

118. Ibid., pp. 37–40.

119. For instance, "under the Herero law the ground belonged to the [group] in common and not even the chief could sell or dispose of it. He could give permission to live on the land, but no sales were valid and no chief ever attempted to sell his people's land." Ibid., p. 51.

120. Dr. Heinrich Göring, a lawyer and first German imperial commissioner in South West Africa, was also the father of Nazi field marshal Hermann Göring. Gugelberger, *Diary and Letters*, p. 7.

121. Drechsler, *Let Us Die Fighting*, p. 43.

122. Letter of Samuel Maharero to Curt von François, quoted in Drechsler, *Let Us Die Fighting*, p. 43.

123. Gugelberger, *Diary and Letters*, p. vi.

124. Ibid., pp. v–viii.

125. Ibid.

126. The circumstances of the death of the settler are still unclear, but historians agree that the death cannot be attributed to Lambert. Great Britain, Parliamentary Papers, *Natives of South-West Africa*, pp. 79–81.

127. Ibid.; also see Drechsler, *Let Us Die Fighting*, pp. 75–77.

128. Great Britain, Parliamentary Papers, *Natives of South-West Africa*, pp. 79–81.

129. Ibid.

130. The Herero classified their cattle as "(a) the sacred specially selected cattle . . . , (b) the Eanda or mother group trust cattle, owned by no particular individual, but the common property of the family group, . . . and (c) the privately owned cattle." Great Britain, Parliamentary Papers, *Natives of South-West Africa,* p. 39.

131. Drechsler, *Let Us Die Fighting,* p. 89.

132. Ibid., p. 84.

133. Bley, *South-West Africa under German Rule,* p. xxvi.

134. The most important were (1) the law relating to jurisdiction for the purposes of punishments and disciplinary control (dated April 23, 1903); (2) the law prohibiting the taking of natives out of the protectorate "for Exhibitions and other purposes" and forbidding natives to travel over the borders without prior permission of the governor (November 30, 1901); and (3) the ordinance of the imperial chancellor regulating legal procedure and jurisdiction in cases between Europeans and natives (July 23, 1903). Great Britain, Parliamentary Papers, *Natives of South-West Africa,* p. 111.

135. Ibid., pp. 111–12.

136. Ibid.

137. Drechsler, *Let Us Die Fighting,* p. 118; also see Great Britain, Parliamentary Papers, *Natives of South-West Africa,* p. 50.

138. In the euphoria created by this ordinance, the German settlers made thousands of unsubstantiated claims against Africans. In the years 1903–4, for instance, they made 106,000 claims against the Herero alone. Great Britain, Parliamentary Papers, *Natives of South-West Africa,* pp. 51; also see Drechsler, *Let Us Die Fighting,* pp. 90–119.

139. Drechsler, *Let Us Die Fighting,* pp. 90–119.

140. The circumstances of the war, leading to the unity of African forces, as well as the reconciliation between Nama and Herero are detailed by the German historian Horst Drechsler in *Let Us Die Fighting.*

141. Jon M. Bridgman, *The Revolt of the Hereros;* Arnold Valentin Wallenkampf, *The Herero Rebellion in South West Africa, 1904–1906: A Study in German Colonialism.*

142. Bley, *South-West Africa under German Rule,* p. xix.

143. Ibid., p. 154.

144. Drechsler, *Let Us Die Fighting,* pp. 132–75.

145. Ibid.; also see Great Britain, Parliamentary Papers, *Natives of South-West Africa,* pp. 61–67.

146. Drechsler, *Let Us Die Fighting,* pp. 132–67.

147. Ibid., pp. 150–54.

148. Bley, *South-West Africa under German Rule,* p. xix.

149. Ibid., p. 93.

150. Gugelberger, *Diary and Letters.*
151. Drechsler, *Let Us Die Fighting,* pp. 179–98.

4. BEHIND THE VEIL OF THE TRUST

1. Harry Hansen, *The Adventures of the Fourteen Points,* pp. 48–70.
2. Raymond B. Fosdick, *Letters on the League of Nations,* p. 3.
3. For instance, the populations of Alsace and Lorraine, which had been ceded by France to Germany as a result of the 1871 Frankfurt Treaty, exercised their right to self-determination through electoral consultation, or plebiscite, and rejected their German status for incorporation into France. See Charles Downer Hazen, *Alsace-Lorraine under German Rule*; Daniel Blumenthal, *Alsace-Lorraine: A Study of the Two Provinces to France and to Germany and a Presentation of the Just Claims of Their Peoples*; and Whitney Warren, "The Question of Alsace-Lorraine."
4. Edith Sandhaus, *Les Mandats C de l'Empire Britannique,* p. 5.
5. Immanuel Geiss, *The Pan-African Movement,* pp. 234–40; also see Oliansanwuche P. Esedebe, *Pan-Africanism: The Idea and Movement 1776–1963,* pp. 75–90.
6. Ian Brownlie, "An Essay in the History of the Principle of Self-Determination," in *Grotian Society Papers,* Charles H. Alexandrowicz, p. 95.
7. Hansen, *Adventures of the Fourteen Points,* p. 107.
8. League of Nations Covenant, Articles 19–23.
9. Woodrow Wilson, quoted in Hamilton Foley, *Woodrow Wilson's Case for the League of Nations,* pp. 164–65.
10. Philippe Dewitte, *Les Mouvements nègres en France: 1919–1939,* pp. 9–13.
11. Paul Gordon Lauren, *Power and Prejudice: The Politics and Diplomacy of Racial Discrimination,* pp. 44–75.
12. Dewitte, *Les Mouvements nègres,* pp. 17–93.
13. The anticolonial movement created various newspapers prior to the end of the war. Some, including *L'Action coloniale* and *Le Libéré,* had wide circulation among French humanists and academics. Dewitte, *Les Mouvements nègres,* pp. 70–90.
14. Ibid.
15. Ibid., pp. 55–70
16. "With the collapse of the Tsarist Empire in March 1917 Russia ceased to be one of the powers who claimed stakes in Asia Minor.... In November 1917 [the Bolshevik successor of the czarist state] declared null and void the agreements on Turkey and by publishing the secret treaties acquainted the peoples of the Near East with the nature and results of the policy actively pursued by Britain during the war." Gerhard Schulz, *Revolution and Peace Treaties: 1917–1920,* p. 80.

17. Lenin and Russian socialists had a great deal of influence in Europe. With the ascendance of Marxists in the socialist movement in Russia, workers' movements throughout Europe began to redefine their relations not only to the state but also to their political allies—usually social democrats and nationalists—within it. Ibid., pp. 49–71.

18. Vladimir I. Lenin, "The Socialist Revolution and the Right of Nations to Self-Determination," pp. 157–66.

19. Yuri Davidov, *Lenin and National Liberation in the East,* introductory note.

20. The declarations of Soviet officials contributed to Western paranoia. During their first congress, in March 1919, party officials declared their intention to incorporate decolonization into a global strategy to undermine the West. Dewitte, *Les Mouvements nègres,* pp. 95–102; also see Lenin, "The Socialist Revolution."

21. Dewitte, *Les Mouvements nègres,* pp. 95–102.

22. Ibid.

23. Ibid.

24. Woodrow Wilson, quoted in Hamilton Foley, *Woodrow Wilson's Case,* pp. 164–65.

25. Harold J. Laski, *Democracy in Crisis,* pp. 62–63 and passim.

26. Sandhaus, *Les Mandats C,* pp. 1–16.

27. The Vigilantes, *Why the League Has Failed,* p. 27.

28. John Harris, *Slavery or "Sacred Trust"?* prefatory note.

29. Ibid., p. v.

30. Sandhaus, *Les Mandats C,* p. 10.

31. Ibid., pp. 10–11.

32. Ibid., p. 5.

33. Norman Bentwich, "Colonial Mandates and Trusteeships," in Grotius Society, *Problems of Public and Private International Law,* pp. 121–22.

34. Benjamin Gerig, "Mandates and Colonies," p. 218.

35. Ibid., pp. 10–11.

36. Charles Gore, *The League of Nations: The Opportunity of the Church.*

37. Georges Cioriceanu, *Les Mandats internationaux: Une des Conséquences des principes fondamentaux de la Société des Nations,* p. 73.

38. According to Benjamin Gerig, "Australia and New Zealand opposed the Open Door in the mandates they were about to receive in order to exclude Orientals and continue their 'White Australia' policy." Benjamin Gerig, *The Open Door and the Mandates System: Study of the Economic Equality before and since the Establishment of the Mandates System,* p. 96.

39. Robert H. Ferrell, *Woodrow Wilson and World War I: 1917–1921,* p. 213.

40. Japan objected to Australia's promotion of the whiteness of its territories through selective naturalization of settlers and the granting of commercial rights solely to people of Anglo-Saxon heritage. Eleven of the nineteen members present voted in favor, but to the astonishment of the delegates, President Wilson ruled that in view of "serious objections on the part of some of us" the amendment should not be carried. Warwick McKean, *Equality and Discrimination under International Law*, p. 19.

41. Lauren, *Power and Prejudice*, pp. 76–101.

42. Foley, *Woodrow Wilson's Case*, p. 47.

43. Cioriceanu, *Mandats internationaux*, p. 6.

44. Ibid.

45. Foley, *Woodrow Wilson's Case*, p. 46.

46. Gerig, *Open Door*, p. 99 and passim.

47. Ibid., pp. 91–93.

48. Under the terms of Articles 118, 119, and 227 of the Versailles Treaty and Article 16 of the Lausanne Treaty, Germany and Turkey relinquished their territorial possessions and all related rights and privileges to the Allied powers. This transfer was to occur without any compensation in the form of credit, payment, or reduction of German debts incurred for damages caused by the war. Turkey also renounced any claims to monetary compensation for the transfer of its dependencies. These legal dispositions laid the basis for the mandate system.

49. Also, France, Great Britain, and the United States had feared the possibility that czarist Russia (later the Soviet Union) might use the weaknesses of its neighbor, Turkey, to its own advantage, that is, against Western European interests. See Lawrence Evans, *United States Policy and the Partition of Turkey, 1914–1924*; S. S. McClure, *Obstacles to Peace*.

50. Foley, *Woodrow Wilson's Case*, p. 154.

51. Hansen, *Adventures of the Fourteen Points*, p. 51.

52. The United States was initially designated the fifth member of the Council, but its failure to ratify the Covenant reduced the number to four. The Assembly made the Union of Soviet Socialist Republics the fifth permanent member on September 18, 1934. The first nonpermanent members of the Council were Belgium, Brazil, Spain, and Greece.

53. Turkey and Japan were the only non-European powers. Japan's position as an imperial power was recognized by a 1919 secret treaty in which Great Britain ceded the Caroline and Marshall Islands to Japanese sovereignty.

54. In effect, the British Empire was made up of formal colonies, which did not belong to the League, and five semi-independent dominions, which did. Foley, *Woodrow Wilson's Case*, pp. 94–101.

55. Ibid., pp. 95–96

56. Ibid., p. 92; also see George Wilson, *The Monroe Doctrine and the Program of the League of Nations*, p. 5.

57. League of Nations, *Covenant and Amendments*, December 16, 1935.

58. Paul Hymans, *La première Assemblée de la Société des Nations*; Lord Cecil Robert, *The First Assembly: A Study of the First Proceedings of the First Assembly of the League of Nations*.

59. In the Armenian case, Lord Robert Cecil noted that "the urgency of the peril and the strength of the ... claim to world consideration seemed to require the direct intervention of the Assembly." Because of the Council's resistance to the idea, it was decided that the League should act through the instrumentality of the Council, and Armenia was not admitted to the League. Robert, *First Assembly*, pp. 231–33.

60. Ferrell, *Woodrow Wilson and World War I*, pp. 124–26, 235–37; also see League of Nations Assembly, *Responsibilities of the League*, p. 14.

61. Ibid., Annex 2 and p. 14.

62. Ibid.

63. Ibid., Annex 4.

64. Ibid. The mandates were allocated in the following manner: Togoland and Cameroon to France and Great Britain; German East Africa to Great Britain; German South West Africa to the Union of South Africa; German Samoan Islands to New Zealand; other German Pacific possessions south of the equator (excluding the German Samoan Islands and Nauru) to Australia; Nauru to Great Britain; and the German islands north of the equator to Japan (Annex 2).

65. The terms of the mandates were discussed in July and August 1919 by a commission appointed by the Allied powers, in conformity with Article 22 of the Covenant. Ibid., pp. 3, 10, and passim.

66. Ibid., p. 17.

67. The role of the commission was limited to examining these reports in order to make recommendations to the Council. League of Nations, "Rules of Procedure in Respect of Petitions Concerning Inhabitants of Mandated Territories," p. 300.

68. Ibid.

69. League of Nations, *Minutes of the Seventh Session of the Permanent Mandate Commission*, p. 133.

70. Hymans, *La première Assemblée*, p. 13.

71. Ibid., p. 13 and passim.

72. Ibid., passim.

73. Solomon Slomin, *South-West Africa and the UN: An International Mandate in Dispute*, pp. 12–14.

74. Bentwich, "Colonial Mandates and Trusteeships," pp. 121–22.

75. For a description of Orientalism and its view of the Orient, see Edward Said, *Orientalism*.

76. This ethnocentric and demeaning portrayal of the other has been labeled the "mosaic model" by critics. See Bryan S. Turner, *Marx and the End of Orientalism*.

77. See, for instance, Robert L. Bradford, "The Origin and Concession of the League of Nations' Class 'C' Mandate for South-West Africa and Fulfillment of the Sacred Trust, 1919–1939."

78. George Antonius, *The Arab Awakening: The Story of the Arab National Movement*.

79. Bradford, "League of Nations' Class 'C' Mandate."

80. Gerig, *Open Door*, p. 85 and passim.

81. Sandhaus, *Les Mandats C*, p. 13.

82. Great Britain, Parliamentary Papers, *Correspondence between His Majesty's Government and the United States Ambassador Respecting Economic Rights in Mandated Territories*, p. 4.

83. Ferrell, *Woodrow Wilson and World War I*, pp. 124–26.

84. Great Britain, Parliamentary Papers, *Correspondence between His Majesty's Government and the United States*, p. 4.

85. Duncan Hall, "The League Mandate System and the Problem of Dependencies," p. 48.

86. Gerig, *Open Door*.

87. Sandhaus, *Les Mandats C*, p. 16.

88. Jan Christian Smuts, *Jan Christian Smuts*, p. 199.

89. Ibid., pp. 199–200.

90. Sandhaus, *Les Mandats C*, pp. 14–16.

91. Ibid.

92. For further reading, see Antonius, *Arab Awakening*.

93. For a history of German economic involvement in Turkey and elsewhere in Asia and the challenge this posed for Britain and France, see McClure, *Obstacles to Peace*.

94. Cioriceanu, *Les Mandats internationaux*, p. 74.

95. Sandhaus, *Les Mandats C*, p. 14.

96. Antonius, *Arab Awakening*, pp. 216–42 and passim.

97. Ibid., pp. 216–42.

98. Cioriceanu, *Les Mandats internationaux*, p. 75.

99. In Palestine, where the mandatory intended to create a Jewish state by partitioning the territory, the expression of nationalism took the form of armed resistance. See Ghassan Kanafani, *The 1936–39 Revolt in Palestine*.

100. League of Nations, *Covenant*, p. 13.

101. South Africa's annexationist policy was mostly supported by Japan, also an annexationist, and by Great Britain and its dominions, specifically Australia and New Zealand.

102. Peter H. Katjavivi, *A History of Resistance in Namibia*, p. 13.

103. Jan Smuts, who championed the annexationist drive, called for a mere integration of South West Africa, New Guinea, Samoa, and other Pacific islands into their respective metropoles.

104. Britain, Lloyd George said, did not object to the military ambitions of France "so long as M. Clemenceau [the French premier] did not train big nigger armies for the purposes of aggression." Cited in Gerig, *Open Door*, p. 98.

105. Japan was not allowed to control any territory south of the equator. Such territorial control would have posed a real or imagined threat to the colonial interests of other powers, especially non-Asians, in the Pacific. German "possessions" north of the equator were eventually assigned to Japan as C mandates. League of Nations, "Text of 'C' Mandate: Japanese Mandated Islands," p. 78; also see Slomin, *South-West Africa and the UN*, p. 17.

106. Bradford, "League of Nations' Class 'C' Mandate," p. 122.

107. An amendment proposed by Mr. Vesnitch of Serbia "designed expressly to facilitate the complete emancipation of the mandated peoples and their admission to the League of Nations was not accepted." Slomin, *South-West Africa and the UN*, p. 35.

108. Bradford, "League of Nations' Class 'C' Mandate."

109. Hall, "League Mandate System," p. 47.

110. The administrator's office in Windhoek compiled a series of carefully worded statements by African leaders that favored British assistance. In point of fact, a number of local leaders made repeated requests for military assistance from the British and Afrikaner settlers during their wars against German colonialists. Great Britain, Parliamentary Papers, *The Wishes of the Natives of the German Colonies as to Their Future Government*.

111. A number of Africans had requested the protection of Britain against German aggression. South West Africa People's Organization, *To Be Born a Nation*, p. 20.

112. Ibid.

113. Health care was essential because of the scarcity of labor resulting from German extermination of the Herero and Nama populations. For further discussion of health policy in the South African mandate, see Keith Gottschalk, "The Political Economy of Health Care: Colonial Namibia 1915–1961."

114. Hall, "League Mandate System," pp. 57–59.

115. UN General Assembly, *Responsibilities of the League*, pp. 14, 17.

116. In a report to the Mandate Commission, the South African government admitted that "full power of administration over South-West Africa is by Act No. 49 of 1919 vested in the Governor General of the Union who by Proclamation (Union) No. 1 of 1921 has delegated executive powers to his agent in the Territory, the Administrator of South-West Africa." Union of South Africa, *Report to the Mandate Commission,* 1946, p. 7.

117. Commissioner for Namibia, *Laws and Practices Established in Namibia by the Government of South Africa,* p. 203.

118. UN Institute for Namibia, *Namibia: Perspectives for National Reconstruction and Development* (1986), p. 36.

119. The extensive powers given to the mandatory over the mandate included the authority to control all indigenous institutions. In fact, "there was no provision in the mandate for its termination or transfer. It constitutes merely an obligation and not a form of temporary tenure under the League of Nations." Hall, "League Mandate System," p. 56.

120. South Africa inherited all "vested German interests" in South West Africa.

121. See UN Institute for Namibia, *Namibia: Perspectives,* p. 40.

122. In 1922, the Native Reserves Commission recommended that 5 million hectares of the "police zone" be set aside for Africans. Ibid., p. 39.

123. For the text of the law, see UN Commissioner for Namibia, *Laws and Practices,* pp. 310–12.

124. Ibid., p. 67.

125. The 1937 act covers, among other things, such items as the "transfer of land; special provisions relating to women; substituted title deeds; change of title by endorsement; townships and settlements; bonds and mortgages; rights in immovable property; leases." Ibid.

126. South African native legislation could be divided into three categories, according to its sources: the acts of the South African Assembly (e.g., the Native Administration Act of 1922); the proclamations of the governor general of South Africa that applied to the "natives" (the Okavango Affairs Proclamation of 1929, the Okavango Native Territory Affairs Proclamation of 1937, the Prohibited Area Proclamation of 1928, the Rehoboth Affairs Proclamation of 1924, the Undesirable Removal Act of 1920, the Vagrancy Proclamation of 1920, etc.); and the ordinances of the South Africa–run Territorial Assembly.

127. The police function was originally assumed directly by South Africa, under the South West Africa Constitution Act. It shifted to the territorial administration and back again to South Africa prior to independence. The decision whether or not to incorporate the territorial police into the South African police was always motivated by political realities

such as popular unrest. UN Commissioner for Namibia, *Laws and Practices*, p. 129.

128. Hall, "League Mandate System," p. 58.

129. Ibid., p. 366; also see UN Commissioner for Namibia, *Laws and Practices*, pp. 364–66.

130. Ibid., p. 256.

131. Ibid., p. 360.

132. South West Africa People's Organization, *To Be Born a Nation*, pp. 20–22.

133. Ibid., pp. 26–28.

134. German settlers disloyal to South Africa were the targets of laws such as the Undesirable Removal Act.

135. South West Africa People's Organization, *To Be Born a Nation*, pp. 26–27.

136. Ibid., p. 21.

137. Ibid., p. 26. By the beginning of World War II, 25 million hectares of land had been redistributed to white farmers.

138. Ibid., p. 21.

139. Horst Drechsler, *Let Us Die Fighting*, p. 47.

140. UN Institute for Namibia, *Namibia: Perspectives*, p. 41.

141. Shell Oil, South West Africa was established in 1920, at the beginning of the mandate. See UN Institute for Namibia, *Reference Book on Major Transnational Corporations Operating in Namibia* (1985), pp. 59–62.

142. Ibid., pp. 7–10.

5. CONSTITUTIONAL PROTECTION AS PRETEXT

1. For a comparison, see Articles 16 and 19 of the General Act, 21 and 22 of the League Covenant, and 73 through 76 of the UN Charter.

2. Paul Gordon Lauren, *Power and Prejudice: The Politics and Diplomacy of Racial Discrimination*, pp. 102–35.

3. Claude Liazu, *Aux Origines des Tiers-Mondismes: Colonisés et anticolonialistes en France 1919–1939*.

4. Philippe Dewitte, *Les Mouvements nègres en France: 1919–1939*, p. 185 and passim.

5. Sally N'Dongo, *Voyage forcé: Itinéraire d'un militant*, pp. 1–22 and passim.

6. Quoted in Dongo, *Voyage forcé*, p. 22.

7. Lauren, *Power and Prejudice*, pp. 137–65.

8. Great Britain, Parliamentary Papers, *Joint Declaration by United Nations* (1942), p. 1.

9. Great Britain, Parliamentary Papers, *Declaration of Principles Known as the Atlantic Charter* (1942), p. 3.

10. Ibid., p. 1.

11. Charles G. Fenwick, *International Law,* pp. 204–10.

12. Ibid.; also Article 3 and 4 of the Charter.

13. Fenwick, *International Law,* pp. 204–10.

14. Lauren, *Power and Prejudice,* p. 157.

15. Ibid., pp. 3–4.

16. The resolutions of the Security Council, along with treaties and international conventions, constitute the primary sources of international law. See Article 38 of the Charter for the traditional sources of international law, and Article 27 for the powers of the Security Council.

17. Quoted in Richard Rhone, "The Behavior of the Eleven-Member United Nations Security Council: Theory and Practice," pp. 22–23.

18. Ibid.

19. United Nations, *Charter and Statutes of the International Court of Justice,* Articles 24 and 25; chapters 6, 7, 8, and 12.

20. The General Assembly elects nonpermanent members to two-year terms on the basis of criteria that include "the contribution of Members … to the maintenance of international peace and security and the other purposes of the Organization, and also to equitable geographical distribution." Ibid., chapter 5, Article 23, p. 17.

21. Rhone, "Behavior of the Security Council," p. 19; also see UN Charter, Articles 48 and 103.

22. Rhone, "Behavior of the Security Council," p. 21.

23. Edwardo Jiminez de Aréchaga, *Voting and the Handling of Disputes in the Security Council,* p. 32.

24. Ibid., pp. 19, 23–25.

25. Since the Four-Power Declaration was neither entered into by other states nor endorsed by any international forum, it has been argued that it is binding only on permanent members of the Security Council. In fact, practice shows that nonpermanent members do not consider themselves to be bound by the agreement. Ibid., p. 12.

26. Ibid., p. 11.

27. Whenever the veto is applied to the preliminary question, it takes effect before the substance of the matter is considered. Effectively, a permanent member not only can veto any decision of the Security Council, it can also determine the question it intends to veto. Ibid., p. 12.

28. Ibid., p. 30.

29. Ibid.

30. There have been many attempts to reduce to a minimum the use of the double veto. One practice has been the tacit assent of the permanent

members to increase the power of the president of the Security Council, who may be independent of the permanent members. Ibid., pp. 1–19.

31. Ibid., p. 33.

32. Quoted in ibid., p. 4.

33. Tae Jin Kahng, *Law, Politics and the Security Council,* pp. 112–20.

34. There is more than one definition of a dispute, but the one retained by the majority of the permanent members can be summarized as follows: "If a State makes a charge against another State, and the State against which it is made repudiates it or contests it, then there is a dispute." Ibid., p. 28.

35. UN Charter, Articles 75 through 85; 86 through 91 for the Trusteeship Council; 73 and 74 with respect to the so-called non-self-governing territories.

36. See Articles 76 and 86 of the Charter.

37. During the eleventh session of the Trusteeship Council, the colonial powers agreed to retain the annual report only if it were in narrative — as opposed to analytical — form. According to this scenario, the report would not specify the obligations to which the trustee powers committed themselves. These objections were made by the representatives of New Zealand, the United Kingdom, France, and the United States, all trustee powers. UN Trusteeship Council, Official Records: *Revision of the Provisional Questionnaire* (June 6, 1952), pp. 11–13.

38. Kahng, *Law, Politics and the Security Council,* foreword.

39. UN, Economic and Social Council, Commission on Human Rights, *Report of the Seventh Session of the Sub-Commission on Prevention of Discrimination and Protection of Minorities to the Commission on Human Rights* (February 1955), pp. 39–42.

40. UN General Assembly, *Report of the Trusteeship Council,* statement by the representative of France, Mr. Leon Pignon (December 1951).

41. Ramadera Nath Chowdhuru, *International Mandates and Trusteeship Systems: A Comparative Study.*

42. Ibid.

43. International Court of Justice, Pleadings, Oral Arguments, Documents, "Rejoinder of South Africa," *South-West Africa Cases: Ethiopia v. South Africa; Liberia v. South Africa* vol. 5 (1966), pp. 380–82.

44. Ibid.

45. Ibid.

46. In 1968, the General Assembly voted to rename the South West Africa territory Namibia. UN Council for Namibia, "Perspective: Namibia," reprinted from *U.N. Chronicle* 20, no. 3 (March 1983), pp. 17–32.

47. International Court of Justice, Pleadings, Oral Arguments, Documents, *International Status of South West Africa* (1950), p. 289.

48. International Court of Justice, Pleadings, Oral Arguments, Documents, *Voting Procedure on Questions Relating to Petitions Concerning the Territory of South West Africa* (1950).

49. International Court of Justice, Pleadings, Oral Arguments, Documents, "Resolution Adopted by the General Assembly at Its 501st Plenary Meeting," *Voting Procedure on Questions Relating to Petitions Concerning the Territory of South West Africa* (1954), p. 9.

50. Ibid. The U.S delegate at the San Francisco Conference agreed in principle with South Africa's position when he stated with regard to the trusteeship that "all rights, whatever they may be, remain exactly the same as they exist—they are neither increased nor diminished by the adoption of the Charter. Any change is left as a matter for subsequent agreements." International Court of Justice, *International Status of South West Africa* (1950), p. 98.

51. International Court of Justice, Pleadings, Oral Arguments, Documents, "Resolution Adopted by the General Assembly at Its 501st Plenary Meeting," pp. 54–69.

52. International Court of Justice, *International Status of South West Africa* (1950), p. 283.

53. For instance, New Zealand did not consider that "the dissolution of the League of Nations and, as a consequence, of the Permanent Mandates Commission will have the effect of diminishing her obligations to the inhabitants of Western Samoa, or of increasing her rights in the territory." International Court of Justice, "Written Statement of the U.S.A," p. 98.

54. International Court of Justice, "Statement by Dr. Steyn," p. 289.

55. Ibid.

56. Ibid., p. 294.

57. Ibid.

58. International Court of Justice, Pleadings, Oral Arguments, Documents, *South-West Africa Cases* vol. 1 (1966), pp. 417–18.

59. Ibid.

60. Ibid.

61. For a comprehensive reading of the court's opinion, see M. Hidayatullah, *The South West African Case.*

62. This resolution received overwhelming support within the General Assembly; only Portugal and South Africa dissented. Great Britain, France, and Malawi abstained. UN Council for Namibia, *Question of South West Africa* (March 1984), p. 32.

63. Ibid.

64. Ibid.

65. Statement by Professor N. J. J. Oliver, a former vice chairman of the Technical Advisory Committee of the Western Cape Committee on Local

Administration, a member of the International Conference on Race Relations in World Perspective (Hawaii, 1954), International Court of Justice, Pleadings, Oral Arguments, Documents, "Rejoinder of South Africa," *South-West Africa Cases* vol. 5, p. 340.

66. Ibid., p. 385.

67. Ibid.

68. Demians d'Archimbaud, quoted in International Court of Justice, Pleadings, Oral Arguments, Documents, "Rejoinder of South Africa," *South-West Africa Cases* vol. 5 (1966), p. 397.

69. Ibid., p. 404.

70. Ibid., p. 406.

71. Ibid., p. 327.

72. Ibid.

73. Ibid., p. 411.

74. Ibid., p. 385

75. Ibid., p. 328.

76. International Court of Justice, Pleadings, Oral Arguments, Documents, "Rejoinder of South Africa" vol. 5, p. 338 and passim.

77. S. C. Saxena, *Namibia: Challenges to the United Nations,* pp. 224–25.

78. International Court of Justice, Pleadings, Oral Arguments, Documents, "Rejoinder of South Africa," *South-West Africa Cases* vol. 5, p. 335.

79. Republic of South Africa, *Report of the Commission of Enquiry* (1964), p. 3.

80. Ibid., passim.

81. Ibid., p. 91.

82. Ibid.

83. The Odendaal report assumed that "there (is) only one sound approach if the ultimate goal of self-determination is to be peacefully attained, and that is to build upon existing traditions and the right of the various groups to their own areas and forms of government." Ibid., p. 515.

84. Republic of South Africa, *Report of the Commission of Enquiry,* p. 515.

85. Reprinted from UN Council for Namibia, "Perspective: Namibia," *U.N. Chronicle* 20, no. 3 (March 1983), pp. 17–32.

86. Catholic Institute for International Relations, "A Future for Namibia: Namibia in the 1980's," p. 32.

87. Yobert K. Shamapande, "Economic Exploitation under the Apartheid Environment and Options for Economic Decolonization of Namibia."

88. Yobert K. Shamapande, "Perspectives for Post-Independence Development in Namibia," p. 3.

89. Republic of South Africa, *Report of the Commission of Enquiry.*

90. The mining industry operated under the umbrella of seventeen foreign-owned companies that competed for "the eighteen odd significant mines in the territory." South-West Africa People's Organization, *To Be Born a Nation*, p. 36; also see Heinz Hunke, *Namibia: The Strength of the Powerless*, pp. 25–30.

91. By 1983, seventy-five U.S. companies and their affiliates operated in Namibia. Sixty-eight businesses had links to Great Britain, twenty-five to West Germany, nineteen to South Africa, twelve to France, and ten to Canada. Companies from the Netherlands, Switzerland, Italy, Austria, Norway, Israel, and Portugal also were doing business in Namibia. See UN Centre on Transnational Corporations, *Role of Transnational Corporations in Namibia* (August 1982), and UN International Conference in Support of the Struggle of the Namibian People for Independence, *List of Transnational Corporations and Other Foreign Economic Interests Operating in Namibia* (April 1983).

92. South West Africa People's Organization, *To Be Born a Nation*, pp. 151–83.

93. Ibid.

94. Ibid., p. 171.

95. Ibid.

96. Ibid., p. 174.

97. Ibid.

98. Ibid.

99. UN Council for Namibia, "Perspective: Namibia," pp. 17–32.

100. For the nationalists in Namibia, the advent of independence in Angola and Mozambique symbolized the successes of armed resistance. SWAPO's decision to escalate the armed struggle inside Namibia was sparked by the introduction of a new version of the contract labor system, but it coincided with the advent of independence in Angola and Mozambique. South West Africa People's Organization, *To Be Born A Nation*, p. 206.

101. Ibid., pp. 206–7, 214–19.

102. The contribution of white Namibians to the political successes of apartheid goes back to the coming of the National Party to power in South Africa. The 1948 victory of the National Party and the advent of official apartheid was the direct result of the power of Afrikanerdom and the support of SWANP for apartheid. The margin of the National Party victory was enlarged by the South West African vote. South West Africa elected six deputies and four senators to the South African legislature. Hunke, *Strength of the Powerless*, p. 58.

103. South-West Africa People's Organization, *To Be Born a Nation*, pp. 214–15.

104. Hunke, *Strength of the Powerless*, pp. 66–70.

105. Ibid.

106. Ibid., pp. 66–70, 158.

107. Geisha Maria Rocha, *In Search of Namibian Independence: The Limitations of the United Nations*, p. 110.

108. Among other things, Security Council resolution 385 (1976) demanded that South Africa "take the necessary steps to effect the withdrawal, in accordance with Security Council resolutions 264(1969), 269(1969) and 366(1974), of its illegal administration maintained in Namibia and to transfer power to the people of Namibia with the assistance of the United Nations." UN Council for Namibia, *Compendium of Major Resolutions, Decisions, and Other Documents Relating to Namibia* (1984), pp. 19–20.

109. Ibid., p. 102.

110. Hunke, *Strength of the Powerless*, pp. 70–71.

111. At the San Francisco conference, the chief delegate of the Philippines proposed, for instance, that "the General Assembly be vested with the legislative authority to enact rules of international law which should become effective and binding upon the members of the Organization after such rules have been approved by the majority vote of the Security Council." The proposal received only one vote, its author's. Richard A. Falk, *The Status of International Law in International Society*, p. 175.

112. The principle of self-determination as a political and legal right for all peoples and nations did not exist prior to the UN Charter. The exercise of self-determination in the form of national autonomy and independence became acceptable state practice when Third World nationalist movements posited it as the basis of their demands. In fact, the League Commission of Jurists had observed, in the Aaland Islands dispute, that international law did not recognize the right of self-determination of dependent peoples to separate themselves from the parent colonial state. See League of Nations, *Official Journal* (1920), Supp. 3 at 3–19.

113. The Soviet Union did not become a permanent member of the League Council until September 18, 1934, only five years before the beginning of World War II. It was the ideological nemesis of Western colonial powers until its dissolution in December 1991. The People's Republic of China (communist China) was not admitted to permanent Security Council membership until 1971.

114. Obed Y. Asamoah, *The Legal Significance of the Declarations of the General Assembly of the United Nations*.

115. Ibid., p. 163.

116. See UN Documents S/PV 1808, October 30, 1974; S/PV 2045, October 31, 1977, with two revised versions; S/PV 2220, August 31, 1981; S/PV 2629, November 15, 1985; S/PV 2686, May 23, 1986; S/PV 2693, June 18, 1986; S/PV 2738, February 20, 1987.

117. The following vetoed drafts directly related to the Namibia question: UN Documents S/PV 1829, June 6, 1975; S/PV 1963, October 19, 1976; S/PV 2277, April 30, 1981, and three revised versions; S/PV 2747, April 9, 1987.

118. Draft resolutions S/PV 1829, 1975; S/PV 1963, 1976; and S/PV 2277, 1987 were vetoed by France, Great Britain, and the United States.

119. See UN Document S/PV 2747, 1987.

120. UN Council for Namibia, *Compendium of Major Resolutions,* pp. 19–26.

121. The formation of such a consultative group is authorized under Article 35 of the Charter. According to this article, "any Member of the United Nations may bring any dispute or any situation of the nature referred to in Article 34 to the Attention of the Security Council or General Assembly." For a more extensive study of the ways in which the Western powers have manipulated this provision of the charter, see Henry J. Richardson III, "Constitutive Questions in the Negotiations for Namibian Independence," p. 86.

122. See also UN Institute for Namibia, *Reference Book on Major Transnational Corporations Operating in Namibia* (1985).

123. Richardson, "Constitutive Questions," p. 86.

124. The initial diplomatic consultations of the Western Five led to the February 1978 "proximity talks" and, later, to Security Council resolution 435. The proximity talks were held in New York. Since the government of South Africa had decided not to hold direct talks with SWAPO delegates, the organizers shuttled between the two groups, who occupied connected rooms; thus the name "proximity talks," in contrast to a third-party-mediated face-to-face talk.

125. Rocha, *In Search of Namibian Independence,* p. 104.

126. Ibid. Also see UN Security Council, *Proposal for the Settlement of the Namibian Situation* (April 1978), p. 2.

127. The Security Council had initially declared that "the territorial integrity and unity of Namibia must be assured through the reintegration of Walvis Bay within its territory." UN Council for Namibia, *Compendium of Major Resolutions,* p. 24.

128. UN Security Council, *Proposal for the Settlement;* also see Richardson, "Constitutive Questions," p. 87.

129. Under the Western plan, other parties to the negotiation process included the representative of the UN general secretary, Mr. Martti Ahtisaari, SWAPO, and the frontline states. Hunke, *Strength of the Powerless,* p. 64.

130. UN Council for Namibia, *Compendium of Major Resolutions,* p. 24.

131. Ibid., p. 6. Also see UN Security Council, *Further Report of the Secretary General Concerning the Implementation of the Security Council Resolutions* (November 1980).

132. UN Council for Namibia, *Documentation on UN Pre-Implementation Meeting on Namibia* (January 1981), p. 8.

133. Ibid.

134. The memorandum, an undated and unsigned document, was circulated in the press room on January 14, 1981.

135. These internal parties were the Liberation Front, the Namibian Christian Democratic Party, the Liberal Party of Namibia, the Progressive Party of Namibia, the Namibia Peoples Liberation Front, and the Federal Party. UN Council for Namibia, *Documentation on UN Pre-Implementation Meeting*, p. 19.

136. Ibid., pp. 119–20.

137. UN Information Service, "Concluding Statement by the Chairman" (January 1981), p. 2.

138. Ibid., p. 45.

139. Ibid., p. 44.

140. TransAfrica, "Namibia: The Crisis in United States Policy Toward Southern Africa," p. 44.

141. Ibid.

142. Ibid., p. 136.

143. Ibid., p. 138.

144. SWAPO did complain about the complexities of the initial electoral procedure because of the illiteracy rate among Africans. The organization also had a preference for proportional representation, as long as the plan did not divide the African population along ethnic lines. SWAPO was willing to accept the single-member constituency system provided that the plan was implemented according to stated procedures, that is, that no extraneous factor be added during its implementation. Statement by Sam Nujoma, president of SWAPO, in TransAfrica, "Namibia: The Crisis in United States Policy," pp. 46–49; also see UN Council for Namibia, "Perspective: Namibia," *U.N. Chronicle*, pp. 17–32.

145. In recent years, the General Assembly has singled out the Western Five and their allies for their obstructionist and neocolonial policies in Namibia. See, for instance, UN Council for Namibia, *Compendium of Major Resolutions*, pp. 88–97.

146. For other references to the "Declaration of Fundamental Rights," ibid., p. 219.

147. For other references to the "Declaration of Fundamental Rights," ibid., p. 219.

244 · NOTES TO CONCLUSION

CONCLUSION: THE CHALLENGES OF POSTCOLONIALISM

1. David Strang, "From Dependency to Sovereignty."

2. Ian Brownlie, "An Essay in the History of the Principle of Self-Determination," in *Grotian Society Papers*, ed. Charles Henry Alexandrowicz, pp. 90–98.

3. Robert H. Jackson, *Quasi-States: Sovereignty, International Relations, and the Third World*, p. 1 and passim.

4. Ibid.

5. Ibid.

6. *Hegemony* is used here in its Gramscian sense, signifying that a society has reached a level of political development such that "the mobilization and reproduction of the political system" is based on the "active consent" of dominated classes. Bob Jessop, "On Recent Marxist Theories of Law, the State, and Juridico-Political Ideology," pp. 342–43. Also see Antonio Gramsci, *Prison Notebooks*, pp. 180–90.

7. Charles Lipson, *Standing Guard: Protecting Foreign Capital in the Nineteeth and Twentieth Centuries*, p. 21.

8. See, for instance, the statement made before the Fourth Committee at its 309th meeting on December 17, 1952, by Mr. Ruben Um Nyobe, representative of the Union des populations du Cameroun in UN General Assembly, *Report of the Trusteeship Council* (December 22, 1952).

9. Jackson, *Quasi-States*.

10. Ibid., p. 21.

11. According to Jackson, "the *grundnorm* of such a political arrangement is the basic prohibition against foreign intervention which simultaneously imposes a duty of forbearance and confers a right of independence on statesmen. Since states are profoundly unequal in power the rule is obviously far more constraining for powerful states and far more liberating for weak states." Ibid., p. 6.

12. The territorial expansion of the more powerful national capitals is the subject matter of Marxist theories of imperialism, even though this expansion occurs in fundamentally precapitalist areas. Robin Murray, "The Internationalization of Capital and the Nation State," p. 86.

13. On the nature and economic functions of the state, see Jessop, "Recent Marxist Theories," pp. 339–68.

14. This scenario was repeatedly used during decolonization in order to incorporate the postcolonial state into the global economic system. See Murray, "Internationalization of Capital."

15. In general, the preindependence conditions included a commitment to respect property rights, to inherit the debt of the colonial state, and to grant amnesty for crimes committed against the persons and properties of

the colonized. More significantly, such conditions have been required by the former colonial powers, acting as guarantors for the postcolonial system.

16. According to Gary Peller, the "dominant legal thought [within the state] merely institutionalizes particular visions of the social world. These visions cannot be justified under legal thought's own criteria of rationality." Peller, "The Metaphysics of American Law," p. 1211.

17. See Eric Cheyfitz's impassioned comments on the importance of translation in colonial transactions, with particular respect to culture and modes of production. Cheyfitz, *The Poetics of Imperialism: Translation and Colonization from the Tempest to Tarzan*, pp. 43–57.

18. Colonialism rested upon ethical and juridico-political forms of representation, property, and entitlements that expropriated Africans. On the effects of liberalism on noncapitalist political forms, see Boaventura De Sousa Santos, "Law and Community: The Changing Nature of State Power in Late Capitalism," pp. 379–97.

19. Samir Amin, quoted in Valentin Y. Mudimbe, *The Invention of Africa: Gnosis, Philosophy, and the Order of Things*, p. 5.

20. Dickason, "Concepts of Sovereignty at the Time of First Contacts," in Green and Dickason, *Law of Nations*, p. 248.

21. Henry Reynolds, *The Law of the Land*, p. 1.

22. Ibid., passim.

23. Dickason, "Concepts of Sovereignty."

24. Richard A. Falk, *The Status of International Law in International Society*, pp. 136 and passim.

25. Ibid., p. 138 and passim.

26. See, for instance, Obed Y. Asamoah, *The Legal Significance of the Declaration of the General Assembly of the United Nations*, and S. C. Saxena, *Namibia: Challenges to the United Nations*.

27. Falk, *Status of International Law*, p. 141.

28. Young, *White Mythologies: Writing History and the West*, pp. 165 and passim.

29. Michel de Certeau, *The Practice of Everyday Life*.

30. Falk, *Status of International Law*, pp. 130–32.

31. Some Third World and newly established states have established foreign rule over or opposed the national aspirations of other dependent territories: Indonesia, for instance, took over the former Portuguese colony of East Timor; Ethiopia annexed Eritrea after defeating Italy; Morocco replaced Spain as the colonial ruler in Western Sahara.

32. See Malcolm Shaw, *Title to Territory in Africa*, pp. 1–26.

33. Umozurike O. Umozurike, *International Law and Colonialism in Africa*.

34. Asamoah, *Legal Significance,* p. 163.

35. UN Council for Namibia, *Compendium of Major Resolutions, Decisions, and Other Documents Relating to Namibia* (1984), p. 31.

36. According to Article 73 (b), the colonial power, and to some extent the international community, must "develop self-government, [taking] ... account of the political aspirations of the peoples, and ... assist them in the progressive development of their free political institutions, according to the particular circumstances of each territory and its peoples and their varying stages of advancement."

37. UN Economic and Social Council, Commission on Human Rights, *Implementation of United Nations Resolutions Relating to the Right of Peoples under Colonial and Alien Domination to Self-Determination* (June 1978), pp. 16–78.

38. UN Document A/C.4/L.180, Annex II (1952), pp. 7–12.

39. UN General Assembly, *Compliance of Member States with the Declaration and Other Relevant Resolutions on the Question of Decolonization, Particularly Those Relating to Territories under Portuguese Administration, Southern Rhodesia, and South West Africa* (July 1968), p. 3, 4–25.

40. UN Office of the Commissioner for Namibia, *Efforts to Implement Decree No. 1 for the Protection of the Natural Resources of Namibia* (n.d.), p. 6.

41. Ibid., pp. 5–7.

42. UN Institute for Namibia, *Prospectus: 1985/1986* (1985), p. 1 and passim.

43. Acting on the assumption that "sovereignty vests in the people of the territory and not in the colonial power," the General Assembly endowed national liberation movements with the interim responsibility to represent the populations of colonial territories until they are free of foreign domination and elect their own officials. Kader Asmal, "Walvis Bay: Self-Determination and International Law," p. 13.

44. UN General Assembly, *Compliance of Member States.*

45. For instance, the Western Contact Group successfully subverted the operations of the UN Council for Namibia to the point of nullifying its relevance to the process of decolonization. See UN, *Namibia Bulletin,* no. 2 (1986), p. 12.

46. UN Office of the Commissioner for Namibia, *Efforts to Implement Decree No. 1,* p. 10; also see pp. 11–12.

47. Great Britain, the United States, France, and Portugal (before 1975) have all been the subject of criticism in the General Assembly for their failure to comply with Article 73, that is, their refusal to transmit information related to territories under their administration. See, for instance, UN Document A/AC.109/300 (September 27, 1968).

48. The Axis Victims League Inc. made similar interpretations of the economic clauses of the Versailles Treaty in advocating compensation for individuals who incurred property losses as a result of Nazi actions. Axis Victims League Inc., "Reparations for Wrongs and Damages Inflicted upon Axis Victims"; also see Siegfried Goldschmidt, *Legal Claims against Germany.*

49. Ibid.

50. Solomon Slomin refers to this resolution in *South-West Africa and the UN: An International Mandate in Dispute.*

51. Francis H. Hinsley, *Sovereignty,* pp. 214–35.

52. UN General Assembly, *Compliance of Member States,* pp. 3, 4–25.

53. It is often argued in theories of hegemony (Gramscian or not) that the use of force should be distinguished from the persuasive role of rhetoric—for example, the appeals of the logical formulation of the law. In fact, in order to understand the hegemony of the dominant discourse, one has to pay attention to the ideological adherence by the dominated others to the dominant legal system and other cultural elements. Yet, one cannot fully explain this adherence by focusing on the internal structure of the legal system or culture. In fact, it can be demonstrated that whether an ideology is transplanted, or adhered to by other cultures, the use of force is an integral part of its imposition and later adherence. Where there is no tradition to sustain the outside ideology, the imperial powers often resort to physical (military) force before "persuasion." See Fredric Jameson, *The Political Unconscious: Narrative as a Socially Symbolic Act,* pp. 281–88.

54. Young, *White Mythologies,* pp. 168–69 and passim.

55. Ibid., p. 169.

56. See Mudimbe, *Invention of Africa.*

57. Felix Houphouet-Boigny, "Sur les thèmes de paix, fraternité et dialogue," Centre de Recherche et de Documentation Africaine (France), *Citations du President Felix Houphouet-Boigny.*

58. Samir Amin, *La Déconnexion: Pour Sortir du système mondial,* pp. 25–34.

59. According to Frantz Fanon, France required Africans' adherence to its models as a prerequisite to maintaining ties between the metropole and the former dependencies in the postcolonial era. Fanon, *The Wretched of the Earth,* pp. 148–205.

60. Felix Houphouet-Boigny, the president of the organization, supported the *désapparentement,* as it was called, because the so-called anticolonialist elements of French society were in no position to lend practical support to postcolonial reconstruction. It was opposed by Gabriel d'Arboussier, the vice president, and other radical anticolonialists. Gabriel d'Arboussier, "Le Problème de l'apparentement," Centre de Recherche et de Documentation Africaine (France), *Reunion du Comité de Coordination du RDA*

à Dakar, and Felix Houphouet-Boigny, "Reponse a d'Arboussier," *Afrique Noire,* no. 27 (July 24, 1952).

61. See Gabriel d'Arboussier, "Le Problème de l'apparentement," and Felix Houphouet-Boigny, "Reponse à d'Arboussier."

62. The International Court of Justice also held that the conditions of a people's admission to the international community are establishment as a territorial entity and admission to the United Nations. Henry J. Richardson III, "Constitutive Questions in the Negotiations for Namibian Independence," p. 91.

63. Gayatri Chakravorty Spivak quoted in Young, *White Mythologies,* p. 168.

64. See UN Trusteeship Council, *Statement Made before the Fourth Committee at its 309th Meeting by Mr. Ruben Um Nyobe;* also see *Statement Made by Joseph Ndzinga at Its 380th meeting.*

65. UN Trusteeship Council, *Statement by Mr. Ruben Um Nyobe.*

66. See Centre de Recherche et de Documentation Africaine (France), *Interventions de Gabriel d'Arboussier à l'Assemblée de l'Union Française; Interventions de Boubou Hama à l'Assemblée de l'Union Française.*

67. Centre de Recherche et de Documentation Africaine (France), *Interventions de Gabriel d'Arboussier.*

68. Crawford Young, *Ideology and Development in Africa.*

69. Amin, *La Déconnexion,* p. 15.

70. The French government, for instance, created special agencies to deal with overseas organizations, including the Service de liaison avec les organisations des territoires français d'outre-mer (SLOTFOM) and the Controle et assistance aux indigenes (CAI). Centre des Archives d'Outre-Mer. SLOTFOM II/94. Also see Philippe Dewitte, *Les Mouvements nègres en France,* pp. 21–27.

71. Dewitte, *Les Mouvements nègres.*

72. Great Britain. Parliamentary Papers, *Joint Declaration by United Nations* (1942), p. 1.

73. Joan Edelman Spero, *The Politics of International Economic Relations,* pp. 200–208.

74. Jackson, *Quasi-States,* p. 131.

75. Ibid.

76. Ibid.

77. Ibid., p. 202.

78. Ibid., passim.

79. Olivier Russbach, *Situation: Journal Bimensuel du Centre de Recherches Droit International* 90, no. 20/21 (July 1993).

80. Ibid., pp. 33–37.

81. Ibid.

82. Fanon, "Racism and Culture," in *Toward the African Revolution*, pp. 25–44 and passim.

83. Claude Marchant, *Nord-Sud: De l'aide au contrat; pour un developpement equitable*, pp. 26–27 and passim.

84. Mudimbe, *Invention of Africa*, p. 5.

85. Samir Amin quoted in ibid., p. 5.

86. Amin, *La Déconnexion*, pp. 17–25.

87. Eden Kodjo, *Africa Tomorrow*, passim and pp. 251–86.

88. Amin, *La Déconnexion*, pp. 312–31.

89. "National Security Review 30: American Policy toward Africa in the 1990s—Key Findings," *Africa News* 37, no. 7–8 (December 21, 1992–January 3, 1993), p. 6.

90. Togo, Conférence Nationale Souveraine, *Rapport Général de la Conférence Nationale Souveraine du Togo* (1991), pp. 17, 23.

Bibliography

BOOKS AND ARTICLES

Abu-Lughod, Janet L. *Before European Hegemony: The World System* A.D. *1250–1350.* New York: Oxford University Press, 1989.

Aichelle, George Jr. *The Limits of Story.* Chico, Calif.: Scholars Press, 1985.

Alexandrowicz, Charles Henry. *An Introduction to the History of the Law of Nations in the East Indies.* Oxford: Clarendon, 1967.

———. *The European-African Confrontation.* Leiden: Sijthoff, 1973.

Alexandrowicz, Charles Henry, ed. *Grotian Society Papers.* The Hague: Martinus Nijhoff, 1970.

Amin, Samir. *La Déconnexion: Pour Sortir du système mondial.* Paris: La Decouverte, 1986.

Amzalak, Moses Bensabat. *Trois Précurseurs portugais.* Paris: Teceuil, ca. 1935.

Anderson, Benedict. *Imagined Communities: Reflections on the Origin and Spread of Nationalism.* London: Verso, 1986.

Antonius, George. *The Arab Awakening: The Story of the Arab National Movement.* New York: Lippincott, 1939.

Aréchaga, Edwardo Jiminez de. *Voting and the Handling of Disputes in the Security Council.* Washington, D.C.: Carnegie Endowment for International Peace, United Nations Series, no. 5, 1950.

Asad, Talal. "Anthropology and the Analysis of Ideology." *Man* 14 (1979).

Asamoah, Obed Y. *The Legal Significance of the Declarations of the General Assembly of the United Nations.* The Hague: Martinus Nijhoff, 1966.

Asmal, Kader. "Walvis Bay: Self-Determination and International Law." Seminar on the 10th Anniversary of the Namibia Opinion. The Hague: June 22–24, 1981.

————. "Juridical Aspects of the Berlin Conference (1884-1885): Contribution to a New Legal Order." Namibia: 100 Years of Foreign Occupation. A conference organized by the British Namibia Support Committee in cooperation with the SWAPO Department of Information and Publicity to commemorate the 100th anniversary of formal colonial rule in Namibia. London: September 10–13, 1984.

Axis Victims League Inc. "Reparations for Wrongs and Damages Inflicted upon Axis Victims." Pamphlet IV. New York, 1945.

Aydelotte, William O. *Bismarck and British Colonial Policy.* New York: Russell and Russell, 1970.

Baker, J. H. *An Introduction to English Legal History.* London: Butterworths, 1979.

Banning, Emile. *La Conférence Africaine de Berlin et l'Association Internationale du Congo.* Brussels: Muquardt, 1885.

Bley, Helmut. *South-West Africa under German Rule: 1894–1914.* London: Heinemann, 1971.

Blumenthal, Daniel. *Alsace-Lorraine: A Study of the Two Provinces to France and to Germany and a Presentation of the Just Claims of Their Peoples.* New York: Putnam, 1917.

Boff, Leonardo. *Jesus Christ Liberator.* Edited by Patrick Hughes. New York: Orbis, 1978.

————. *Liberating Grace.* Edited by John Drury. New York: Orbis, 1979.

Bradford, Robert L. "The Origin and Concession of the League of Nations' Class 'C' Mandate for South-West Africa and Fulfillment of the Sacred Trust, 1919–1939." Ph.D dissertation, Yale University, 1965.

Brantlinger, Patrick. "Victorians and Africans: The Genealogy of the Dark Continent." *Critical Inquiry* 12, no. 1 (Autumn 1985).

Bridgman, Jon M. *The Revolt of the Hereros.* Berkeley: University of California Press, 1981.

Brumfitt, J. H. *The French Enlightenment*. London: Macmillan, 1972.

Brunschwig, Henri. *Enlightenment and Romanticism in Eighteenth Century Prussia*. Translated by Frank Jellinek. Chicago: University of Chicago Press, 1974.

Casas, Bartolome de las. *The Devastation of the Indies: A Brief Account*. Translated by Herma Briffault. Baltimore: Johns Hopkins University Press, 1992.

Catholic Institute for International Relations. "A Future for Namibia: Namibia in the 1980s," no. 1, 1986.

Chapman, James. *Travels in the Interior of South Africa: 1849-1863*. Edited by E. C. Tabler. Cape Town: Balkema, 1971.

Cheyfitz, Eric. *The Poetics of Imperialism: Translation and Colonization from the Tempest to Tarzan*. New York: Oxford University Press, 1991.

Chowdhuru, Ramadera Nath. *International Mandates and Trusteeship Systems: A Comparative Study*. The Hague: Martinus Nijhoff, 1955.

Cioriceanu, Georges. *Les Mandats internationaux: Une des Conséquences des principes fondamentaux de la Société des Nations*. Paris: Vie Universitaire, 1921.

Comisetti, Louis. *Mandats et souveraineté*. Paris: Receuil Sirey, ca. 1932.

Condorcet, Marie-Jean-Antoine-Nicolas, marquis de. *Oeuvres Complètes*. Edited by M. F. Aragot and A. C. O'Connor. Paris, 1847.

Congo Reform Association. *Indictment against the Congo Government: Report of the King's Commission of Inquiry and the Testimony Which Compelled It*. Boston: Tremont Temple, 1904.

Coquet, Jean-Claude. *Le Discours et son sujet*. Vol. 1. Paris: Klincksiek, 1984.

Courcel, Geoffrey de. *L'Influence de la Conférence de Berlin sur le droit colonial international*. Paris: Internationales, 1935.

Crowe, S. E. *The Berlin West Africa Conference: 1884–1885*. Westport, Conn.: Negro University Press, 1942.

Culler, Jonathan. *On Deconstruction: Theory and Criticism after Structuralism*. Ithaca, N.Y.: Cornell University Press, 1982.

Davidov, Yuri. *Lenin and National Liberation in the East*. Moscow: Progress Publishers, 1978.

Davidson, Basil. *Black Mother, Africa: The Years of Trial.* London: Victor Gollancz, 1961.

de Certeau, Michel. *The Practice of Everyday Life.* Berkeley: University of California Press, 1984.

de Man, Paul. *Allegories of Reading.* New Haven, Conn.: Yale University Press, 1979.

Derrida, Jacques. *Margins of Philosophy.* Translated by Alan Bass. Chicago: University of Chicago Press, 1982.

Dewitte, Philippe. *Les Mouvements nègres en France: 1919–1939.* Paris: L'Harmattan, 1985.

Dongo, Sally N'. *Voyage forcé: Itinéraire d'un militant.* Paris: Maspero, 1975.

Doyle, Arthur Conan. *The Crime of the Congo.* New York: Doubleday, Page and Company, 1909.

Drechsler, Horst. *Let Us Die Fighting.* Berlin: Akademie-Verlag, 1966.

Engelhardt, Edouard P. *Etude de la Déclaration de la Conférence de Berlin relative aux occupations africaines.* Brussels: Librarie Europeenne C. Muquardt, 1887.

d'Entrèves, A. P. *Natural Law: An Introduction to Legal Philosophy.* London: Hutchinson University Library, 1951.

Esedebe, Oliansanwuche P. *Pan-Africanism: The Idea and Movement 1776–1963.* Washington, D.C.: Howard University Press, 1982.

Esterhuyse, J. H. *South West Africa 1880–1894: The Establishment of German Authority in South West Africa.* Cape Town, 1968.

Evans, Lawrence. *United States Policy and the Partition of Turkey, 1914–1924.* Baltimore: Johns Hopkins University Press, 1965.

Fabian, Johannes. *Time and the Other: How Anthropology Makes Its Objects.* New York: Columbia University Press, 1983.

———. "Hindsight: Thoughts on Anthropology upon Reading Francis Galton's Narrative of an Explorer in Tropical Africa (1853)." *Critique of Anthropology* 7, no. 2 (1984).

Falk, Richard. "Regime Dynamics: The Rise and Fall of International Regimes." *International Organizations* 36 (Spring 1982).

Falk, Richard A. *The Status of International Law in International Society*. Princeton, N.J.: Princeton University Press, 1970.

Fanon, Frantz. *The Wretched of the Earth*. Translated by Constance Farrington. New York: Grove, 1968.

——. *Toward the African Revolution*. Translated by Haakon Chevalier. New York: Grove, 1969.

Fenwick, Charles G. *International Law*. New York: Appleton Century-Crofts, 1965.

Ferrell, Robert H. *Woodrow Wilson and World War I: 1917–1921*. New York: Harper and Row, 1985.

Fetter, Bruce, ed. *Colonial Rule in Africa: Readings from Primary Sources*. Madison: University of Wisconsin Press, 1979.

Fief, J. du. *La Question du Congo depuis son origine jusqu'aujourd'hui*. Brussels: Société Royale Belge de Geographie, 1885.

Foley, Hamilton. *Woodrow Wilson's Case for the League of Nations*. Princeton, N.J.: Princeton University Press, 1929.

Forrest, Derek W. *Francis Galton: The Life and Work of a Victorian Genius*. London: Paul Elek, 1974.

Fosdick, Raymond B. *Letters on the League of Nations*. Princeton, N.J.: Princeton University Press, 1966.

Foucault, Michel. *The Order of Things: An Archaeology of the Human Sciences*. Edited by R. D. Laing. New York: Vintage, 1973.

Freitas, Seraphin de. *Justification de la domination portugaise en Asie*. Translated by A. Guichon de Grandpont. Paris: J.P. Aillaud, Guillard & Co., 1882.

Friedman, Lawrence M. *A History of American Law*. New York: Touchstone, 1973.

Galeano, Eduardo. *Memory of Fire: Genesis*. Edited by Cedric Belfrage. New York: Pantheon, 1985.

Galton, Francis. *Tropical South Africa*. London: John Murray, 1853.

——. *Memories of My Life*. London: Methuen, 1908.

Geiss, Immanuel. *The Pan-African Movement*. New York: Africana, 1974.

Gerig, Benjamin. "Mandates and Colonies." *World Organization: A Balance Sheet of the First Experiment.* Washington, D.C.: American Council on Public Affairs, n.d.

————. *The Open Door and the Mandates System: Study of the Economic Equality before and since the Establishment of the Mandates System.* London: Allen and Unwin, 1930.

Gifford, Prosser, and Wm. Roger Louis, eds. *The Transfer of Power in Africa: Decolonization, 1940–1960.* New Haven, Conn.: Yale University Press, 1982.

————. *Decolonization and African Independence: The Transfers of Power, 1960–1980.* New Haven, Conn.: Yale University Press, 1988.

Goldschmidt, Siegfried. *Legal Claims against Germany.* New York: Dryden, 1945.

Gore, Charles. *The League of Nations: The Opportunity of the Church.* New York: Doran, ca. 1919.

Gottschalk, Keith. "The Political Economy of Health Care: Colonial Namibia 1915–1961." *Social Science and Medicine* 26, no. 6. (1988).

Gould, Stephen Jay. *The Mismeasure of Man.* New York: Norton, 1981.

Gramsci, Antonio. *Prison Notebooks.* Translated by Quintin Hoare and G. N. Smith. New York: International, 1971.

Green, L. C., and Olive P. Dickason. *The Law of Nations and the New World.* Alberta: University of Alberta Press, 1989.

Grimsley, Ronald. *From Montesquieu to Laclos: Studies on the French Enlightenment.* Geneva: Droz, 1974.

Grotius, Hugo. *The Freedom of the Seas; or, The Right Which Belonged to the Dutch to Take Part in the East Asia Trade.* Translated by Ralph Van Deman Magoffin. New York: Oxford University Press, 1916.

Grotius Society. *Problems of Public and Private International Law.* Vol. 32. London: Longmans, Green, 1947.

Gugelberger, Georg M., ed. *Diary and Letters of Nama Chief Hendrik Witbooi: 1884–1894.* Boston: African Studies Center, 1984.

Gutierez, Gustavo. *The Power of the Poor.* Edited by Robert R. Barr. New York: Orbis, 1979.

Hall, Duncan. "The League Mandate System and the Problem of Dependencies." Washington, D.C.: Carnegie Endowment for Peace, 1945.

Hall, Stuart. "The Problems of Ideology: Marxism without Guarantees." *Journal of Communication Inquiry* 10, no. 2 (Summer 1986).

Hansen, Harry. *The Adventures of the Fourteen Points*. New York: Century, 1919.

Harris, John. *Slavery or "Sacred Trust"*? London: Victor Gollancz, 1938.

Harris, Norman Dwight. *Europe and Africa*. Boston: Houghton Mifflin, 1927.

Hazen, Charles Downer. *Alsace-Lorraine under German Rule*. New York: Holt, 1971.

Headrick, Daniel R. *The Tools of Empire: Technology and European Imperialism in the Nineteenth Century*. New York: Oxford University Press, 1981.

Hidayatullah, M. *The South West African Case*. New York: Asia Publishing, 1967.

Hinsley, Francis H., *Sovereignty*. Cambridge: Cambridge University Press, 1986.

Horwitz, Morton J. *The Transformation of American Law: 1780–1860*. Cambridge, Mass.: Harvard University Press, 1978.

Hulme, Peter. *Colonial Encounters: Europe and the Native Caribbean, 1492–1797*. London: Methuen, 1986.

Hume, David. *An Inquiry Concerning Human Understanding*. 3d ed. Edited by P. H. Nidditch. Oxford: Clarendon, 1975.

———. *Treatises on human Nature*. Edited by L. A. Selby Bigge. Oxford: Clarendon, 1896.

Hunke, Heinz. *Namibia: The Strength of the Powerless*. Rome: IDOC International, 1980.

Hymans, Paul. *La première Assemblée de la Société des Nations*. Geneva: Payot & Cie, 1921.

Jackson, Robert H. *Quasi-States: Sovereignty, International Relations, and the Third World*. Cambridge: Cambridge University Press, 1991.

Jameson, Fredric. *The Political Unconscious: Narrative as a Socially Symbolic Act*. Ithaca, N.Y.: Cornell University Press, 1981.

JanMohamed, Abdul R. "The Economy of Manichean Allegory: The Function of Racial Difference in Colonialist Literature," *Critical Inquiry* 12, no. 1 (Autumn 1985).

Jellnek, Georg. *L'Etat moderne et son droit*. Paris: Giard et Briére, 1913.

Jennings, R. Y. *The Acquisition of Territory in International Law*. London: Manchester University, 1963.

Jessop, Bob. "On Recent Marxist Theories of Law, the State, and Juridico-Political Ideology." *International Journal of the Sociology of Law* 8 (1980).

Kahng, Tae Jin. *Law, Politics and the Security Council*. The Hague: Martinus Nijhoff, 1964.

Kanafani, Ghassan. *The 1936–1939 Revolt in Palestine*. Committee for Democratic Palestine, n.d.

Kant, Immanuel. *Critique of Pure Reason*. Translated by F. Max Muller. New York: Anchor, 1966.

Katjavivi, Peter H. *A History of Resistance in Namibia*. London: James Currey, 1988.

Keith, Arthur Berriedale. *The Belgian Congo and the Berlin Act*. London: Oxford University Press, 1919.

Kelly, J. M. *A Short History of Western Legal Theory*. Oxford: Oxford University Press, 1992.

Kodjo, Eden. *Africa Tomorrow*. Translated by E. B. Khan. New York: Continuum, 1987.

Krasner, Stephen. "Structural Causes and Regime Consequences: Regime as Intervening Variable." *International Organizations* 36 (Spring 1982).

Laski, Harold J. *Democracy in Crisis*. Chapel Hill: University of North Carolina Press, 1933.

Lauren, Paul Gordon. *Power and Prejudice: The Politics and Diplomacy of Racial Discrimination*. Boulder, Colo.: Westview, 1988.

Lenin, Vladimir I. "The Socialist Revolution and the Right of Nations to Self-Determination." In *Selected Works*. New York: International, 1971.

Lentricchia, Frank, and Thomas McLaughlin. *Critical Terms for Literary Study*. Chicago: University of Chicago Press, 1983.

Liazu, Claude. *Aux Origines des Tiers-Mondismes: Colonisés et anticolonialistes en France 1919–1939*. Paris: L' Harmattan, 1982.

Lindley, M. F. *The Acquisition and Government of Backward Territory in International Law*. New York: Longmans, Green, 1926.

Lipson, Charles. *Standing Guard: Protecting Foreign Capital in the Nineteenth and Twentieth Centuries*. Berkeley: University of California Press, 1985.

Locke, John. *Human Understanding*. Oxford: Clarendon, 1924.

———. *Two Treatises of Government*. Edited by Peter Laslett. New York: New American Library, 1965.

Lorimer, Douglas A. *Colour, Class and the Victorians*. Leicester: Holmes and Meir, 1978.

———. *Race, Class and the Victorians*. New York: Holmes and Meir, 1978.

Lorimer, James. *The Institutes of Law: A Treatise of the Jurisprudence as Determined by Nature*. London: Blackwood, 1880.

———. *The Institutes of Law: A Treatise of the Jural Relations of Separate Political Communities*. London: Blackwood, 1883.

Malchow, H. L. "Frankenstein's Monster and Images of Race in Nineteenth-Century Britain." *Past and Present* 139 (May 1993).

Marchant, Claude. *Nord-Sud: de l'aide au contrat; pour un développement équitable*. Paris: Syros Alternatives, 1991.

Mason, Peter. *Deconstructing America: Representation of the Other*. London: Routledge, 1990.

McClure, S. S. *Obstacles to Peace*. Boston: Houghton Mifflin, 1917.

McKean, Warwick. *Equality and Discrimination under International Law*. Oxford: Clarendon, 1983.

Miller, Christopher. *Blank Darkness: Africanist Discourse in French*. Chicago: University of Chicago Press, 1985.

Montesquieu, Charles Louis de Secondat, baron de la Brède. *Oeuvres complètes*. Edited by Roger Callois. Paris: Gallimard, 1951.

———. *Lettres persanes*. Edited by Paul Verniere. Paris: Garnier Frères, 1960.

Mudimbe, Valentin Y. *The Invention of Africa: Gnosis, Philosophy, and the Order of Things*. Bloomington: Indiana University Press, 1988.

Murray, Robin. "The Internationalization of Capital and the Nation State." *New Left Review*, no. 67 (1971).

Pagden, Anthony, ed. *The Languages of Political Theory in Early-Modern Europe.* London: Cambridge University Press, 1987.

Payne, Harris C. *The Philosophes and the People.* New Haven, Conn.: Yale University Press, 1976.

Peller, Gary. "The Metaphysics of American Law." *California Law Review,* no. 73 (1985).

Pierantoni, Riccardo. *Le Traité de Berlin de 1885 et l'état independant du Congo.* Paris: Librairie Nouvelle de Droit et de Jurisprudence, 1901.

Reiss, Hans, ed. *Kant's Political Writings.* Cambridge: Cambridge University Press, 1985.

Reynolds, Henry. *The Law of the Land.* 2d ed. Victoria, Australia: Penguin, 1992.

Rhone, Richard S. "The Behavior of the Eleven-Member United Nations Security Council: Theory and Practice." Ph.D dissertation, Pennsylvania State University, 1973.

Richardson, Henry J. III. "Constitutive Questions in the Negotiations for Namibian Independence." *American Journal of International Law* 78, no. 1 (January 1984).

Robert, Lord Cecil. *The First Assembly: A Study of the First Proceedings of the First Assembly of the League of Nations.* London: Macmillan, 1921.

Robinson, Ronald. *Africa and the Victorians: The Official Mind of Imperialism.* London: Macmillan, 1961.

Rocha, Geisha Maria. *In Search of Namibian Independence: The Limitations of the United Nations.* Boulder, Colo.: Westview, 1984.

Rodney, Walter. *How Europe Underdeveloped Africa.* Washington, D.C.: Howard University Press, 1982.

Rousseau, Jean-Jacques. *Oeuvres complètes.* Vol. 3. Edited by B. Gagnebin et al. Paris: 1959.

Russbach, Olivier. "Légalité des armes nucleaires: L'OMS s'addresse à la Haye," *Situation: Journal Bimensuel du Centre de Recherches Droit International* 90, no. 20/21 (July, 1992).

Said, Edward. *Orientalism.* New York: Vintage, 1979.

Sale, Kirkpatrick. *The Conquest of Paradise.* New York: Knopf, 1990.

Sandhaus, Edith. *Les Mandats C de l'Empire Britannique.* Grenoble: Saint-Bruno, 1931.

Santos, Boaventura De Sousa. "Law and Community: The Changing Nature of State Power in Late Capitalism." *International Journal of the Sociology of Law,* no. 8 (1980).

Saxena, S. C. *Namibia: Challenges to the United Nations.* Delhi: Sundeep Prakashan, 1978.

Schmidt, Steffen W. Appendix A of *American Government and Politics Today.* Minneapolis/St. Paul: West, 1993.

Schulz, Gerhard. *Revolution and Peace Treaties: 1917–1920.* Translated by Marian Jackson. London: Methuen, 1972.

Segal, Ronald, and Ruth First, eds. *South West Africa: Travesty of Trust.* London: Andre Deutsch, 1967.

Shamapande, Yobert K. "Perspectives for Post-Independence Development in Namibia." Unpublished paper presented at the International Conference on Namibia. London, September 1984.

————. "Economic Exploitations under the Apartheid Environment and Options for Economic Decolonization of Namibia." Unpublished paper presented at the Conference of Namibian Students. New York, December 1985.

Shaw, Malcolm. *Title to Territory in Africa.* Oxford: Clarendon, 1986.

Shropshire, Dennis W. T. *The Church and Primitive Peoples.* New York: Macmillan, 1938.

Sibley, Mulford Q. "The New Testament and Early Christianity." In *Political Ideas and Ideologies: A History of Political Thought.* New York: Harper and Row, 1970.

Singham, A. W., and Shirley Hune. *Namibian Independence.* Westport, Conn.: Lawrence and Hill, 1986.

Slade, Ruth M. *King Leopold's Congo.* London: Oxford University Press, 1962.

Slomin, Solomon. *South-West Africa and the UN: An International Mandate in Dispute.* Baltimore: Johns Hopkins University Press, 1973.

Smuts, Jan Christian. *Jan Christian Smuts.* New York: Morrow, 1952.

South West Africa People's Organization. *To Be Born a Nation.* London: Zed, 1981.

Spero, Joan Edelman. *The Politics of International Economic Relations.* 2d ed. New York: St. Martin's, 1981.

Stanley, Henry M. *In Darkest Africa.* Vol. 2. New York: Scribner, 1890.

Strang, David. "From Dependency to Sovereignty: An Event History Analysis of Decolonization, 1870–1987." *American Sociological Review* 55 (December 1990).

Todorov, Tzvetan. *La Conquête de l'Amérique: La question de l'autre.* Paris: Seuil, 1982.

TransAfrica. "Namibia: The Crisis in United States Policy Toward Southern Africa." Washington, D.C., 1983.

Trubek, David. "Where the Action Is: Critical Legal Studies and Empiricism." *Stanford Law Review* 36, nos. 1 & 2 (January 1984).

Trubek, David M., and John Esser. "'Critical Empiricism' in American Legal Studies: Paradox, Program, or Pandora's Box?" *Law and Social Inquiry* 14, no. 1 (Winter 1989).

Turner, Bryan S. *Marx and the End of Orientalism.* London: Allen and Unwin, 1978.

Umozurike, Umozurike O. *International Law and Colonialism in Africa.* Enugu, Nigeria: Nwamife, 1979.

Vedder, Heinrich. *South West Africa in Early Times.* Translated by Cyril G. Hall. London: Cass, 1966.

Verzijl, J. H. W. *International Law in Historical Perspective.* Vol. 7: *State Succession.* Leiden: Sijthoff, 1974.

Vigilantes, The. *Why the League Has Failed.* London: Gollancz, 1938.

Wallenkampf, Arnold Valentin. *The Herero Rebellion in South West Africa, 1904–1906: A Study in German Colonialism.* Ph.D. dissertation, University of California, Los Angeles, 1969.

Warren, Kay B. *The Symbolism of Subordination.* Austin: University of Texas Press, 1978.

Warren, Whitney. "The Question of Alsace-Lorraine." Lecture at Aeolian Hall, New York, March 14, 1917.

Westlake, J. *International Law*. Cambridge: Cambridge Unviversity Press, 1904.

White, James Boyd. *Heracles' Bow: Essays on the Rhetoric and Poetics of the Law*. Madison: University of Wisconsin Press, 1985.

Wilson, George. *The Monroe Doctrine and the Program of the League of Nations*. Washington, D.C.: World Peace Foundation, 1916.

Young, Crawford. *Ideology and Development in Africa*. New Haven, Conn.: Yale University Press, 1982.

Young, Robert. *White Mythologies: Writing History and the West*. London: Routledge, 1990.

OFFICIAL DOCUMENTS

International Organizations

International Court of Justice, Pleadings, Oral Arguments, Documents. "Written Statement of the United States of America." *International Status of South West Africa*. 1950.

———. *Voting Procedure on Questions Relating to Petitions Concerning the Territory of South West Africa*. 1950.

———. "Statement by Dr. Steyn, Representative of the Republic of South Africa." *International Status of South West Africa*. May 1950.

———. "Resolution Adopted by the General Assembly at Its 501st Plenary Meeting." *Voting Procedure on Questions Relating to Petitions Concerning the Territory of South West Africa*. 1954.

———. "Observations of the Governments of Ethiopia and Liberia." *South-West Africa Cases: Ethiopia v. South Africa; Liberia v. South Africa*. Vol. 1. 1966.

———. "Rejoinder of South Africa." *South-West Africa Cases: Ethiopia v. South Africa; Liberia v. South Africa*. Vol. 5. 1966.

League of Nations. *Official Journal*. 1920.

———. Document. "Text of a 'C' Mandate: Japanese Mandated Islands." Appendix III-A. December 1920.

———. *Responsibilities of the League Arising out of Article 22* (Mandates). Document no. 20/48/161. December 6, 1920.

———. "Rules of Procedure in Respect of Petitions Concerning Inhabitants of Mandated Territories." *Official Journal*. No. 4. C.P.M.36(1), 1923, IV.

———. *Minutes of the Seventh Session of the Permanent Mandate Commission.* C.648, M.237. 1925.

———. *Covenant and Amendments.* December 16, 1935.

UN Document. A/C.4/L.180, Annex II, 1952.

UN Document. A/AC.109/300. September 27, 1968.

UN Document. *U.N. Chronicle* 20, no. 3 (March 1983).

United Nations. *Charter and Statutes of the International Court of Justice.* D.I.l.-24.

———. Centre on Transnational Corporations. *Role of Transnational Corporations in Namibia.* August 1982.

———. Commissioner for Namibia. *Laws and Practices Established in Namibia by the Government of South Africa.* Prepared by Elizabeth Landis. December 18, 1975.

———. Council for Namibia. *Documentation on UN Pre-Implementation Meeting on Namibia.* Geneva. January 7–11, 1981.

———. Council for Namibia. "Perspective Namibia." *UN Chronicle* 20, no. 3 (March 1983).

———. Council for Namibia. *Question of South West Africa.* Res. 2145 (XXI). A/AC.131. 1984.

———. Council for Namibia. *Compendium of Major Resolutions, Decisions, and Other Documents Relating to Namibia.* A/AC.131/1984/CRP. March 17, 1984.

———. Economic and Social Council. Commission on Human Rights. *Report of the Seventh Session of the Sub-Commission on the Prevention of Discrimination and Protection of Minorities to the Commission on Human Rights.* E/CN.4/711/sub.s/170.4. February 1955.

———. Economic and Social Council. Commission on Human Rights. *Implementation of United Nations Resolutions Relating to the Right of Peoples under Colonial Rule and Alien Domination to Self-Determination.* E/CN.4/Sub.2/405. June 20, 1978.

———. General Assembly. *Report of the Trusteeship Council.* A/C.4/.166. December 1951.

———. General Assembly. *Report of the Trusteeship Council.* A/C.4/226/Add.1. 22 December 1952.

———. General Assembly. *Compliance of Member States with the Declaration and Other Relevant Resolutions on the Question of Decolonization, Particularly Those Relating to Territories under Portuguese Administration, Southern Rhodesia, and South West Africa.* A/AC.109. July 11, 1968.

———. General Assembly. International Conference in Support of the Struggle of Namibian People for Independence. *List of Transnational Corporations and Other Foreign Economic Interests Operating in Namibia.* A/Conf.120/8. April 4, 1983.

———. Information Service. "Concluding Statement by the Chairman." Press Release NAM/36. January 14, 1981.

———. Institute for Namibia. *Reference Book on Major Transnational Corporations Operating in Namibia.* 1985.

———. Institute for Namibia. *Prospectus: 1985/1986.* 1985.

———. Institute for Namibia. *Namibia: Perspectives for National Reconstruction and Development.* 1986.

———. Office of the Commissioner for Namibia. *Efforts to Implement Decree No. 1 for the Protection of the Natural Resources of Namibia.* n.d.

———. Security Council. *Proposal for the Settlement of the Namibian Situation.* S/12636. April 10, 1978.

———. Security Council. *Further Report of the Secretary General Concerning the Implementation of the Security Council Resolutions.* S/14266. November 24, 1980.

———. Trusteeship Council. Official Records. *Revision of the Provisional Questionnaire.* 11th Session. June 6, 1952.

———. Trusteeship Council. *Statement Made before the Fourth Committee at its 309th Meeting by Mr. Ruben Um Nyobe.* A/C.4./226/add.1. December 22, 1952.

———. Trusteeship Council. *Statement Made by Joseph Ndzinga at its 380th Meeting.* A/C.4/225. November 28, 1953.

Government Documents

France. Centre des Archives d'Outre-Mer. *SLOTFOM II/94.* 1928–1932.

France. Centre de Recherche et de Documentation Africaine. *Interventions de Gabriel d'Arboussier à l'Assemblée de l'Union Française.* Itp 7.16/br.

France. Centre de Recherche et de Documentation Africaine. *Interventions de Boubou Hama à l'Assemblée de l'Union Française.* Itp 5.16/br.

France. Centre de Recherche et de Documentation Africaine. *Réunion du Comité de Coordination du RDA à Dakar.* 3.48/br. 1. October 2–3, 1948.

France. Centre de Recherche et de Documentation Africaine. *Citations du President Felix Houphouet-Boigny.* No.1.45/doss.7.

Great Britain. Parliamentary Papers. *Natives of South-West Africa and Their Treatment by Germany.* Cmd. 9146 (1918).

Great Britain. Parliamentary Papers. *The Wishes of the Natives of the German Colonies as to Their Future Government.* Cmd. 9210 (1918).

Great Britain. Parliamentary Papers. *Correspondence between His Majesty's Government and the United States Ambassador Respecting Economic Rights in Mandated Territories.* Cmd. 1226, misc. no. 10 (1920).

Great Britain. Parliamentary Papers. *Joint Declaration by United Nations.* Treaty series no. 5, Cmd. 6388 (1942).

Great Britain. Parliamentary Papers. *Declaration of Principles Known as the Atlantic Charter.* Treaty series no. 5, Cmd. 6388 (1942).

United States Government. "National Security Review 30: American Policy toward Africa in the 1990's—Key Findings," reprinted in *AfricaNews* 37, no. 7–8 (December 21, 1992).

United States Senate. *Message from the President of the United States Transmitting a Report of the Secretary of State Relative to Affairs of the Independent State of the Congo.* Executive Document no. 196, 49th Congress. Ca. 1885.

Republic of South Africa. *Report to the Mandate Commission.* 1946.

Republic of South Africa. *Report of the Commission of Enquiry.* R.P. no. 12, 1964.

Togo. Conference Nationale Souveraine. *Rapport Général de la Conférence Nationale Souveraine du Togo.* August 28, 1991.

Index

Abolitionists, on African emancipation, 39
Abu-Lughod, Janet, on world systems, 18–19
Accords of cession, 74
Adjudication, according to precedents, 64
Adventurers, as agents of discourse, 4
Africa: as dark continent, 38, 215 n.113; discursive appropriation of, 8; as a fiction, 6; salvation, 34
African: chiefs, 92; collaborators, 93; crises, 199; diaspora, 112; emancipation, 78; Moors, 7; Paris meeting, 112; right, 88, 92
African elites: in French National Assembly, 197; on black cultures, 196; ideologies, 144; initiatives, 197; juridical capacity, 218 n.42; and liberalism, 196; performance, 199; political attitudes, 195; postcolonial associations, 197; radicalism,

201; renouncing radicalism, 196; struggle for national independence, 145; views of interdependence, 197, 207
African rulers: chiefs, 92; collaborators, 92; and German crown, 99
African sovereignty: claim to, 88; negation of, 99
African territory: aquisition, 74, 221 n.117; as colonial property, 221 n.110
African troops, *dette de sang,* 114
Africans: *dette de sang,* 113–14; enlightened vs. barbaric, 39; European paternalism, 39; *evolués,* 113; mental endowment, 4; mental powers of, 38; opposition to German rule, 104; organization, 114; Pan-Africanism, 115; paternal protection, 77; political rights, 118; primitives, 49; radical exploitation, 77; right to dispose of themselves, 87; status, 77; subhumans, 4

Siba N'Zatioula Grovogui received a Ph.D. in political science, with a minor in international law, from the University of Wisconsin-Madison. Having previously earned a law degree and practiced in his native Guinea, he selected a dissertation topic that integrated his juridical interests in international organizations with his new training. His dissertation, entitled "Conflicting Selves in International Law: Colonialism and Decolonization in Namibia," was nominated for the Helen Dwight Reid Award of the American Political Science Association in 1989. He currently teaches at Johns Hopkins University and has embarked upon a second book that examines the responses of Francophone African intellectuals to the post-World War II international systems and their visions of alternative international orders.

1) THROUGH THIS READING OF
THE DISCOURSE OF POWER
HOW SHOULD WE VIEW
POSTMODERNISM? IT'S BROAD
DEFINITION OF POWER ETC?
CAPITOL OFF THE HOOK (62-63)

2) HOW DO WE CHANGE WESTERN
PERCEPTIONS OF PROPERTY. RIGHT
ETC?

3) 74-75 ANALYZES THE PROCESS
OF LAND STEALING BY EUROPEANS
HOW WAS THIS DONE?
TECHNOLOGY PLAYS A ROLE...

4) PG 86 RATIONALE OF 'IMPROVEMENT'
IN ALLOCATION OF PROPERTY